ABOUT THE EDITOR

Tommy M. Tomlinson has been a senior associate with the U.S. Department of Education in the Office of Educational Research and Improvement (OERI) and its predecessor, the National Institute of Education, since 1973. He began his career in 1962 as a clinical psychologist in the Department of Psychology at UCLA after graduating from the University of Wisconsin, Madison, under the aegis of Carl R. Rogers. He was a member of the team that produced the touchstone study of the Los Angeles Riot of 1965. In 1970 he shared the Gordon Allport Intergroup Relations Prize for his paper on the political and social views of Los Angeles blacks and their attitudes about the 1965 riot. In 1968 Tomlinson joined the Office of Economic Opportunity in Washington, D.C., where he initiated study of the behavioral correlates of poverty and the psychological and social dimensions of anti-poverty strategies such as income maintenance and equal educational opportunity.

In 1973 Tomlinson moved from the OEO to the newly created National Institute of Education (NIE) as chief of the intramural research and policy studies program. During his tenure at NIE/OERI he served as director of elementary and secondary education research for the National Commission on Excellence in Education, and participated in the publication of the Commission's landmark report on educational reform, *A Nation At Risk*. He was a principal contributor and editor for the first (1986) edition of *What Works*, a compendium of practical results growing out of educational research. He is co-editor with Herbert Walberg of *Academic Work and Educational Excellence*, an anthology of papers about students' role in learning prepared for the National Commission on Excellence in Education, and wrote *Class Size and Public Policy: Politics and Panaceas*, a review of the political and educational implications of research on class size. The present volume reflects his continuing interest in the social and cultural politics of effort and the role of academic work in the education of American children.

MOTIVATING STUDENTS TO LEARN

The Series on Contemporary Educational Issues
Kenneth J. Rehage, Series Editor

The 1993 Titles

Motivating Students to Learn: Overcoming Barriers to High Achievement,
edited by Tommy M. Tomlinson
Educational Leadership and School Culture, edited by Marshall
Sashkin and Herbert J. Walberg

The Ninety-second Yearbook of the National Society for the Study
of Education, published in 1993, contains two volumes:

Gender and Education, edited by Sari Knopp Biklen and Diane Pollard
Bilingual Education: Politics, Practice, and Research, edited by
M. Beatriz Arias and Ursula Casanova

All members of the Society receive its two-volume Yearbook.
Members who take the Comprehensive Membership also receive
the two current volumes in the Series on Contemporary
Educational Issues.

Membership in the Society is open to any who desire to receive its
publications. Inquiries regarding membership, including current
dues, may be addressed to the Secretary-Treasurer, NSSE, 5835
Kimbark Ave., Chicago, IL 60637.

The Society's Committee for the Series on
Contemporary Educational Issues

Daniel U. Levine and Herbert J. Walberg, cochairs
Edgar G. Epps   Kenneth J. Rehage
John J. Lane   Diana Slaughter-Defoe

Board of Directors of the Society — 1992–93
David C. Berliner   Jeannie Oakes
Larry Cuban   A. Harry Passow
Joyce Epstein   Penelope L. Peterson
Kenneth J. Rehage, ex officio

MOTIVATING STUDENTS TO LEARN

OVERCOMING BARRIERS TO HIGH ACHIEVEMENT

Edited by

Tommy M. Tomlinson

Office of Educational Research and Improvement
U.S. Department of Education

McCutchan Publishing Corporation
2940 San Pablo Ave., P.O. Box 774, Berkeley, CA 94701

ISBN 0–8211–1909–5
Library of Congress Catalog Card Number 92–81780

Printed in the United States of America

CONTENTS

v

CONTRIBUTORS

B. Bradford Brown is a professor in the Department of Educational Psychology and research scientist at the Wisconsin Center for Educational Research at the University of Wisconsin-Madison. Brown is widely known for his study of adolescent behavior and teenage peer pressure.

Martin Covington is a professor of psychology and research psychologist in the Institute of Personality Assessment and Research at the University of California, Berkeley. Covington's imaginative research has explored the social meaning and implications of academic ability and effort and their motivational consequences for student achievement.

Antoine M. Garibaldi is Vice-President for Academic Affairs and professor of education at Xavier University in Louisiana. He has been a teacher and administrator in elementary and secondary schools and was a researcher with the U. S. Department of Education's National Institute of Education between 1977 and 1982.

Thomas Good is a professor in the College of Education and research associate at the Center for Research in Social Behavior in the Graduate School at the University of Missouri. Good is the editor of the *Elementary School Journal*.

Sandra Graham was a former social studies and English teacher at a junior high school, was recently a fellow at the Center for Advanced Study in the Behavioral Sciences at Stanford University, and is now professor in the Graduate School of Education at the University of California, Los Angeles.

James Guthrie is a professor of education at the University of California, Berkeley, and is well known for his study of educational policy.

Guthrie was selected in 1990 as the American Educational Research Association's first senior fellow, and has recently assisted the U. S. Department of Education's National Center for Education Statistics in developing a strategic plan for future statistical studies.

Robert L. Hampel is an associate professor in the College of Education at the University of Delaware. Hampel is the author of *The Last Little Citadel: American High Schools since 1940*.

Mary McCaslin is an associate professor of curriculum and instruction in the College of Education at the University of Missouri.

Sharon Nelson-LeGall is a professor of psychology at the University of Pittsburgh and a nationally recognized researcher and scholar in the area of social-cognitive and personality development in the preschool through early adolescent years.

Lois Peak performs comparative international research at the National Center for Education Statistics of the U.S. Department of Education. She is the project officer for the Third International Mathematics and Science Study. She is the author of *Learning to Go to School in Japan*.

John W. Thomas is an independent educational researcher, a visiting scholar at the University of California, Berkeley, and a consultant to the Beryl Buck Institute for Education in Novato, California. Thomas is currently focusing on the relationship among course features, student characteristics, and students' study activities.

Tommy M. Tomlinson is a senior associate at the Office of Educational Research and Improvement, U.S. Department of Education, Washington, D. C. Tomlinson assisted in the preparation of *A Nation At Risk* and co-edited with Herbert Walberg *Academic Work and Educational Excellence*, a collection of background papers prepared for the National Commission on Excellence in Education.

Florence Webb is completing work for her Ph.D. in educational policy analysis at the University of California, Berkeley.

Bernard Weiner is a professor of psychology at UCLA and a leading scholar in the development of motivation theory. Weiner was a Guggenheim Fellow and recently received the Distinguished Research in Social Psychology Award from the American Psychological Association.

Rhona S. Weinstein is a professor of psychology at the University of California, Berkeley, and director of the Clinical Psychology Training Program and its associated Psychology Clinic. Weinstein has been studying the dynamics of teacher expectations and self-fulfilling prophecies in elementary school classrooms from the child's point of view.

PREFACE

On October 29–30, 1990, almost coincident with the conference from which the chapters in this volume were taken,* the U.S. Department of Education sponsored a conference entitled "The Promise and Peril of Alternative Assessment." Two apparently contradictory themes emerged from that conference that also concern us in this examination of the development and maintenance of academic motivation and its operant, academic work.

On the one hand, many observers at the conference on assessment thought that schooling must shift from an instructional economy based on ability to one based on effort. That is, rewards in school should be based more nearly on how hard one works, and less on how smart one is. The aim is to foster persistent engagement by all students in the tasks of learning, regardless of their ability. The reason is simple: other things equal, if children do not study, they will not learn, and if effort goes unrewarded, academically burdened children may stop trying. What we now have is some children of ability working hard and doing very well (unless they lose interest), more children working just enough to beat the average, and many children of more modest aptitude working too little, because, their interest notwithstanding, their effort goes unrewarded.

On the other hand, save for grade hungry college-bound students, there simply is no presently active incentive or system of incentives that either justifies or compels hard work by all students. There is certainly nothing close to the effort necessary to realize the educational goals this society has set for its children, especially the disadvantaged ones.

---

*The conference, entitled "Hard Work and High Expectations: Motivating Students to Learn," was sponsored by the Office of Educational Research and Improvement and held on November 7–8, 1990.

The solution is not self-evident. The students who must work hardest are those for whom academic achievement is the most difficult; they get the least amount of learning in return for a unit of their effort. For them the rewards of learning are typically few no matter how hard they try. In contrast, the return to the academic effort of bright students substantially exceeds that of less talented students, and one would expect them to work harder because the rewards are greater. Ironically, they often do not. Indeed, because meeting the standards is easier for them, many seem to treat their advantage as an opportunity to avoid work by expending only enough effort to pass at an acceptable level.

Thus, as things now stand, we seem to be at cross purposes at every turn. Academic ability remains a critical determinant of academic performance and recognition, even though we have tried to suppress or finesse its effects by altering instructional formats and forbidding practices that might emphasize ability differences. Effort itself is suspect because we are not sure how much work we should expect from our children, especially the disadvantaged ones. High-stakes incentives, including gatekeeping examinations, lag because we cannot agree on the stakes themselves, much less on the morality of having them, even though their absence eliminates most of the motivating punch of higher standards and expectations.

But make no mistake, we must find some way to boost academic effort if we are to see higher achievement. Absent the methods and the incentives to assure a widely distributed increase in academic effort, meeting the national goal of a 90 percent graduation rate may force only a further erosion of standards. Nor will equality be a natural product of an effort-based school economy; individual and group differences will remain just as pronounced as they are now. The benefits, however, will be widespread and worthwhile: a rise in the overall level of achievement by all students, fewer failure-induced dropouts, and better job prospects for many more otherwise ineligible students.

The contents of this book will not resolve these issues, but they will help us to better understand the issues. Each chapter will spell out some of the self-defeating practices in which schools, teachers, and students engage on a regular basis and that prevent the realization of the academic goals we seek. Many of the papers will also dwell long on practices and procedures that are consistent with an effort-based curriculum and assessment and that may turn instruction and the classroom experience of students in a more profitable direction.

Tommy M. Tomlinson

Part I
The Context for Academic Achievement

Chapter 1

EDUCATION REFORM: THE UPS AND DOWNS OF GOOD INTENTIONS

Tommy M. Tomlinson

Ask any group of students what it takes to do well in school and almost every one will place ability and effort at the top (see Chapter 8 in this volume). Ask whether they would prefer to be called smart or hard working and they will likely say smart. Indeed, students who study hard risk two distinctly unattractive attributions: low ability or excessive ambition. Not that high ability may be flaunted; rather it must be kept in check lest one's friends be shown up as less intelligent. Students must learn to cope with this complex relationship, striking, if they can, a balance between the extremes of achievement, not too high and not too low (see Chapter 4). Most do it by adopting an attitude of apparent, if not real, indifference to hard work, a stance that implies both confidence in their own ability and a casual attitude toward academic success.

The most troubling part of all this is how pervasive is the indifference of U.S. students to high achievement or even to doing their best. Not only do low-ability and low-achieving students study the least, even though they need to study the most just to keep up, but U.S. public school students, high ability or low, are collectively not committed to high academic achievement.

How bad can it get? A recent story in the Washington *Post* (Huff and Greenberger, 1990) quotes Sam Jones, the former Boston Celtic basketball great and subsequently the athletic director for the Interhigh League in the District of Columbia. Jones, after complaining that too few male students are turning out for football to field the

3

teams, says, "I can see the time when there won't be anymore football in the interhigh if things keep going the way they are. I think we have to do away with the 2.0 rule (minimum GPA). There are kids who want to play, but can't because of the rule. Basically, the time has vanished when a kid would do anything to play sports. There are too many other things to do." Subsequent *Post* stories told of continued decline in interest and participation in D.C. interhigh sports (Brubaker, 1992), and a similar decline and predicted loss of interhigh sports was reported in Los Angeles, California (Wilbon and Seinin, 1992). In both cases, the situation had been further complicated by the threat of gang violence at athletic events and had led to forfeited games and the imminent loss of night football.

Plainly, for these benighted urban students—mostly male and mostly minority—staying eligible to play ball is no longer a motivational force for meeting academic standards. By all evidence, they are beyond reach of such innocent justifications for keeping up their grades. If participation in sports requires that time and effort be spent studying to stay eligible, never mind, these students think they have more important things to do.

While this condition may be extreme, it is not altogether out of line with tradition. The fact is that Americans have always been ambivalent about schoolwork and the worth of academic achievement, and they have always pursued extracurricular interests at the expense of academic achievement in school (see Chapter 2). Only the unexpected rejection of organized athletics by urban males and the consequent loss of sports as an incentive to meet minimum standards of academic achievement are new. In matters intellectual the middle ground has always been more to the nation's egalitarian taste. On the one hand, we admire high achievers, even as we ridicule them as grinds and nerds and mad scientists. On the other, we ridicule low achievers as dunces and worse, even as we excuse them with stories about Einstein, a genius who did poorly in public school. The "Gentleman's C" has long served to remind us that it is unseemly to do too well lest we shame our less talented or motivated friends or appear to take pleasure or pride in a display of unearned ability.

Yet, the number of students who are driven to engage in face-saving underachievement in order to evade censure for displaying academic talent is hardly the stuff of a national emergency. Moreover, many of the distractions that beset American students and appear to compete for their attention have always been with us, yet students today seem uniquely susceptible to their influence. Something is different about American schools and our system of education that is starkly antagonistic to the dedicated effort that a rigorous academic curriculum requires.

THE UPS AND DOWNS OF REFORM

In general, schools have traditionally been expected to accomplish two tasks: to offer a basic education to everyone who attended, and to identify and encourage academically promising students. If ability was unequally distributed, equal effort was expected of all. If the best students combined ability and effort in high degree, there was still plenty of room for hard-working but less talented children. To be sure, less talented children would have to work harder to measure up, but if they did, most teachers believed their sustained effort would enable them to at least master the basics.

Most educators still subscribe to this belief. Yet, many of them believe their view is not widely shared by the rest of society, especially by students and their parents. They may be right. The responsibility—or the blame—for the shortfall in learning has fallen largely on the schools and, in particular, on the teachers. Consequently, most reforms to date have assumed that students were not using their ability effectively because of poor teachers or poor textbooks, and achievement would rise if the quality of instruction was improved. Left out of this conception, of course, was the possibility that student achievement as well as the success of the reforms might be jeopardized by deficiencies in the amount or quality of student effort.

This is not to imply that schools have been failing to see ever-increasing numbers of students through to a diploma. On the contrary, despite concerns about dropouts and at-risk children, the present rate of high school completion, particularly for minority children, is one of the signal, if unsung, educational accomplishments of the past twenty-five years. In 1990, 78 percent of nineteen- and twenty-year-old black students completed secondary school, up from 50 percent in 1965. Blacks are now approaching parity with whites, who themselves moved from 70 percent in 1965 to 87 percent in 1990. Indeed, by age twenty-three or twenty-four, blacks and whites have narrowed the gap to less than 5 percent, as over 85 percent of blacks and 90 percent of whites have completed their high school education. Only Hispanics have lagged, with a graduation rate of 60 percent, but even that is 10 percent higher than it was fifteen years earlier (Kaufman and McMillen, 1991).

However, there is an unwanted and apparently unanticipated downside to this story. Graduation rates measure how many students pass through the system, not how much they learn along the way. As the body count of graduates was building, many students received diplomas for little more than staying the course. Indeed, the high school diploma has become one of the weakest of recognized achievement indicators, and its slide from respectability is easily documented.

As graduation rates were burgeoning in the late 1960s and throughout the 1970s, achievement test scores were in their sharpest decline, a relationship that casts doubt on the academic integrity of the schooling and the diploma. In fact, many observers believed that the equalization of graduation rates was succeeding only because the standards of competence required of all students were being reduced (Resnick and Resnick, 1985). In so doing, the appearance of equality provided by the higher and merging graduation rates of blacks and whites masked the dilution of content that accompanied the putative improvement.

The problem was particularly serious for disadvantaged minorities. For them, high school graduation and the diploma had become a critical symbol of the nation's commitment to educational and economic equality. Regrettably, symbolism overrode substance because many educators and advocates believed that poor children should not be denied graduation simply because they had not met some arbitrary criterion of academic achievement. Keeping students, especially disadvantaged minorities, in school at almost any cost became widespread, and dropout-prevention programs proliferated as alternatives to school. In most instances, the first casualty was academic learning, since the "irrelevance" of learning and the time and effort it required were high on the list of reasons students offered for dropping out. The practice of keeping students in school spread as dropout prevention became a national concern and educators struggled to find methods and practices that would reduce student alienation from the conventional academic experience (General Accounting Office, 1986; 1987).

This de-emphasis on academic learning led the National Commission on Excellence in Education (NCEE) to observe in 1983 that the curriculum had become a shambles and performance standards a laughing stock. In the widespread absence of formal course requirements and an academic core, students were writing their own tickets, and unsurprisingly, many were taking the easy way out. White students in large numbers had voluntarily abandoned the academic curriculum in favor of a curricular smorgasbord called the general curriculum, and minority students continued to opt for and remained crowded in academically weak programs. All the while graduation rates were rising.

A Nation At Risk (NCEE, 1983) recommended a number of reforms for states to adopt that would bolster the academic content of their high school curricula and increase graduation requirements. The states took steps to comply, and over the past ten years most have raised their graduation requirements, reemphasized the academic core, and instituted policies that emphasize the importance of higher achievement. For example, the 1991 *Digest of Education Statistics* reported that in 1987,

1. The proportion of students receiving credit for courses of the kind and amount recommended for all high school students in *A Nation At Risk* leapt from 4.6 percent in 1982 to 28 percent in 1987 (National Center for Education Statistics [NCES], 1991, p. 130, Table 132).
2. The average number of Carnegie units earned by high school graduates increased from 21.2 in 1982 to 23.0 in 1987 (NCES, 1991, p. 128, Table 130).
3. Thirty-two states now require that students meet minimum curricular standards (NCES, 1991, p. 146, Table 150).
4. Ninety percent of schools had instituted programs to reduce absenteeism, 66 percent of which were initiated since 1982–83 (NCES, 1991, p. 146, Table 149).
5. Seventy-seven percent of schools provide programs of instruction in study skills, 61 percent of which were started after 1983 (NCES, 1991, p. 146, Table 149).

Yet, there was a catch to the reforms. Education reformers assumed that the higher standards would be met with harder work by the students, but by all evidence their effect on the study habits of students was as weak as it was on achievement.

To be sure, the news was not all bad. According to the National

Assessment of Educational Progress (NCES, 1991, p. 111, Table 104) between 1979–80 and 1987–88, the number of thirteen-year-olds who spent no time at all on homework dropped from about 38 percent to 21.5 percent, and the number of seventeen-year-olds who did no homework dropped from over 43 percent to 34 percent. The reforms seem to have inspired more effort from those students who customarily avoided it completely, but their effects on the more industrious workers were modest at best. Among "hard workers," thirteen-year-olds who studied two or more hours a day increased from slightly more than 7 percent to about 11 percent, and seventeen-year-olds who studied that much moved from slightly less than 10 percent to 12 percent. Improvement of a kind, but it was also true that in 1987–88 over 60 percent of American students were still studying less than one hour per day, and 20 percent of these students still did no homework whatsoever. Only about 10 percent of all students studied at least two hours a day. By any calculation, American students do not take much time from their day to study. But then, as it turns out, so long as they graduate, they have little reason to do so. Traditional sources of motivation—parental pressure, workplace requirements, and college admission—have all accommodated to the situation by expecting less of high school graduates; indeed, students have learned that, beyond the diploma, few doors are opened or closed to them by their record of high school achievement or their academic work ethic.

Parental Pressure

Parental pressure appears to have declined in company with test scores. In the 1950s and early 1960s, SAT scores were climbing toward their peak, but graduation rates had not yet begun their inflationary ascent. Students then complained about the pressure they were under to get good grades so that they could get into college. The pressure came from their parents, who took steps to ensure that their children studied their lessons and brought home acceptable grades. Today, according to a recent student survey (Sylvan Learning Centers, 1992), just 14 percent of U.S. students believe their parents are heavily involved in preparing their children for school and schoolwork. Moreover, students believe that parents provide their best help when they assist their children with their homework and set rules that make sure their children will study. By all evidence, today's parents must be falling down on the job, since so many students spend so little time cracking their books. The prospects for more parental attention also seem slim, since working parents and single heads of household now compose an overburdened majority of American parents with schoolage children.

Workplace Requirements

As for the workplace, everyone knows that a high school diploma is the first thing employers ask about. But usually the last thing they ask about is the candidate's academic record. The workplace is not interested in high school students' transcripts or the courses students have taken; only the diploma makes a difference. Corporations do not offer entry-level jobs that vary in pay, quality, or desirability as a function of how well the student did in high school. Grades of As and Bs are indistinguishable from Cs and Ds on most diplomas, and high school transcripts are seldom requested or available for employer inspection (Bishop, 1990; Rosenbaum, 1989).

College Admission

If high school achievement standards have been compromised in the interest of achieving higher graduation rates, the results of the compromise have had similar effects on admission standards for postsecondary education as well. Studying hard in order to qualify for college is largely unnecessary. Academic preparation is distinctly secondary to society's desire that any student who wants to go to college should not be denied the opportunity. Most community colleges and many state colleges and universities are customarily open to all residents regardless of their high school GPAs, although, as in California, students may be routed to less prestigious campuses within a state system, depending on their entering qualifications. Even highly selective universities, which attract a miniscule fraction of the college-going population and pride themselves on the academic quality of their student body, often find ways around weak high school transcripts for students who add the diversity of background and talent most premier universities seek. The upshot is that access to postsecondary education in some form or another is assured, and while most observers consider this to be a testimony to the ideals of equality and opportunity, the academic consequences have been distinctly negative.

In 1991, grade inflation reached an all-time high when 23.5 percent of entering college students reported an "A" average, compared to 12.5 percent in 1969 (Dey, Astin, and Korn, 1991). Contrary to this specious sign of accomplishment, college professors have complained bitterly about record numbers of unprepared freshmen. The Carnegie Foundation for the Advancement of Teaching (1990) found that 75 percent of college faculty held the belief that incoming high school students were unprepared and that colleges spend too much time teaching the things that should have been learned in high school. Eighty-five percent of community college faculty, whose schools specialize in low-cost, open enrollment for the academically undistinguished, believed entering students were seriously unprepared.

Some of the professors in the Carnegie survey used harsh words in their ascription of blame. Fifty-five percent believed that their students work only hard enough to get by and 43 percent thought students were more willing to cheat to get good grades. As a consequence, two-thirds believed the shortfall in preparation was responsible for an erosion of standards at the universities, a process that could be stopped only if the standards at the secondary level (and before) were raised and rigorously followed.

In sum, the reforms of the past fifteen years or so seem to have spoken to the worst instincts in our students, who were being asked to work harder, but given no reason for doing so. More to the point, students were held harmless from failure if they refused to go along with the plan. The lesson for students was plain: Whether they chose to engage in schoolwork or not, so long as they stayed in school and graduated they would be meeting the first criterion of success that the society had set for them. Hard work or high achievement was not required.

What's Left?

Where does this catalog of structural disincentives leave us in our search for sources of academic motivation? Unless students want to learn for reasons of their own, they are not obliged, nor are they made to feel obliged, to meet the evidently fanciful academic expectations of their school. Absent reasons or experience to the contrary, students are free to believe that school counts little in their lives and that they can do almost as little schoolwork as they choose without harm to their prospects. What is left to inspire study?

Ironically, as we have taken steps to lighten the burden of learning and promote the cause of equality, we have contrived a situation where little, save love of learning and the voluntary effort it assumes, is available to inspire serious levels of academic work. This is ironic because love of learning, sometimes called intrinsic motivation, finds students working and studying because they want to, not because someone insists they must. Evidence testifying to the effort and dedication of students when they are in an intrinsically motivated state (Csikszentmihalyi, 1990) has been hailed by educators as a beacon for our schools. It is also true, however, that the examples educators cite are those that have an attraction based on student talent and intrinsic interest, and not merely on the quotidian characteristics of school life. If every child has a talent, one to which they willingly would give most of their waking minutes, they must nevertheless also give time to those features of school life for which they have little talent or taste.

After twenty-five years of trying to fix things, it is perhaps time to face a few facts of human nature: setting higher standards and expectations is one thing; persuading students to try harder is another. Yet, educational reforms that do not change the study habits and behavior of students are unlikely to improve achievement.

MOTIVATING STUDENTS TO LEARN: AN OVERVIEW

American students are neither stupid nor lazy, and their parents, rich and poor, still place great store in the value of education and want the best they can get for their children. The public remains convinced that schooling is the foundation of society. Why then has school become a corrosive experience for some students and why do so many students put so little into their schoolwork?

Reasons abound, of course, and include the students' favorite explanations: boring courses and bad teachers. Complaints of this kind have been leveled at schools and teachers for generations, and even today they are seldom accepted by educators or the public as justifications for not studying. Rather, other features of school life and society are also contributing to the erosion of student performance. Despite the best intentions of teachers, policymakers, and reformers, the energies of large numbers of American students remain beyond the reach of academic purpose, prey to endless competing alternatives.

Competing Social Values

Most parents say that they want their children to do well in school and get good grades. They also want their children to have friends and to participate in after-school activities. Teenagers, in particular, are encouraged to learn not only their academic lessons but also lessons about personal freedom, love, and employment.

Indeed, American society actively diverts the attention of students away from academic pursuits. Schools are willing participants in these nonacademic pursuits, sponsoring athletic events, providing meeting rooms for after-school clubs, and arranging student schedules to accommodate work as well as sport and debate. Admissions officers in selective colleges give preference to well-rounded applicants with outside interests and accomplishments as well as, and sometimes instead of, good grades.

And that is where the conflict arises. So long as we are ambivalent about the comparative importance of education, we shall continue to underwrite academic mediocrity. As Lois Peak (Chapter 3) puts it in contrasting U.S. and Japanese views of adolescence, "We encourage freedom of choice for our adolescents, forgetting that this means students are free to choose not to devote themselves to schooling. We encourage adolescent social activities and romance, forgetting that students will spend the school day thinking of their friends instead of algebra. American business annually spends billions of dollars developing magazines, fashions, movies, and recreation specifically targeted toward adolescents, forgetting that this means students will want to give short shrift to their homework or leave school early to go to work to earn spending money to enjoy them."

Peak also contrasts the educational practices of the Japanese and Americans. She observes that students in both cultures watch a lot of T.V.; in fact, Japanese students average three hours more per week than Americans. However, she continues, Japanese schools and parents are very careful to keep other distractions low. They believe that students should not hold jobs if they are doing poorly in school; they discourage adolescent dating and parties; they emphasize the importance of effort and perseverance in learning; and, moreover, they believe that effort and perseverance are matters of habit that can be trained. In sum, Japanese culture is organized to reinforce the importance of schooling and the value of academic work.

American society believes that extracurricular activities and social development are essential components of our children's total education, as valuable as doing well academically. However, in the competition for time among attractive alternatives, academics may get less than the share necessary to meet high academic expectations. Yet, the conflict itself implies that students have wide discretion in their use of time, and a great deal of time is available that could be used for learning at little cost to student growth. It is up to American parents and teachers, however, to set the priorities if students are to understand that achievement is to be the first order of their school lives.

THE POLITICS OF EFFORT

Ambivalent, inconsistent, and sometimes cynical messages that mock the value of serious study and academic achievement are daily fare in most schools. These messages inflict substantial damage on the credibility and integrity of the school and the academic work ethic. Of late, policymakers have attempted to reestablish the importance of schooling and study by devising measures that will force otherwise indifferent scholars to attend to their education. Bradford Brown (Chapter 4) cites athletics and the "glorification of jocks" as an example of a bargain that sends the wrong academic message to everyone.

Carrots and Sticks

Jocks enjoy high status not only among their peers but among teachers, school administrators, and the surrounding community as well. Students often complain that jocks are not graded as hard as other students and that they get away with violations of school rules that are enforced for other students. While jocks may regard this arrangement as a fair trade between their privileged status and conventional expectations, it trivializes the integrity of learning and the credulity of students who do work hard to meet graduation and college admission standards.

To remedy the consequences of bargains such as these, Florence Webb, James Guthrie, and Martin Covington (Chapter 5) discuss the interventions (carrots and sticks) that have been designed to return the system and its alienated members to desirable standards of integrity and performance. Aiming to correct these perceived abuses, some states have taken steps to force students to exert the necessary effort to learn. So-called "no pass, no play" policies, for example, have been imposed in a number of states, a step backed both by the National Collegiate Athletic Association's stand against athletic participation of academically unprepared college freshmen and by the high school's efforts to prepare athletes for that contingency.

While "sticks" such as these appeal to policymakers who believe that the horse can be forced to drink, they have limited application. For example, athletes compose a small fraction of the student body, and an even smaller fraction of them are likely to abuse academic standards. In addition, as the Sam Jones quotation implied, loss of athletic eligibility has become an empty threat to high school students who in other times might have gone out for football, but who now think they have better ways to spend their time.

As a source of motivation, sticks are problematical for a variety of reasons, not the least of which is the element of coercion coupled with uncertainty about the legitimacy of the apparent aversion. Students leave school early for a variety of reasons, often not of their own choice, and other students stay for no other reason than the benefit they must forfeit if they leave. In short, an incentive program that depends on a stick for its effect may punish students who deserve better treatment.

Far better, say Webb, Guthrie, and Covington, to create educational situations that enable students to voluntarily choose to engage in the pursuit of learning than to place them in a situation of forced compliance. With this as guiding theory, policy based on incentives, or "carrots," that reward desirable behavior is likely to be more effective in achieving educational goals than is policy based on punishments, or sticks, that threaten to deprive students of a favored activity unless they engage in the desired behavior. Examples of incentive-based policy are programs such as Eugene Lang's "I have a dream" and state-sponsored tuition guarantees for students who complete high school and achieve acceptable grades.

Peer Pressure

But athletes and ineffective and alienating interventions are not the only problems. Research tells us that one of the biggest disincentives to academic effort can be schoolwide peer pressure. For many children, the school's chief virtue is the opportunity it presents to make and be with friends. By the time most children reach adolescence, their need to belong to a crowd with similar interests and values is paramount. Moreover, fear of being cut off from the crowd is a powerful incentive to conform to its views, including those regarding academic achievement.

While teens report some pressure from their peers to get good grades and finish school, few peer groups value academic excellence. Most students resent "brains" for wrecking the grading curve and may exact their revenge by excluding them from social activities. Consequently, students with high academic aptitude may suppress their apparent interest as well as their actual achievement in order to preserve their social standing.

To fully understand how peer pressure affects student motivation, however, Brown says one must look at the phenomena of peer crowds. His studies show that the student's crowd may set limits on academic achievement for a variety of reasons. Among the more complex examples, Brown cites research showing that high-achieving minority students may be accused by their peers of "acting white" and of rejecting their less accomplished classmates when they excel in school.

In other groups, academics are important but not as important as other activities and interests. Members of these crowds, Brown says, "must be careful that academic efforts do not distract from activities and interests that are more central to their status in the peer group." Members of groups that spurn school altogether—such as the "druggies" and the "toughs"—must be doubly careful not to show too great an interest in school or classes.

Any attempt to inspire greater effort in students must take account of these powerful and prevalent disincentives to effort. "Greater awareness of the dynamics of peer groups," Brown maintains, can help teachers understand why a student might cringe at a teacher's public praise for a job well done, for example, or why one group of students might work better together than another. Certainly these influences must be understood and confronted in the planning and design of alternative educational experiences.

Classroom Practices: High School

Disincentives to effort and learning also take place within the classroom. For a variety of reasons, including protecting students from failing, teachers may not insist that students work to their full potential. Teachers may offer challenging work, but, as John Thomas notes (Chapter 7), instead of providing the kind of supports—clear instructions, constructive feedback, and the like—that can help students reach those higher expectations, too many high school teachers undercut their expectations by offering students an alternative and easier way out.

For example, teachers who provide students with summaries of the main ideas of a course without discussion relieve the students from the important task of puzzling them out for themselves. Giving students multiple-choice tests instead of essay questions places a premium on recall and obviates the need for students to make connections between principles or to apply them in new situations. Giving students the questions, sometimes even the answers, that will appear on the next test means that students have no excuse for failing the test, but they also have no incentive for mastering the material.

Other educational researchers note an increase in teacher-student bargains—usually tacit, but sometimes explicit, agreements in which teachers lower their standards in exchange for classroom cooperation. Robert Hampel (Chapter 2) contends that teachers engage in these agreements not only to maintain order but also because society holds them responsible for fulfilling its educational goals. Since high graduation rates are the indication that those goals are being met, bargains embodying lower standards let teachers and students "off the hook without wholly abandoning the appearance of serious work," Hampel says.

Some teachers may set lower goals for students they perceive to be of lower ability because they simply do not believe they are able to perform at higher levels. As Antoine Garibaldi points out (Chapter 6), low expectations from teachers are a particular problem for black males, who may be disproportionately assigned to the lower-ability groups and whose self-images often are affected from an early age by negative stereotypes. In his study of black male students in a Louisiana school district, Garibaldi found little evidence of low aspirations: fully 95 percent expected to go on to college, and 40 percent said that their teachers did not set high enough goals for them and should push them harder. A random sample of the teachers, on the other hand, showed that nearly 60 percent did not believe these students would go on to college.

The data on rates of college attendance by black males would, of course, support the teachers' belief. Whether the low attendance rate is in part a result of these beliefs remains an open but popular surmise. Evidence presented in this volume supports the view that teachers can convey their low expectations to their students, often, albeit, in unwitting and unintended ways. Teachers also make judgments about the academic promise of their students, of course, and even when their assessments are consistent with other estimates of the child's academic aptitude, they may still be the end result of a self-fulfilling prophecy. In light of these uncertainties, perhaps the point to emphasize is that teachers and their students share the view that harder work could lead the students to higher achievement.

Classroom Practices: Elementary School

When children do poorly in school, most teachers seek an explanation. Too little ability or too little effort? Those are the questions teachers customarily ask. How they answer them may determine the child's future. Many teachers will excuse low-ability children from trying hard, some because they think it hopeless and some because they think it unfair. Paradoxically, teachers who try to protect less able children from failure by asking less effort from them may only ensure that the children will not acquire needed academic skills. In the long run, such tender mercies may actually harm rather than enhance self-esteem.

Sandra Graham and Bernard Weiner (Chapter 8) observe that well-intentioned teachers at the elementary level who try to protect or improve the self-esteem of their low-achieving students by praising their success on easy tasks, expressing sympathy following failure, or offering gratuitous help, may inadvertently discourage children from trying to succeed. Children "read" these well-intentioned—indeed, compassionate—acts as cues that they lack ability. Graham and Weiner further believe that these messages are a particular problem for disadvantaged minority children. Because their teachers often feel great sympathy for them and concern to protect their self-esteem, they may offer a diet of praise and help that children know is not deserved and, however well-intentioned, implies inability and stifles the hard work so necessary to learning.

Not all teachers are so well intentioned, however, and not all ability cues are so subtle. Rhona Weinstein (Chapter 9) offers a variety of commonplace classroom events that convey information to children about the ability of their classmates. She notes that even in first grade, children believe that teachers are likely to watch low achievers more closely and scold them more often about their effort, yet expect less of them and give them less challenging assignments and fewer opportunities to lead classroom activities or guide their own learning. On the other hand, children also noted that high-achieving children seem to enjoy a better life in the classroom; they get to do things independently, they work on more difficult and prestigious material, and they get called on more often. Weinstein also describes classroom practices that vary in the degree to which they surface and emphasize ability differences, and she concludes that those which reduce ability comparisons among the children preserve both their self-esteem and their willingness to work.

From experiences such as these, children make inferences about their ability, and those who conclude they are not smart enough to please the teachers or master the material will often cease trying very hard to learn. It is not enough, however, to merely withhold these gratuitous offers. Whether, when, and what kind of help children should be encouraged to seek is another critical feature of classroom life.

Sharon Nelson-LeGall (Chapter 10) observes that children who persist unsuccessfully might be called hard workers, but they are certainly not benefiting from their effort. Indeed, children who persistently try only to fail will in time also stop trying. To avoid this result, children who are trying without success should, of course, be encouraged to seek help. However, the kind of help and the circumstances under which teachers give it are important features to distinguish. First, the child must *seek* the help, and second, the help should enable the child to produce the answer independently. Offering help and giving answers may seem a kindly and efficient thing to do, but not at the risk of undercutting the children's sense of their own competence and independence. Help that requires work to produce the answer promotes the habit of effort as well as the boost to self-esteem and competence that accompanies success through one's own effort.

Plainly, effort alone is not enough; children must also learn how to learn. For youngsters who learn slowly and only with great effort, learning to study effectively can be the difference between self-sustaining success and helpless failure. Yet, classroom instruction sometimes works against the development of learning skills. For example, elementary school children are unsophisticated learners and the slowest among them have more than their share of trouble developing reliable and effective study habits. Accordingly, they are often subjected to rigidly programmed instructional routines that are designed to obviate the need for self-regulated study. Because the method reinforces obedience and dependence rather than self-regulation and autonomy, students may fail to develop their own study capabilities and may become unable to learn effectively when they are on their own.

Not that educators are unaware of the distinction. Teachers have long noted that classrooms filled with children who regulate their own behavior are likely to be more productive than those where children must be coerced into cooperation. Yet, goals such as these have been elusive, especially in schools that serve a disadvantaged clientele and rely heavily on imposed control to maintain orderly classrooms. However, the conditions that foster a sense of efficacy and that sustain effort, though complex, are by no means impossible to create and establish. Mary McCaslin and Thomas Good (Chapter 11) describe a system of "preventive" classroom management that they believe will reduce student misbehavior and advance the likelihood that students will become self-sustaining and self-regulating learners.

Preventive classroom management offers teachers an alternative to traditional, but ever less effective authority as the principal method to win the attention and cooperation of students. Indeed, modern management strategies are being developed that engage students as a cooperative social group in which they learn to regulate their own behavior without the imposition of external authority. The eventual goal is that students become responsible for much of their own learning and the selection of many of their academic tasks.

The key to the management strategy, and to a similar parenting strategy, is captured in the phrase "authoritative teaching." In contrast to "authoritarian" methods, which are essentially non-negotiable demands for obedience, authoritative management offers a plan of continuous negotiation of control and responsibility contingent on the demonstrated self-control and adaptive capabilities of the maturing child. When combined with appropriate strategies of parenting, schools can offer students a consistent set of experiences designed to develop internal control and self-regulation.

Taken together, the contents of this volume offer a timely and insightful explanation of the academic work habits of American students. The reader will discover that common sense is insufficient to cope with many of the motivational barriers that burden the achievement of our children. Indeed, there is much that is counterintuitive, and the unanticipated consequences of good intentions gone awry are a common problem. Accordingly, readers are urged to read each chapter in its turn, with the assurance that upon completion they will better understand why our children learn less than they can and should and what can be done to mate hard work with high expectations on behalf of higher achievement.

REFERENCES

Bishop, John. "The Productivity Consequences of What Is Learned in School," *Journal of Curriculum Studies* 22, no. 2 (1990): 101–126.

Brubaker, Bill. "Where Are All the Athletes?" Washington *Post*, 29 March 1992, p. A 1.

The Carnegie Foundation for the Advancement of Teaching, *The Condition of the Professoriate: Attitudes and Trends, 1989.* Lawrenceville, N.J.: Carnegie Foundation for the Advancement of Teaching, 1990.

Csikszentmihalyi, Mihaly. "Literacy and Intrinsic Motivation," *Daedalus* 119, no. 2 (1990): 115–140.

Dey, Eric L.; Astin, Alexander; and Korn, William. *The American Freshman: Twenty-five Year Trends.* Los Angeles: Cooperative Institutional Research Program, American Council on Education, University of California, 1991.

General Accounting Office. *School Dropouts: The Extent and Nature of the Problem.* Washington, D.C.: General Accounting Office, June 1986.

General Accounting Office. *School Dropouts: Survey of Local Programs.* Washington, D.C.: General Accounting Office, July 1987.

Huff, Donald, and Greenberger, Neil H. "Interhigh Schools See Football Fadeout," Washington *Post*, 11 October 1990.

Kaufman, Phillip, and McMillen, Marilyn M. *Dropout Rates in the United States: 1990.* Washington, D.C.: National Center for Education Statistics, 1991.

National Center for Education Statistics. *Digest of Education Statistics: 1990.* Washington, D.C.: National Center for Education Statistics, 1991.

National Commission on Excellence in Education. *A Nation At Risk.* Washington, D.C.: National Commission on Excellence in Education, 1983.

Resnick, Lauren, and Resnick, Daniel. "Standards, Curriculum, and Performance: An Historical and Comparative Perspective," *Educational Researcher* 14, no. 4 (1985): 5–20.

Rosenbaum, James. "What If Good Jobs Depended on Good Grades?" *American Educator* 13, no. 4 (Winter 1989): 10–43.

Sylvan Learning Centers and the National Association of Secondary School Principals. *Voices from the Classroom.* New York: Kechum Public Relations, 1992.

Wilbon, Michael, and Sheinin, Dave. "Gangs Suit Up in Sportwear, Leaving Games Behind." Washington *Post*, 25 May 1992, p. C 1.

Chapter 2

HISTORICAL PERSPECTIVES ON ACADEMIC WORK: THE ORIGINS OF LEARNING

Robert L. Hampel

Americans like to believe there was a Golden Age when dutiful students learned tough subjects from talented teachers. In orderly classrooms attentive youngsters supposedly turned in their homework, did sight translations from long Latin poems, and recited from memory all the helping verbs. Such nostalgia mistakes the quiet regimentation that marked many schools for the hard work that has usually been in short supply. It is wishful thinking to imagine a time when nearly all American students threw themselves into their studies with the intensity we now admire in Japanese youth.

It is also true that many American students throughout this century have in fact worked hard, respected knowledge, even liked their time in school. Understanding why certain students push hard (and are pushed by teachers) when others avoid (and are allowed to avoid) hard work is a central purpose of this chapter. I seek this understanding by examining several major themes in the history of American schools, especially the expansion of what once was a small and selective "system."

First I will define *academic work ethic*. Each word in this phrase can be construed in various ways. *Academic* is not necessarily the same as *intellectual*. Many fine private schools stress academics—mandatory homework, peer pressure to study, few if any fluff electives, great interest in college "placement" (a telling word)—without celebrating the life of the mind as good in itself. The press on students is to live off, not for, ideas (to use Richard Hofstadter's [1963] distinction).

21

Although I have tried to focus on an academic rather than an intellectual work ethic, the fragility of the distinction is apparent when *work* is defined. If we take that word in reference to a frame of mind, temperament, or disposition, it is obvious that schoolwork can be fun, playful, and occasionally joyous, instead of unrelieved toil and strain. In itself, solving a tricky geometry problem can be satisfying, regardless of external advantage gained now or later by the new skill. Even if the little mathematician never goes to graduate school, the work can be delightful. The third word, *ethic*, could be a habit or pattern of behavior, but it could also entail values, beliefs, and commitments. In *The Vocation of a Teacher*, Wayne Booth discusses the moral obligation of scholars, and his list of moral traits includes honesty, courage, persistence, consideration, and humility (Booth, 1989). In this chapter I focus on issues pertaining to a more modest definition of academic work ethic.

Throughout the nineteenth century, most American children left school after six to eight years of elementary education (and those years were shorter school years than September to June, our current calendar). Once a child knew the rudiments of literacy, numeracy, and civics, there seemed to be no compelling reason to forego work for school, especially when a family needed another field hand or paycheck. Some children picked up another year or two in an academy, normal school, or commercial school, institutions usually less rigorous and more expensive than a good public high school. Some started high school, but the dropout rate was terrific. Economics was not the only reason to leave school. A great many students found formal education unattractive. Often novice teachers, young and ill-prepared, struggled to get and keep order. The devices they relied on—corporal punishment, parental pressure, or humiliations like dunce caps—did not whet the appetite for more school days. The steady diet of drill and recitation, memorization and recall, contained dry facts and formulas from dreary textbooks. Teachers assumed that "students were neither able nor willing to acquire the fundamentals of literacy without external compulsion" (Finkelstein, 1989, p. 95). Opportunities for self-expression were rare in this catechismic approach to learning. Writing, for instance, featured penmanship learned by copying a particular style from a text instead of using language to shape or communicate personal feelings or thoughts. It is true that periodically teachers gave students class time to solve problems, translate passages, or do a writing assignment. Recitations followed, with the teacher correcting mistakes and explaining errors. Straight lecturing was much rarer than today, so the burden on students to puzzle things out on their own was greater than now, when the lecturers often do some of the students' work for them. But if the old regimen bolstered the work ethic of the bright and the successful, it was terror for the less swift. Each recitation meant the possibility of another display of shortcomings in front of fellow classmates. All in all, the routines struck many youngsters as oppressive and, past a certain point, useless.

Even where secondary education offered tangible benefits, hard work was uneven. The flagship high school in mid to late nineteenth-century Philadelphia, Central High, admitted only half of the applicants, who all took a written entrance exam. Only 25 percent of that select group eventually graduated. Social class, remarkably, was not correlated with graduation rates. The attrition occurred even though students knew the diploma was "a commodity whose most important characteristic was that it could be exchanged for something useful like a good job" (Labaree, 1988, p. 62).

In another elite enclave, the best eastern boarding schools, the life of the mind mattered less than other goals. Many wealthy Americans sent their sons to prep schools to form or reinforce personal traits, particularly self-control, sportsmanship, and leadership. The Lawrencevilles and the Andovers did not ignore hard work; they coached many students well enough to pass the written entrance exams required for admission to top colleges. Yet many of those same students avoided books as much as possible as soon as they got to Harvard, Yale, or wherever. Sports, clubs, parties, and friendships often overshadowed classes (Fass, 1977; Saveth, 1988). By the early twentieth century, the epithet "grind," originally referring to mediocre students who worked overtime, became "greasy grind," and applied to any unusually conscientious college student (Lowell, 1934).

What these examples suggest is the absence of a Golden Age in the nineteenth century. Even before the great expansion of enrollments, strong commitment to schoolwork was not widespread. The high attrition, the focus on textbooks, the pedagogy of memorize/recite, and the teachers' willingness to punish severely—those might create an illusion of engagement without a deep transformation of youngsters' attitudes toward schooling. The surface penetration of much education is suggested by the persistent nineteenth-century view of advanced learning as ornamental, a gracious accoutrement for display in polite society. The "polish" of speaking French or playing the piano impressed others whom one wanted to impress, rather than expressing personal absorption and fascination. Too much of that would supposedly unfit a man for practical life.

As enrollment in elementary schools rose throughout the nineteenth century, the curriculum, teaching methods, and textbooks changed very little. In contrast, the surge of high school enrollment, which doubled every decade between 1870 and 1940, did bring about some major changes. In regard to the academic work ethic, it seems that most high schools differentiated more and more sharply between those students with the wit and will to do serious work and the horde of others deemed unsuited for academic exertions.

As educators watched enrollments climb, they knew the dizzying expansion stemmed from many causes, and love of learning was not the least common denominator. Labor market changes were vital, particularly the restrictions on hiring unskilled child labor and the growth of respectable white-collar jobs—salesmen, accountants, clerks—available to high school graduates. Economic opportunity and prolonged schooling seemed to go hand in hand.

Passage of compulsory attendance laws corralled some otherwise errant youngsters, although in most states enrollments soared before those laws passed. Another reason attendance rose was the spread of the new notion of a phase of life called adolescence, a rocky time of turmoil best endured in a sheltered place apart from the marketplace. Still another reason enrollments skyrocketed was a snowballing effect brought on by peer pressure as students stayed in school simply because more and more of their friends were there. Furthermore, the surge would not have been as dramatic if educators had not welcomed and thus accelerated the expansion. They were thrilled that one new high school opened every day, on balance, between 1900 and 1920.

Early in the boom it was clear that educators were not distraught that a thirst for knowledge drove so few of their new recruits. They felt sure the high school could and should offer something useful and interesting to nearly all. To do so, not everyone could be asked to take the same large doses of classical language, mathematics, science, and other traditional nineteenth-century requirements. Different students supposedly needed different courses of study. It seemed undemocratic to do otherwise. A typical high school of 1910 offered academic, commercial, and technical/vocational "tracks" designed to route students to college or to work; the undecided students could take the "general" track, usually a hodgepodge of unrelated courses. With the exception of a few demanding technical specializations, only the academic track featured intellectually strenuous work. Elsewhere the demands were modest—business mathematics, not algebra; general science, not biology; social studies in place of ancient history. In many big high schools, administrators scheduled students for different sections of the same course on the basis of their intelligence or achievement, so "ability grouping" also classified students as bright, dim, or average.

The proliferation of easier, practical courses reflected a widespread assumption that many of the newcomers *could not* take on serious academic work. They seemed to lack the innate intelligence necessary for reasonable performance. The tidal wave of immigration, from the 1890s through World War I, seemed to flood the corridors with unpromising material, particularly the children of eastern Europeans. Educators also doubted the capacities of blue-collar workers' offspring, mistaking their demeanor, clothes, and speech for feeble or mediocre intelligence. By 1920, educators could buttress their impressions with statistical evidence from the new and wildly popular field of intelligence testing, where crude early examinations reported very low scores for many groups already suspect as inferior (Gould, 1981; Chapman, 1988).

Moreover, quite a few educators openly said that many high school students *need not* stretch their minds. Why should future housewives take French or chemistry when they could learn cooking and consumer mathematics? Why should a plumber bother with the pluperfect? Immediately applicable lessons, on topics like hygiene, recreation, and the family budget, educated for real life; Latin III led only to Latin IV. Democratic ideals were said to be hollow if, in an institution with an increasingly diverse clientele, a majority walked away without the know-how they would later need more than old notes on *Julius Caesar*. Administrators could claim to be efficient businessmen, scientifically gearing their products for the market (vocational guidance was the counselors' first beachhead in the schools). Vocational schools usually received students already disenchanted with traditional instruction and curricula; faced with chronically high dropout rates, vo/tech administrators hesitated to require more of the subjects their students wanted to avoid. And where technical students relished academics, in the few elite selective admissions schools for future engineers, the curriculum resembled traditional academic fare more than interweaving shop work with academics (Kantor, 1988).

Furthermore, many early-twentieth-century educators believed that there were students who simply *would not* undertake rigorous studies. Some skeptical, indifferent, or openly hostile youngsters had to stay in school because the job market, parents, or the law insisted. Eager to leave, they saw no good reason to push themselves to do much. Alienated or embittered by the early years of elementary schooling, their appetite for schoolwork was gone by the time coursework moved beyond the rudiments. It seemed hard enough to keep them quiet and orderly (Hollingshead, 1949). A less pesky yet still disengaged group consisted of able youngsters who seemed to lack the maturity or the motivation to do the work they were capable of doing. Most high schools did not force every clever student to take top track or honors courses, a reluctance that alarmed former Harvard President James Conant when he examined who took what in the mid-1950s. He saw that high-ability students could sleep in peace in general track courses and graduate; if they later realized what they could do, no doors to challenging education had been permanently closed. Conant recommended that those students be more forcefully guided to demanding coursework (Hampel, 1986).

A third and much larger batch of students seemed indifferent because they were caught up in the seemingly inevitable and largely healthy preoccupations most adolescents find hard to resist: friendships, dating, personal physical and emotional changes. At the turn of the century, the burgeoning field of psychology viewed adolescence as tumultuous. Buffeted by all sorts of new and intense emotions, teens were thought to deserve "a removal of pressures for adult-like behavior" (Kett, 1977, p. 217), and this message from the pioneers of child and adolescent psychology reinforced the nineteenth-century fears of debilitation and nervous exhaustion among adolescents who studied too much. Whereas nineteenth-century reasoning had emphasized the physical damage wrought by too much time poring over books, the later opinion of G. Stanley Hall, a very well-known developmental psychologist specializing in adolescent development, stressed the emotional effects of rushing youth into adulthood.

UNWISE CANDOR

Schooling for all and education for some: that was the way Americans accommodated the growing diversity of students. We assumed that scads of youngsters either could not, need not, or would not take up demanding coursework. As David Cohen has shown, we did so rather cheerfully (Cohen, 1988). Early-twentieth-century administrators celebrated inclusiveness and touted prolonged schooling as a cure for the social, economic, and political ills of the society. The modestness of the average child's intellectual needs and abilities presented wonderful opportunities, not disheartening setbacks. Many educators inflated their own importance as they underestimated their charges' cognitive reach. They carried on rhapsodically about their vital role in "adjusting" youth (on the assumption that neither teens nor their families could be relied on to do the job adequately) to be wise shoppers, good husbands, sportsmen, or vitamin takers.

It is important to stress that when the rhetoric became too transparent, educators drew a lot of fire. To broadcast frankly and merrily a low estimate of people's intelligence and diligence was foolish, as were the pronouncements that ordinary students required extraordinary pedagogy to learn rather simple stuff. The brief "Life Adjustment" initiative in the late 1940s hurt itself badly by ridiculing academic fare and urging all teachers to stress their subjects' practical applications. The adjusters claimed, loudly, that every student deserved and needed lessons on effective living, family life, and wholesome personal relations. Since students already cared about subjects like dating and acne, teachers were told they would easily win their students' rapt attention by setting adolescent priorities at the center of each period.

Soon after they began to promote their programs, the life adjusters drew vigorous criticisms. Books like Arthur Bestor's *Educational Wastelands* and Albert Lynd's *Quackery in the Public Schools* excoriated life adjustment as pretentious and vapid. Lynd (1953) asked why "something like Progress in Democratic Smoke Abatement is closer to a child's real needs than subjects like Latin and French and English poetry" (p. 17). Bestor (1953) wondered whether "the American people have lost all common sense and native wit so that now they have to be taught in school to blow their noses and button their pants" (p. 64).

The candor of the adjusters was not only unwise strategy; it was also unnecessary. The benefits of getting along pleasantly with others were widely recognized by mid-century. High school students ranked social skills ahead of basic skills as the most important point to secondary education. College students also put "gets along well with others" ahead of "brains" when asked why some people succeed. Furthermore, many schools already offered a few of the adjusters' favorite courses. Enrollments in classes like orientation, group guidance, occupations, hygiene, consumer buying, and family life rose during the 1930s and 1940s. Particularly well subscribed were several hands-on courses. In the areas of the curriculum with gadgets, driver education led the way. Almost nonexistent during the Depression, driver education in some form was offered in nearly all American high schools by 1953, and four of every five schools offered the course for credit. Typewriting and home economics enrollments also rose strongly. Although film study credits were not yet available, the proliferation of audiovisuals let technology colonize the academic areas, especially social studies. One study in 1951 reported that history teachers used audiovisuals more often than they assigned library research projects. Cars, typewriters, kitchens, and projectors were less preachy than the life adjustment rhetoric, but each gadget gave the student the opportunity to avoid some serious academic demands (Hampel, 1986).

Despite those reasons to keep a low profile, life adjusters agitated noisily for their programs. Between 1947 and 1953 over a hundred articles appeared with life adjustment somewhere in the title, and several books on the subject were manuals for curricular revisions. Topics usually reserved for family discussions were brought into the classrooms as suitable for a "useful" curriculum. Opponents were scorned as traditionalists or penny-pinchers (Ravitch, 1983).

In contrast to the obvious curricular changes promoted by supporters of life adjustment courses, the academic demands on students had long been modified with more subtlety and less criticism by setting graduation requirements as credits accumulated. That is, the diploma was not awarded whenever a student could demonstrate a particular set of competencies, through oral or written examination, portfolios of work, or other methods of assessment. Educators did not define specific outcomes that all high school seniors had to know or do in order to finish. What was required was taking courses, earning "credits" by passing the course, and piling up the necessary number of credits to graduate. Each course was defined in terms of time, meeting for X periods each week for Y minutes daily, and getting enough credits almost always required the same stretch of time of all students—twelve grades, twelve years.

This time-and-credits arrangement is so familiar, so taken for granted, that we sometimes fail to appreciate its profound ramifications. All kinds of courses receive equal valuation in regard to the diploma, as do unequal grades within the courses. So hard work for an A in physics "counts" the same as a C in horticulture. Savvy students and parents do understand the competitive edge of physics and top grades in the scramble for admissions to selective colleges, which means that no one can say the time-and-credits setup utterly abandons standards. But it does establish a rather modest standard, perseverance. Showing up, behaving, and exerting at least some effort is usually enough to get a D (schools vary greatly in awarding attendance+quiet+effort more than that). Persistence is the minimum standard. The only students hurt are those recalcitrants who will not show up, behave, and try.

What are the consequences of the time-and-credit arrangement for the academic work ethic? Without an annual or final comprehensive examination integrating the various courses, and with little if any need to remember and use the course material once the term is over, the students easily lose much of what they "covered" each year. They may have the illusion that their learning is cumulative, in light of their larger heap of credits, but they mistake the means (the course) for the end (education). As President Lowell (1934) of Harvard University said,

At present the credit for a course is treated like a deposit in a savings bank, without a suspicion that the deposit is not of gold that can be drawn upon at its face value, but of a perishable article. To change the metaphor, we treat it like wheat poured into a grain elevator, whereas it is often more like the fruit in a cold storage plant without the means of refrigeration. Indeed, it is sometimes more like the contents of an incinerator. [P. 140]

The upshot is that work focused on this course right now, even if it yields high grades, may in time come to only a hodgepodge of disjointed and fragmented information. The psychologists tell us that learning in that way—picking up a grab-bag of bits and pieces of unrelated facts—does not reinforce an academic work ethic (*Daedalus*, Spring 1990). Yet the credit-counting tradition in America is tenacious and respectable, and seems less hostile to intellect than the life adjustment courses.

Another consequence is the upward extension of the elementary schools' premium on effort. In the earliest grades, a dutiful child who tries will usually pass. But being involved often means following rules, obeying, cooperating, and perhaps stifling curiosity and questioning (two characteristics helpful to an academic work ethic). Effort translates as patience, passivity, and compliance (Jackson, 1968; Johnson, 1985). Furthermore, effort usually means a *bit* of effort rather than pushing to one's limits. "Do your best" is a facile command easier said than measured. From time to time, schools have computed an achievement/I.Q. ratio in an attempt to evaluate children by individual metrics, but those grading systems have been controversial and hard to justify to puzzled or angry parents.

It is also noteworthy that "follow the rules" and "do your best" win fewer and fewer high grades and gold stars as the student moves through junior high and high school. The rules for winning the academic games begin to change as students get older, and rarely do teachers make plain just how and why those rules shift. For example, a middle school language arts assignment might ask for an "opinion" of something, and two coherent paragraphs earn a good grade. Somewhere in high school (at least in the better ones) mere opinion is no longer enough. Interpretation backed by evidence is now required, not just a tidy paper with reasonable sentence structure. Alternatively, the "research" paper in high school for which a dozen articles were summarized strikes a college professor as unoriginal rehash. The baffled student wonders why the work that earned an A two years earlier is now unsatisfactory. The boom recently in freshman orientation programs, many with study skills modules, testifies to the confusion and anxiety many college freshmen feel when they realize, often dimly, that the ground rules have changed, and the burden is on them to figure out the changes (Rose, 1989; Sternberg, 1990).

The point is that we let some students get a high school diploma with a very modest commitment to work—a bit of effort. And for others who are willing to push themselves, we keep changing, and often without full explanations of the changes, their earliest understanding of the work necessary to get high marks. For motivated and unmotivated students alike, those practices hamper the development of a strong academic work ethic. And yet, there is no popular outcry against the practices. The silence on this matter is striking. The traditions I have described satisfy many thoughtful people as reasonable expectations—figuring out what is expected is part of learning, and later in life no one hovers around patiently explaining the rules of the game to the unwary.

AFTER MID-CENTURY

Many of my comments so far have referred primarily to developments before 1950. In this section I stay with the same themes discussed earlier, but do so with reference to changes since mid-century.

The steady expansion of enrollments each decade leveled off by the 1950s, when nearly every young adolescent started high school and roughly three-fourths of them graduated, with substantial and persistent differences according to color, class, and geography. The number of adolescents in secondary schools has not changed significantly since then, notwithstanding a slew of programs to boost graduation rates. The numbers tell us that *on balance* high schools were inclusive by mid-century, and have remained so during the last forty years.

What the averages do not reveal is the diversification of students in many individual schools. In rural areas the ongoing consolidation of very small schools mixed youngsters from different and sometimes hostile towns. In some suburbs and in many cities, where high schools were already large, it was not consolidation but rather integration and busing that heightened diversity, with a later influx of immigrants further diversifying some places. The arrival of outsiders, both welcome and unwelcome, was not the only path to diversification. The provision of special services for particular kinds of students increased the heterogeneity. The growth of discrete programs for gifted and talented youth, for handicapped and disabled students, and for "at risk" students made more visible the variety that may or may not have been there before, but was not as easy to see or treat sympathetically.

One might think that greater diversity would have prompted more and more people to write off a considerable proportion of the students as unable to do serious academic work. But it is striking that so many educators, particularly from the mid-1960s on, rejected or at least questioned the old belief that a lot of youngsters cannot learn very much of any substance. The new optimism drew from several rather different sources. On the one hand, the widely acclaimed work of Benjamin Bloom, Jerome Bruner, Howard Gardner, Robert Sternberg, and others lent scientific support to the notion that all children can learn, even if (or because) they did so in somewhat different ways. On the other hand, the hopeful creed seemed politically correct. Denunciations of the biases of traditional schooling suggested that the losers had been victims of a narrow and prejudiced system. Those who had previously struggled or failed were not at fault; the system that middle-class white males built and perpetuated was supposedly the culprit (Murray, 1984).

For proof that all students could learn, educators pointed to a wide range of successful programs. Several inner-city schools were celebrated as models for achieving great gains against great odds. The "effective schools" literature of the late 1970s and the 1980s publicized those remarkable places and held out the promise that their successes could be duplicated elsewhere. The shifts in some vo/tech programs also seemed encouraging. Shop specialties could be demanding and desirable, with small class size, selective admissions, and modern equipment, although not every vo/tech school was so blessed. Changes in special education seemed particularly heartening. Under favorable conditions—active parents, well-enforced legislation, careful diagnostic testing, individualized education plans, caring teachers, and ample resources—many students once cast away as dolts turned in decent performances. The fastest growing segment of special education, the learning disabled, indicated the reluctance to brush aside children whose achievement did not match their innate ability. Your child is not dumb, lazy, or slow; she is learning disabled.

If nearly all youngsters can work at academic tasks, need they do so? Do their future lives necessitate diligence during high school? In the labor markets, some old practices continued. Having the credential mattered more than racking up high grades in hard courses. Few employers asked graduates for copies of their transcripts, grade-point averages, rank in class, coursework taken, or other evidence of academic accomplishments. Many employers tacitly discouraged harder work in school by hiring high school students to work part time, also without regard to the students' academic achievements. For more prestigious jobs, the buying power of the credential continued to slide as most white-collar jobs required some college, if not a degree or two. Street smarts and stamina rarely led to even the first rung on a career ladder. Alternative paths that once beckoned, especially apprenticeships, came to require more, not less, formal education.

As the high school diploma by itself bought less and less, was it still valued as the stepping-stone to the diploma of value, the college degree? The expansion of higher education after World War II certainly opened up access to college. Attendance rose swiftly in the 1950s and 1960s, and even in the 1970s, despite bleak projections. There were more colleges and universities, especially public institutions with modest tuitions, and much more financial aid in both public and private schools. Although there have always been places that would accept a high school graduate able to pay, it was easier to get in somewhere after World War II, particularly when the fastest growing segment of higher education was the community college. High school students can do mediocre or shoddy work and still find some college that will accept them. Reluctant to make early and irrevocable sortings, Americans are more willing than many other nations to allow second and third educational chances for the persistent.

The boom in college and university enrollments has had three other noteworthy effects. First, the college-prep track in high school is no longer as special as it once was. The honors and advanced placement sections attract top students who at one time were less likely to be in separate sections. The vast populations now in college-prep courses are astonishingly varied, including students headed for private out-of-state selective colleges alongside classmates bound for unselective in-state public colleges. A college-prep course is not necessarily rigorous.

Second, as colleges after 1950 increasingly demanded either SAT or ACT scores from applicants, students knew that ho-hum grades could be partially offset by a standardized test score that provided evidence of their innate talent. Aptitude tests promised to gauge the candidate's ability to do good work in the future regardless of the quantity or caliber of work already done. Bright students in dreadful high schools would therefore not suffer, nor would rich but dull students in prep schools have major advantages. James Conant, in his autobiography, recalled this creed: "The aptitude, not the schooling, was what counted" (Conant, 1970, p. 424). The older syllabus-specific entrance exams (common at selective schools before the 1940s) exerted more pressure then on the secondary schools than an SAT or ACT test does now. A student simply had to know the course materials because the college entrance tests gauged mastery of a curriculum, not innate capacity.

Third, as college years rather than high school years became the last stop before adulthood responsibilities for more and more youth, high schools could become more relaxed. There was less pressure to ready students for the demands of the workplace, and more willingness to let them enjoy themselves. Later on the serious business can take over; why rush that and thus deprive kids of the chance to have some fun? (Cohen and Neufeld, 1981). The unhurried pace of elementary schools crept into many high schools, but without the curiosity and excitement students in a lively elementary school display.

The job and college markets clearly told ambitious and competitive students that the most desirable slots did indeed require hard work. Many eager students knew very well the price of admission to the best places. But the payoff for seeking those prizes lay in the far future. The path of least resistance offered a fast-food job now, and tomorrow a place in the local community college.

Since mid-century the old reasons for believing that many youngsters simply would not exert effort continued to seem plausible. Many students still came to high schools frustrated or dejected by their elementary or middle school experiences. Some actively disliked schooling and misbehaved; many more were docile and apathetic, so much so that they often blamed themselves entirely, and just wanted to drift along quietly and painlessly rather than clamor for better service or smash things up. A second group, the above-average students uninterested in schoolwork, diminished a bit with the growth of gifted and talented, advanced placement, and honors offerings, but it did not disappear. Whether from peer pressure (Greene, 1988; Leahy, 1988; Welsh, 1986), lack of parental pressure (Freedman, 1990), or other reasons, quite a few did just enough to get by.

The third and largest contingent, those distracted by the natural and healthy preoccupations of adolescents, remained sizable, but it was not as clear that their rites of passage were as wholesome as they had seemed before the 1950s. In the 1950s and early 1960s, adolescent recreation seemed more raucous and less amenable to adult control, but compared to the late 1960s and afterwards, the earlier developments were tame. At that time, smoking cigarettes, drinking beer, rock and roll music, and unchaperoned parties explored but rarely exceeded the boundaries of middle-class propriety. Knowing when to stop remained an important norm through the mid-1960s. The later changes struck many adults as more ominous, especially drug use and sexual activity. Kids seemed to grow up faster, crossing thresholds sooner than their parents had or finding new ones Mom and Dad never even knew about (Winn, 1983).

While more parents worried about out-of-control children, they also felt less empowered to order their young to do this or that. Some parents were so caught up in their own curiously adolescent behaviors—identity crises, career shifts, marital realignments—that they empathized with rather than criticized their children's experimentations. Others hesitated to be old fashioned and out of step with what "all the other mothers do." Whatever the situation (and there were many), the old balance of power seemed changed by the mid-1970s, although certainly many families still closely resembled their counterparts a generation earlier.

Those same issues of authority and power relations between adults and youth marked most schools after the late 1960s. If a student resisted learning, teachers hesitated to give immediate orders or bark commands. There were legal issues to consider, with the sudden rise of concern about the rights of students and of parents. There were psychological issues also—maybe a sleepy student had worked until 2:00 A.M., or was struggling to stay off drugs, or lived with abusive parents.

The basic point is that even absent a surge of apathetic students, teachers and administrators by the early 1970s felt less entitled to tell indifferent students to work hard, pay attention, and stick to it (Grant, 1988). Although that less directive style meant considerable relaxation of the rigidity and austerity of many classrooms, it also marked a waning of educators' power to enforce their notions of what was educationally desirable (alongside greater intrafaculty disagreement over those notions). Frequently, the burden was on the students to take what the school or teacher had to offer—"it's all here but you have to make the move to get it"—on the debatable assumption that students were mature and savvy enough to choose wisely (Powell et al., 1985).

The erosion of the older foundations of teachers' authority encouraged more negotiations with students. Sometimes overt, usually tacit, the "treaties" students and teachers struck let each other off the hook without wholly abandoning the appearance of serious work. Relying on worksheets, accepting single-word answers, tolerating digressions, starting the period late and ending early: these are some common tactics to let everyone disengage quietly without veering away totally from the curriculum. None of these strategies is brand new, some are merely bad pedagogy, and others occasionally surface in a good teacher's practice. But in the past twenty years they do seem to have become more common as tactics to negotiate authority and strong enough to prevent conflict. In the wake of the unrest of the late 1960s, teachers were eager to find means of control that, although very different from the old unilateral treaties inside more regimented classrooms, nevertheless kept the peace.

The pressure to reach treaties agreeable to all parties is heightened by the expectation that all children can learn. That assumption, however noble, puts nontrivial pressure on teachers. Unlike other practitioners in various fields of human improvement (psychotherapy, social work, and exercise, for example), teachers are held responsible for the outcomes of their instruction. Although we see a patient in analysis as a co-producer of the changes achieved, carrying much of the responsibility for whatever occurs, rarely do we view contemporary American students that way. For teachers, that bind "encourages them to redefine success in terms acceptable to most clients" (Cohen, 1988, p. 68), and that, in turn, breeds treaties.

The classroom bargains have become more visible, at least to educational researchers, in the past ten years. The surge of qualitative studies of classrooms and schools yielded many glimpses of quid pro quos. Although they are not yet as widely known as the life adjustment crusade was, the quiet and largely private deals are no longer any secret. What was once harder to discern is now easier to see, and we even have a book summarizing the first wave of studies of the topic (Sedlak et al., 1986). Books by students, or ex-students posing as students, also pulled back the curtain (Owen, 1981; Crowe, 1981). It is unlikely that exposure will discourage the practices as swiftly as the early-1950s' outcry undermined life adjustment. Many of the treaties stem from the constraints of the current school day, especially its crowded and rushed schedule. It is misleading and unjust to trace treaties to the nastiness or dimness of teachers. Many fine teachers also strike treaties but on behalf of hard work and intensity. And many treaties are due to the lack of compelling incentives in the wider world to work harder, including the job market, college admissions, and youth culture influences I mentioned earlier.

Treaties are only one reason why an academic work ethic will be hard to establish firmly and widely in the immediate future. Even if the incentives in the wider world pressed students to do more, and if the country valued the life of the mind more than it has, there would still be the sheer strain of prolonged thinking. Learning does not always come easily. As Abraham Flexner once said, "In a vague way the general public wants education and believes in it; but of its difficulties and severities it has no comprehension" (Flexner, 1930, p. 50). Energy, perseverance, and tolerance for failure are necessary, and the less able students may need more of those traits to keep pace with brighter peers. Faith that exertions now will later be worthwhile is also helpful, but success itself can bring about a difficult sloughing off of a former self, which is not necessarily what family and friends expect or value (Cohen, 1988; Rodriguez, 1982; Rose, 1989).

To build a compelling case we may need to link the academic work ethic to other deeply rooted American values. Such linkages help explain why Japanese students work as strenuously as they do. Their exertions are wrapped around notions of virtuous behavior, proper mother-child relations, and correct individual-group relations (White, 1987). It is not just a college admissions system that explains Japanese students' intensity. Nor was it merely the desire for money that accounted for the work ethic in mid-nineteenth-century America, when work was seen as the center of a moral life, signaling self-discipline, emotional control, and a sense of duty (Rodgers, 1978).

It is surprising that in a country so keen on profits and pleasure, we are reluctant, even embarrassed, to spell out how using your mind well can have big financial payoffs. We do see the raw statistics on how the average college graduate earns more money, but those recitals never feature vivid and dramatic examples of how reasoning, analysis, logic, and so on can lead to large gains. It is even more striking, in light of the country's nearly universal enthusiasm for sports and recreation, that we have not built the case that thinking can be profoundly pleasurable, notwithstanding the strain and pain it involves. To establish firmly a work ethic may require new notions of work: playfulness, cooperation, immediate and visible results, feedback, chances to practice and improve. Much of that already happens now in schools, but it is in the sports competitions and various extracurricular activities. To get more work we might need to watch how our students play.

REFERENCES

Bestor, Arthur. *Educational Wastelands.* Urbana: University of Illinois Press, 1953.

Booth, Wayne. *The Vocation of a Teacher.* Chicago: University of Chicago Press, 1989.

Chapman, Paul. *Schools as Sorters.* New York: New York University Press, 1988.

Cohen, David. "Teaching Practice: Plus Que Ça Change." In *Contributing to Educational Change: Perspectives on Research and Practice,* edited by Philip W. Jackson. Berkeley, Calif.: McCutchan, 1988.

Cohen, David, and Neufeld, Barbara. "The Failure of High Schools and the Progress of Education," *Daedalus* 100 (Summer 1981): 69–89.

Conant, James. *My Several Lives.* New York: Harper and Row, 1970.

Crowe, Cameron. *Fast Times at Ridgemont High.* New York: Simon and Schuster, 1981.

Daedalus. Special Issue on Literacy, vol. 119 (Spring 1990).

Fass, Paula. *The Damned and the Beautiful.* New York: Oxford University Press, 1977.

Finkelstein, Barbara. *Governing the Young: Teacher Behavior in Popular Primary Schools in Nineteenth Century United States.* New York: Falmer Press, 1989.

Flexner, Abraham. *Universities.* New York: Oxford University Press, 1930.

Freedman, Samuel. *Small Victories.* New York: Harper and Row, 1990.

Gould, Stephen. *The Mismeasure of Man.* New York: Norton, 1981.

Grant, Gerald. *The World We Created at Hamilton High.* Cambridge, Mass.: Harvard University Press, 1988.

Greene, Bob. *Be True to Your School.* New York: Atheneum, 1988.

Hampel, Robert. *The Last Little Citadel.* New York: Houghton Mifflin, 1986.

Hofstadter, Richard. *Anti-Intellectualism in American Life.* New York: Random House, 1963.

Hollingshead, August. *Elmtown's Youth.* New York: Wiley, 1949.

Jackson, Philip. *Life in Classrooms.* New York: Holt, Rinehart, and Winston, 1968.

Johnson, Norris. *West Haven.* Chapel Hill, N.C.: University of North Carolina Press, 1985.

Kantor, Harvey. *Learning to Earn.* Madison: University of Wisconsin Press, 1988.

Kett, Joseph. *Rites of Passage.* New York: Basic Books, 1977.

Labaree, David. *The Making of an American High School.* New Haven, Conn.: Yale University Press, 1988.

Leahy, Michael. *Hard Lessons.* Boston: Little Brown, 1988.

Lowell, A. Lawrence. *At War with Academic Traditions in America.* Cambridge, Mass.: Harvard University Press, 1934.

Lynd, Albert. *Quackery in the Public Schools.* Boston: Little Brown, 1953.

Murray, Charles. *Losing Ground.* New York: Basic Books, 1984.

Owen, David. *High School*. New York: Viking, 1981.

Powell, Arthur; Farrar, Eleanor; and Cohen, David. *The Shopping Mall High School*. Boston: Houghton Mifflin, 1985.

Ravitch, Diane. *The Troubled Crusade*. New York: Basic Books, 1983.

Rodgers, Daniel. *The Work Ethic in Industrial America, 1850–1920*. Chicago: University of Chicago Press, 1978.

Rodriguez, Richard. *Hunger of Memory*. Boston: David Godine, 1982.

Rose, Mike. *Lives on the Boundary*. New York: Free Press, 1989.

Saveth, Edward. "Education of an Elite," *History of Education Quarterly* 28 (Fall 1988): 367–386.

Sedlak, Michael; Wheeler, Christopher W.; Pullin, Diana C.; and Cusick, Philip A. *Selling Students Short: Classroom Bargains and Academic Reform in the American High School*. New York: Teachers College Press, 1986.

Sternberg, Robert. "Prototypes of Competence and Incompetence." In *Competence Considered*, edited by Robert Sternberg and John Kolligian. New Haven, Conn.: Yale University Press, 1990.

Welsh, Patrick. *Tales Out of School*. New York: Viking, 1986.

White, Merry. *The Japanese Educational Challenge*. New York: Free Press, 1987.

Winn, Marie. *Children without Childhood*. New York: Pantheon, 1983.

Chapter 3

ACADEMIC EFFORT IN INTERNATIONAL PERSPECTIVE

Lois Peak

Student effort is important to parents and teachers around the world. Teachers throughout history have known that to progress, students must exert themselves to learn and remember what they are taught. A Japanese proverb says, "Without perseverance, nothing is accomplished." Shantideva (1976), a great first-century Indian philosopher, stated more poetically:

> Having patience, one must develop diligence.
> For accomplishment will dwell only in those who exert
>   themselves.
> Just as there is no movement without wind,
> So, success does not occur without diligence. [P. 52]

Although student diligence and effort are universally recognized as important, different cultures impart different meanings to the concept. To what degree should school-related activities be part of a child's daily life? How much academic effort is appropriate for children of different ages? What should teachers do to induce children to work harder? Cultures have various answers to these questions.

Students' academic effort must be seen within the broad context of all the activities societies allow and urge on their children. I will consider three ways in which cultural messages about effort are transmitted to children and students: legal mandates, cultural beliefs and expectations, and habit training.

Examples and data will be drawn from the cross-national research of Harold Stevenson and his colleagues, from the International

41

Association for the Evaluation of Educational Achievement (IEA), from my own two years of fieldwork in Japanese classrooms, and from research of others in Japanese schools.

Japan is a good case study for cross-national comparison with the United States. Its standard of living, economy, and style of life are similar. Japanese children listen to the same popular music groups and watch similar television programs. In fact, they average two or three hours more television viewing per week than U.S. students (Stevenson and Lee, 1990, p. 43).

Although many in the United States have had their interest dulled by numerous stories in the popular press that portray Japanese schools as humorless, intensely competitive places where anxious parents and teachers push children to their limits in the race for the best universities, the reality of schooling in Japan is not like this. Entrance examinations are a major hurdle for only about half of the one in five students who go on to the university (Leestma, August, George, and Peak, 1987, p. 46). If one looks beyond the media stereotypes, the lives and feelings of individual Japanese children are largely typical of children throughout the industrialized world.

When discussing cultural differences, it is convenient to state in verbal shorthand that "the Japanese" do this, and "the Americans" do that. This is not to suggest that all people in either country are the same, and should not imply that there are not important subcultural variations within each of these countries. The task of this paper is to consider the beliefs and values held to a greater or lesser degree by most Americans and Japanese. Some of these are already consciously apparent to members of the culture, and others become obvious only in cross-cultural comparison, or when viewed by an outsider.

There are fundamental differences between Japan and the United States in cultural attitudes and values, and education is one of the areas in which these attitudes are most different. Comparing the two cultures brings into sharp relief the cultural priorities and value judgments that we take for granted in everyday life. By examining our own beliefs in cross-cultural perspective, we can better understand the effect of American culture on our children's academic effort.

LEGAL MANDATES CONCERNING ACADEMIC EFFORT

School Attendance

Laws are the most fundamental way in which societies regulate student academic effort. Laws regulating the amount of time children of certain ages must spend in school are obvious indications of the minimum expectations of a society. As a measure of expectations, school attendance laws must be considered alongside the other activities society provides as legal alternatives to school.

We easily forget that compulsory schooling for all youth is a recent phenomenon. It has been only within the past one hundred years that most of the world's adults have believed formal schooling sufficiently important that they have been willing to pay for schooling and to compel their children to spend most of their childhood and adolescence in formal education.

At the most basic level, the number of days per year that a society pays to provide school attendance for its children can be seen as a rough measure of the degree to which the society believes school should be the central activity of children's lives. How does the length of the U.S. school year compare to that of other nations in this regard?

The average length of the school year for the twenty national school systems that participated in the 1986 IEA mathematics achievement study was 194 days. The average length of the school year in the United States is 180 days. Only French and Flemish Belgium require their children to spend fewer days in school than does the United States (McKnight et al., 1989, p. 52). Furthermore, the scheduling of a long, uninterrupted summer vacation in the United States enculturates our children in the habit that for a quarter of the year, they may completely disassociate themselves and their minds from school.

This is in contrast to other nations such as Japan, where the school year of 240 days is the longest of the nations studied. Japanese children go to school for ten months per year, five and a half days a week (Leestma et al., 1987, p. 10). The eight weeks of vacation are broken up throughout the year, such that no single vacation is longer than three weeks. Even during the three-week summer holiday, school buildings remain open, homework projects are assigned, and student activity clubs continue to meet. Japanese children are trained never to completely disassociate their minds from school.

Employment

The age at which a culture allows children to work full time is a good indication of how strongly the culture believes that school is its children's primary job. In semischooled preindustrial societies, schooling is in direct competition with productive work. In such societies, adolescents in the prime of their strength are an important economic asset to the family, and are frequently kept from school by their parents either to assist with family enterprises or to take wage labor to supplement the family income.

In fully industrialized societies, child labor laws, higher educational requirements for meaningful employment, compulsory schooling, and different family expectations combine to keep young children out of the labor force. Sometime during adolescence, however, employment becomes a viable alternative to schooling for children. The age and circumstances under which children are allowed to go to work vary according to cultural priorities.

In the United States, children under the age of fourteen can be employed only in very limited circumstances. Children of fourteen and fifteen are allowed to be employed in nonhazardous agricultural, retail, food service, and gasoline service establishments. According to federal law, however, they cannot work during school hours, more than three hours a day on school days, or late at night and early in the morning (U.S. Department of Labor, 1990, p. 2). Through these explicit legal requirements that schooling takes precedence over work, American society clearly establishes schooling as children's primary duty through the age of fifteen.

The picture changes for sixteen- and seventeen-year-olds, however. Whether or not a child is in school, full-time work is allowed without restriction, except in the most hazardous of occupations. Indeed, some sectors of American business depend heavily on the easy availability of teenage minimum wage employees. Custom and popular values support work as an alternative to school for teenagers. Most American schools cooperate with local business by rearranging schedules so that students can be dismissed early or arrive late, by setting up work-study programs, and by otherwise providing students easy access to the labor market. Most parents cooperate by giving their children permission to accept part-time jobs during high school.

Japanese national labor law is similar to that of the United States. Japanese children between the ages of twelve and fifteen are legally allowed to take light work outside of school hours in certain specified occupations. Both the provision allowing twelve- and thirteen-year-olds to work and the wider range of approved occupations make the law somewhat more liberal than that of the United States. However, Japan recognizes the school's first right to children's time and effort by requiring employers of children under fifteen to keep on file in the workplace a written consent from the parents and a certificate from the principal of the child's school certifying that employment does not hinder the child's education (Japanese Ministry of Labor, 1990). For children between fifteen and eighteen years of age, a broad range of full-time employment is allowed within nonhazardous occupations.

Although the letter of the Japanese law is more lenient, custom and popular values do not as readily sanction competition between employment and schooling for children's time and energy as in the United States. In Japan, most schools establish their own strict regulations designed to discourage student employment. Many academic high schools completely prohibit part-time work during the school term, and allow students to accept jobs during summer vacation only if they are approved by the school. Either job or employer may be vetoed by the school. Commercial and vocational high schools are less likely to prohibit part-time jobs completely because their students spend less time in study, as most are not planning to go to college. Even in these schools, however, restrictions on the types of jobs and the necessity of obtaining permission still apply.

Japanese schools and parents support each other in their efforts to keep adolescents out of the workplace and loosely confined to the more sheltered environments of family and school. In contrast to the United States, work is not seen as valuable in developing an early sense of responsibility. Instead, it distracts children's minds and energies from their primary job of gaining an education. Adolescents best acquire a sense of responsibility by applying themselves to their studies within the school context, it is believed. Furthermore, association with dubious adult influences in the workplace and the possession of personal spending money is seen as too heady a mix for students whose sense of morality and long-term goals is still developing (Rohlen, 1983, p. 197).

Despite the comparatively liberal Japanese national law concerning adolescent employment, the coordinated efforts of Japanese parents and schools have a very real effect in keeping students focused on their studies instead of being out in the workforce. Only 21 percent of Japanese high school students report having held any type of part-time job, compared to 63 percent of students in the United States (Leestma et al., 1987, p. 46). This is an example of the power of cultural values to create and enforce informal rules about children's behavior that are stricter than the letter of the legal sanctions.

CULTURAL BELIEFS AND EXPECTATIONS CONCERNING STUDENT EFFORT

Effort Versus Ability

Among the many values and beliefs that exist in every society, some reinforce and others undermine student academic effort. Some of the most important of these beliefs and values concern the relationship of effort to success. Most cultures acknowledge that academic success is influenced by a combination of effort and innate ability, but the relative emphasis placed on effort and ability differs. Stevenson and Lee (1990) note:

> The greater the cultural emphasis on effort, the more likely it is that parents and teachers will believe that they can be instrumental in aiding children in their academic achievement. This belief is transmitted to children, and they, too, come to believe that diligence will lead to success. If, however, adults believe that innate ability imposes critical limitations on children's progress in school, it seems unlikely that they would be motivated to make such strong efforts at assistance. [P. 7]

Stevenson and his colleagues compared the opinions of mothers and teachers in Minneapolis, Taipei, and Sendai (Japan) concerning the relative contributions of effort and ability to academic success. They asked mothers to apportion ten points among four factors that influence children's school performance: ability, effort, difficulty of schoolwork, and luck.

On the average, mothers in the three countries assigned the same average rank orders to the items: effort was the most important, ability second, task difficulty third, and luck fourth. However, mothers in the United States scored effort and ability more nearly equal than mothers in Japan and China. U.S. mothers assigned effort an average score of 3.9, and ability a score of 3.4. Taiwanese mothers assigned effort a 4.4 and ability 2.6, and Japanese mothers assigned them 5.1 and 2.4, respectively. U.S. mothers also tended to agree more strongly with statements suggesting that their children were born with their mathematics and reading abilities, and less strongly with statements that any student can be good at reading or mathematics if he or she works hard enough (Stevenson and Lee, 1990, p. 61).

Schools mirror the beliefs of mothers. In Japanese schools, effort is so consistently portrayed to children as the key to success that ability is rarely mentioned. Mottos and slogans adorn the walls of Japanese classrooms: "Become a child who can persevere," "If you try, you can do it," and the like. Many times a day, children are encouraged "gambatte" (hang in there), and "gaman shite" (persevere).

In keeping with Japanese belief that effort is much more critical to academic success than ability, ability grouping is not used in Japanese schools. Elementary and junior high classrooms are organized into a series of small mixed-ability groups similar to Scout patrols, which are required to spend much of the school day helping each other with assignments and working together. Even in high school, where students are separated into academic and vocational high schools on the basis of their earlier academic performance, within-school tracking or ability grouping is not used. All students are believed to be able to master the curriculum if they try hard enough, and those who are ahead of their peers should exert their effort toward helping their friends.

This is in marked contrast to the United States, where ability is believed to be so crucial to academic performance and potential that it is standard practice to separate children during the first weeks of first grade into ability groups for reading and sometimes for other subjects. Ability grouping continues throughout a student's school career, becoming more elaborate and encompassing more subjects as the child progresses through the system.

Japanese schools provide many opportunities for the public recognition of outstanding diligence and effort. In fact, there are no public academic awards in Japanese schools. Instead, at the year-end ceremony, students are given awards for perfect or near-perfect attendance, along with the principal's praise for their diligence and perseverance in continuing their studies in the face of minor illnesses and occasional discomfort. During the annual sports day, all students, no matter how unathletically inclined, must participate in the events, and two awards are given for the various events: the winner, and the contestant who displayed the most effort.

What are American concepts of effort and ability? In contemporary American classrooms, exhortations to "diligence" and "perseverance" have almost a mawkish and old-fashioned sound. While teachers do encourage students to "do their best," individuals are rarely given public recognition for exemplary effort, in isolation from high scores. In fact, students who try very hard despite low or average ability are typically given labels of opprobrium, ranging from "nerd" and "grind" in the popular lexicon, to "overachiever" in psychological jargon. Mirroring this, it is not surprising that American students seem to exhibit a generally lower level of effort.

Homework

Homework is important to the discussion of student effort for two reasons. First, the amount of homework teachers assign indicates the degree to which teachers believe that extra effort improves academic performance. Second, the amount of homework students do indicates how much effort students are willing to invest in their studies.

How do U.S. students rank in terms of the amount of homework they do? An analysis of mathematics homework in the twenty national school systems who participated in the second IEA mathematics achievement study showed that at both the eighth- and twelfth-grade levels, the United States is about average in both the amount of homework teachers report that they assign and the amount students report that they do (McKnight et al., 1989, pp. 72–73).

Some other countries, such as Japan and Taiwan, assign a great deal more homework, however, even to elementary students. Stevenson and his colleagues asked mothers of children in the first and fifth grades in Minneapolis, Taipei, and Sendai to estimate how much homework their children did each week. Differences between the countries were striking. First-grade children in Minneapolis were reported to spend an average of 1.2 hours on homework, in Sendai 3.9 hours, and in Taipei 8.2 hours per week. The differences continued at the fifth grade, where the U.S. students were reported to spend 4.2 hours, Japanese students 6.0 hours, and Chinese students 12.9 hours per week. These results suggest that even in elementary school, Japanese and Chinese children spend at least twice the amount of time and effort on homework that U.S. children do (Stevenson and Lee, 1990, p. 43).

The fact that American students do less homework than their counterparts in Japan and Taiwan is not their own fault. American teachers assign less homework and believe it to be less valuable. Teachers in the three cities were asked to rate sixteen methods such as quizzes, individual instruction, use of praise, and homework on a scale of one (low) to nine (high) to indicate how useful it was to students' academic development. Homework was rated fairly high (7.3) by Taiwanese teachers, average (5.8) by Japanese teachers, and low (4.4) by American teachers. In fact, the only method American teachers ranked as less useful than homework was physical punishment (Stevenson and Lee, 1990, p. 90).

Homework not only reflects the strength of teachers' belief that extra practice makes a difference and students' willingness to exert extra effort on behalf of their studies. It also reflects the culture's emphasis on training in good study habits and self-disciplined effort toward a long-term goal.

American parents do not appear to consider good study habits as critical to academic success as do parents in Asia. Mothers in Minneapolis, Sendai, and Taipei were asked if their child's academic performance had improved or declined between the first and fifth grades, and if so, what they believed to be the reason. The Chinese and Japanese mothers were much more likely to attribute changes in academic performance to better or worse study habits.

Forty percent of Taipei mothers, 27 percent of Sendai mothers, and only 9 percent of Minneapolis mothers cited study habits such as working harder, possessing better study skills, or applying oneself more effectively as the reason for their child's improvement. Poor study habits were cited as the reason for decline in academic performance by 31 percent of the Japanese and 27 percent of the Chinese mothers. So few American mothers (8 percent) thought that their child's performance had declined that the data were not broken out into separate answers (p. 80). Apparently, not only is homework a lower cultural priority in the United States, but American mothers are less likely to believe that good study habits make a great deal of difference to their children's academic success.

Children's academic performance is influenced by their parents' expectations for achievement, which are in turn influenced by cultural expectations concerning how much academic effort is appropriate for children of various ages. Compared to parents in Japan and Taiwan, American parents seem to be well satisfied with their children's academic performance. Almost 90 percent of the mothers of Minneapolis fifth graders said that they were satisfied with their child's academic performance, compared to only about 60 percent of Japanese and Taiwanese mothers. Parental satisfaction does not seem to be closely related to how much children know; although the American mothers were more satisfied, their children performed much more poorly on cross-national tests of arithmetic and reading (Stevenson and Lee, 1990, p. 76).

Not only are American mothers satisfied with their children's academic performance, they are satisfied with their children's schools as well. Ninety-one percent of mothers in Minneapolis believed that the school was doing an "excellent" or "good" job of educating their child, compared to 41 percent of mothers in Taipei and 39 percent of mothers in Sendai (p. 79). In reflecting on their data, Stevenson and his collaborators note:

Minneapolis mothers were positive and enthusiastic about their child's education. Those in Taipei and Sendai were much more critical. We believe that the difference . . . stemmed from the lower academic standards of the American mothers than those held by the Chinese and Japanese mothers. . . . American mothers were less critical, and they expected less of their children and of the schools. . . . Another possible explanation is the American mothers' lower emphasis on academic achievement. It is much easier to be satisfied with moderate levels of performance when it is not deemed to be of critical importance to a child's future. [P. 81]

As Americans, we should recognize that our students' relative lack of academic effort is not primarily our children's fault. It is a reflection of the beliefs and values of our society. From an international perspective, it can fairly be said that comparatively low academic expectations are a culturally institutionalized part of American life.

What is the appropriate place of academic pursuits in children's lives? Everywhere in the world, after school is over for the day, students engage in a combination of academic and nonacademic activities. They do homework, watch television, meet with their friends, and interact with family members. Mothers in the three cities Stevenson studied all reported that after school, their first- and fifth-grade children spent more time engaged in nonacademic activities such as play and watching television than they spent in academically related activities such as homework and reading (Stevenson and Lee, 1990, p. 43).

Which of these various pursuits do cultures single out as most significant? Which of children's various activities are worthy of their parents' notice and description? This is one of the ways in which students learn their culture's perspective on the relative significance of the many activities that fill their daily lives. When asked to describe their child's after-school activities, virtually all (99 percent) mothers of first graders in Minneapolis described nonacademic activities, such as playing with friends, socializing with family members, watching television, participating in sports, and taking music lessons. Slightly less than half (47 percent) described the academic activities their child engaged in after school, such as doing homework, reading, or playing academically related games. In Sendai, almost all mothers (93 percent) also chose to mention nonacademic activities, but academic activities were considerably more likely to be mentioned (74 percent) than in the United States. In Taipei, mothers chose to describe their child's academic activities (85 percent) more commonly than their nonacademic activities (73 percent).

By the fifth grade, Asian parents are much less likely to discuss their child's nonacademic activities. Although mothers still estimate that their children spend more after-school time in nonacademic pursuits than in academic activities, nonacademic pursuits were less frequently chosen by mothers when they were asked to describe what their child did after school. Only 38 percent of mothers in Taipei and 55 percent of mothers in Sendai discussed nonacademic activities, compared to virtually all the mothers (96 percent) in Minneapolis. Minneapolis mothers mentioned academic activities much less commonly (68 percent) than mothers in Sendai (85 percent) and in Taipei (89 percent).

Americans believe that it is important for children to be involved in activities that potentially compete with school, such as sports, friends, and hobbies. This emphasis grows by the time children enter the teenage years, a time in many cultures when students are expected to engage seriously in their studies to prepare for adult life. American high schools reflect the belief that social life, entertainment, and employment are important channels for children's energies in addition to studies and homework. Rohlen, author of a two-year ethnographic study of Japanese high schools (1983), writes:

> Americans, when they think of adolescence, think first of a virtual explosion of peer group activities. Parents expect that their adolescent sons and daughters will hardly be present after school and during weekends. Parties, jobs, cars, romance, and just "hanging out" are what we deem natural. [P. 276]

In contrast, Japan carefully maintains the school and family as the center of students' lives. The culture of adolescence and peer-group relationships, which is such a hallmark of growing up in America, is much more subdued in Japan. Rohlen notes:

> Recreational time with one's peers is almost a residual category in the Japanese case. At the most, it averages about fifteen hours per week if commuting [on bicycles or public transportation] and club activities are included. In United States surveys, no inclusive category of peer group activities is used, therefore precise comparisons are not possible. Nevertheless, there is no question that a major difference between the two nations exists. Nearly half of all American seniors report going on at least one date weekly, and parties on weekends are commonplace in the lives of an even larger percentage. Neither activity would engage as many as one in twenty Japanese adolescents in any week. American teenagers spend much weekend and vacation time together. They stay overnight regularly at homes of their friends. This rarely happens in Japan. I would estimate peer recreation time in the United States to average more than thirty hours a week, double the most liberal estimate for Japan. [P. 278]

In Japan, early experimentation with the pleasures and vices of adult life, such as romance, driving, pocket money, fashions, and the excitement and glamour of city night life, are carefully held in abeyance. Schools have rules against frequenting shopping centers, coffee shops, video and pinball houses, and other places in which students might be inclined to waste their time and neglect serious study. In many communities, parents cooperate with the head of the school counseling section in patrolling the neighborhood after school and on weekends, to ensure that students comply with regulations (Leestma et al., 1987, p. 46).

Japanese schools and parents concur in their desire to keep high school students' physical freedom comparatively limited. Automobile licenses are not granted to those under eighteen years of age, and most schools strictly prohibit their students from owning or riding motor bikes. Students must commute to school on foot, by public transportation, or by a standard three-speed bicycle (Rohlen, 1983, p. 46). Few hold jobs, and because regular weekly allowances are not a custom, students have limited pocket money.

Relations between high-school-age boys and girls in Japan are characterized by extreme shyness. Dating is rare and is generally limited to a secret meeting in an out-of-the-way coffee shop or public park. Rohlen notes:

Compared with American high school hallways and schoolyards, sprinkled with flirtations and intense boy-girl discussion, the circumspection and reticence of Japanese students is striking. "Our youth are modest and naive," I was told by a Japanese teacher who had visited American high schools for a year. Asked his opinion of American teenage relationships and pressed to be more than polite, he confided in being shocked and bewildered by the degree of open and active sexuality in American high schools. He said he had the uncomfortable feeling that he was witnessing something very primitive. Conversely, American exchange students in Japanese high schools find their counterparts "young" and "immature" in boy-girl relations. [P. 289]

Our culture values adolescence as an opportunity for children to branch out to the world outside the home and school to learn their first lessons about personal freedom, life, love, and leisure. Chemistry and Shakespeare are only a part of the larger cultural curriculum. The textbooks that purvey the wider lessons are the instruments of mass culture: teen magazines, television, youth music, and shopping malls. Parents and teachers both sympathize and agonize as they watch children learn to keep their head above water in the turbulent stream of contemporary American culture.

The United States has chosen high school as the appropriate age for students' introduction to adult culture. In Japan, these lessons are postponed until students enter the university, vocational training school, or their first job. It is only after the majority of students have finished their schooling that young people begin to date, drive, hang around in the city, drink, and come home late at night. Students in high school remain sheltered and protected, and the society conspires to keep their minds focused on study.

Our culture sends mixed messages to adolescents, encouraging them to devote their energy and enthusiasm to academic study, but at the same time to experiment with free time and adult habits. Children read the dual message, and most dutifully go through the motions at school, but reserve their enthusiasm for friends, parties, music, and shopping malls. Confronted with the glittering array of contemporary American youth culture and new to the exercise of freedom, it is not surprising that adolescents make academic effort a comparatively low priority.

Cultural values and priorities are usually described in terms of their intended constructive goals. Yet these same values automatically entail a less frequently acknowledged destructive counterpart. We encourage freedom of choice for our adolescents, forgetting that this means students are free to choose not to devote themselves to schooling. We encourage adolescent social activities and romance, forgetting that students will spend the schoolday thinking of their friends instead of algebra. American business annually spends billions of dollars developing magazines, fashions, movies, and recreation specifically targeted toward adolescents, forgetting that this means students will want to give short shrift to their homework or leave school early to go to work to earn spending money to enjoy them. Although we may not welcome both the positive and negative consequences of our values, American adolescents' assignment of a comparatively low priority to academic effort is an accurate reflection of our wider culture.

HABIT TRAINING

If the low priority American students assign to academic effort is an unintentioned by-product of other cherished cultural values, what hope is there for those who expect more from our students' educational performance? Although cultural values are not immutable, their change requires decades, and the slow development of a nationwide consensus.

Meanwhile, what can parents and teachers do to remedy lack of student effort? The answer derives from various countries' folk theories about the causes of academic effort, and their beliefs about what to do when confronted with a lack of it. In the United States, student academic effort is generally held to reflect motivation and interest in the subject matter. Teachers can overcome disinterest or a lack of effort by enlivening the material and its presentation so that students pay attention and study out of curiosity and enthusiasm.

Not too long ago in the history of American schooling, student effort was seen to be an expression of good character and moral virtue. Lack of effort was termed laziness, and teachers attempted to overcome it with punishment and by inducing a strong fear of failure. Although the era of the dunce cap and switch for those who forgot their lessons is behind us, contemporary American education retains a sense of conviction that lack of effort is a character fault for which students are to blame.

The Japanese have a different folk theory of effort. They believe that it is a combination of well-practiced personal habits and properly acquired attitudes. Diligence can be inculcated through the practice of efficient routines. The remedy for lack of effort is correct training in proper daily habits. Japanese elementary schools see this as one of the most important of their teaching goals. The key elements in this training are perseverance, a well-disciplined daily routine, and concentration skills. Although families' help is solicited in this regard, schools believe they also carry a heavy responsibility for this training.

An elementary school handout for parents of new first graders summarized this philosophy:

Children must develop the perseverance to accomplish the tasks that they are assigned. From this they come to understand "I have to do this even though I don't really want to." Unless the habit of diligence and the strength to continue are developed, children soon get tired of tasks and lose interest. We will do our best to train these habits through the daily life of the school, and we request your assistance at home through the following three activities: (1) Assign a chore and see that your child continues to perform it. (2) Don't help too quickly when your child has difficulty. (3) Raise your child according to the proverb "Scold twice and praise three times." [Genchi Elementary School, 1983, p. 6]

In the early elementary grades, schools teach effort by emphasizing physical perseverance. This is done by encouraging children to push themselves beyond what they expect they can do. Long hikes and challenging activities in physical education classes are common lessons in this. Children are not urged to compete with each other, but to keep logs and compete against their own previous records. In the winter, classrooms are only minimally heated and parents are encouraged to send their children to school dressed in shorts, in the belief that this helps children learn to develop perseverance against the cold. Teachers accompany such activities by frequent references to the importance of perseverance and effort and publicly praising and encouraging individual children who they can see are struggling to expand the psychological and physical limits of their endurance. Children come to realize that with disciplined effort, they are capable of much more than they thought they could do.

Perseverance is soon extended to academic subjects as well. Daily homework is an important part of this training. Developing the habit of setting personal resolutions and planning how to work toward them is another. An exercise relating to this that I have frequently witnessed in Japanese elementary schools occurs at the beginning of each new term. Students are encouraged to think about their past performance and set a personal goal for the coming term. Next they are encouraged to adopt a plan about how they will reach it. Students write down their goals and plans and post them on the classroom wall, and are periodically assigned a brief essay describing progress in their program of self-improvement. At the end of the term, students write a final essay describing the successes and difficulties they encountered, and they read it to the class. At the end of each student's reading, the teacher finds a few words of praise and the entire class applauds.

Japanese believe that responsible and disciplined daily habits are the root of diligence and sustained effort. A wholesome daily routine is the cornerstone of this. Children are encouraged to determine a fixed time each day at which they sit down to do their homework. Japanese schools' emphasis on daily routine extends far beyond this, however.

Teachers at all levels devote considerable class time to discussing with their students the importance of going to sleep and arising early and at the same time each day, and carefully following an invariant morning routine of toothbrushing, face washing, and breakfast. Students are also encouraged to develop an evening routine of checking their book bag and equipment to be sure that everything necessary for the next day is ready, then laying out the uniform and clothing for the next day before they go to sleep. This emphasis on developing and maintaining proper daily habits is believed not only to increase the likelihood that children will come to school properly prepared each day, but also to foster self-discipline and discourage procrastination and overindulgence in time-wasting activities.

Although so much public emphasis on personal resolutions and tidy daily routines may strike Americans as bordering on priggish, Japanese teachers and parents take it very seriously, and it seems to rub off on Japanese children. Even popular teen magazines carry articles on these subjects. Next to double-page glossy photos of rock stars and television idols are articles with comical illustrations and question-and-answer columns about how to get up on time in the morning and how to arrange one's study time most effectively, and advertisements for home-study courses on how to improve your penmanship.

To supplement perseverance and good daily habits, Japanese teachers also believe that concentration and mindfulness in academic activities is a habit that can be taught. Particularly in the classroom, academic effort translates into the ability to listen carefully and remember what the teacher said. In Japanese elementary classrooms, the habit of listening is broken down into a series of small routines, which children practice until they become habit and then continue until they become second nature.

During the first weeks of first grade, students are taught a series of steps by which they prepare themselves for study. First, they learn how to lay out materials on their desk, with pencil, notebook, and textbook each arranged in a particular place. Again and again, the teacher has students lay out their materials and put them away again, checking their desks until all students can do it rapidly and correctly. Cueing the routine and checking the desks is then delegated to the daily student monitor.

Similarly, children learn a routine for coming to order in their seats, which involves a precise arrangement of feet on the floor, hands in their laps, faces forward, mouths closed, and eyes on the blackboard. Students practice this routine again and again, just as a drill team practices making an about-face, until the class is able to come instantly to order on the teacher's cue. Checking this routine is again delegated to the student monitor, who cues it thereafter at the beginning of each class period.

Concentration exercises are also common in the early grades, to lengthen students' ability to listen to the teacher (Peak, 1986, p. 120). After bringing the students to order, the teacher challenges the class to remain silent and unmoving for as long as possible, with their eyes on a circle on the blackboard. In the manner of a coach training a group of beginning athletes, initial efforts are lavishly praised, but demands are short and gradually lengthened as students develop their skill. A daily record is kept of the amount of time the class is able to maintain the silent focus. After several months of practice, even first graders become able to join the rest of the student body in standing in formation at attention in school assemblies without talking or moving for as long as ten minutes.

In order to help children develop the habit of remembering what they are taught, most Japanese elementary schools begin teaching children how to take notes during the second term of first grade. Each subject has its own notebook, which is to be put on the desk along with the textbook at the beginning of each class. Teachers train children how to use these and structure their lessons so that use of the notebook is an integral part. Each day, children are trained to date a new page and copy the words that the teacher outlines on the blackboard. The notebook also contains individual notes and all homework in that subject. By the fifth or sixth grade, Japanese students use these notebooks as conscientiously as most American graduate students. Japanese teachers believe that these notebooks are very important not only for developing good study habits, but also for providing the child with a record of his or her academic progress.

Although American cultural beliefs about student effort are not based on the Japanese assumption that academic effort derives from habits that can be trained, there seems to be much common sense in the Japanese approach. Americans are typically reluctant to invade the personal independence of individuals to recommend the correct time to get up and when to pack one's bookbag for school. Yet our desire to encourage children's personal independence and autonomy is purchased at the price of having American students live their lives much more as they choose. A comparative lack of emphasis on academic effort is part of the bargain.

CONCLUSIONS

The lack of student effort we decry in the United States is frequently ascribed to a breakdown in or absence of values. I have argued, however, that the cause is not an absence of values, but rather the inevitable consequence of the conflict between academic effort and the other cherished values we have chosen for our society.

In the United States, doing well in school is only one of the many goals we have for our children. Compared to Japan and other Asian cultures, we want our children to be interested and involved in sports, part-time jobs, friends, and hobbies. A childhood and youth focused on homework and school seems colorless, boring, and lacking important opportunities to enjoy life. Because our culture emphasizes other priorities in addition to school, the inevitable result is that few students reserve their best efforts for study.

Do Americans care enough about improving our students' academic effort to campaign long and hard enough to change our cultural priorities? Are we willing to do this at the risk of de-emphasizing some of our other cultural values? These questions are not easy to answer. However, those who wish to help the students under their care exert a bit more effective effort might borrow some ideas from the Japanese approach to habit training and encourage American children to also develop daily routines and classroom habits that are more conducive to study.

REFERENCES

Genchi Elementary School. "Educational Goals for First Graders." Matsumoto, Nagano Prefecture, Japan: Genchi Elementary School, 1983.

Japanese Ministry of Labor. *Labor Standards Law*, Article 56, Provision on Youth Employment, Chapter VI. Tokyo: Ministry of Labor, 1990.

Leestma, Robert; August, Robert L.; George, Betty; and Peak, Lois. *Japanese Education Today*. Washington, D.C.: U.S. Government Printing Office, 1987. ERIC ED 275, 620.

McKnight, Curtis C.; Crosswhite, F. Joe; Dorsey, John A.; Kifer, Edward; Swafford, Jane O.; Travers, Kenneth J.; and Cooney, Thomas J. *The Underachieving Curriculum: Assessing U.S. School Mathematics from an International Perspective*. Champaign, Ill.: Stipes Publishing Co., 1989.

Peak, Lois. "Training Learning Skills and Attitudes in Japanese Early Education Settings." In *Early Experience and the Development of Competence*, edited by William Fowler. New Directions for Child Development, No. 32. San Francisco: Jossey–Bass, 1986.

Rohlen, Thomas. *Japan's High Schools*. Berkeley: University of California Press, 1983.

Shantideva. *A Guide to the Bodhisattva's Way of Life*. Dharmasala, India: Library of Tibetan Works and Archives, 1976.

Stevenson, Harold, and Lee, Shin-Ying. "Contexts of Achievement: A Study of American, Chinese, and Japanese Children," *Monographs of the Society for Research in Child Development* 55, Nos. 1–2 (1990): 1–119.

U. S. Department of Labor. *Child Labor Requirements in Nonagricultural Occupations under the Fair Labor Standards Act*, Publication WH-1330. Washington, D.C.: Wage and Hour Division, Employment Standards Administration, U. S. Department of Labor, 1990.

Part II
Motivating Students in Secondary Schools

Chapter 4

SCHOOL CULTURE, SOCIAL POLITICS, AND THE ACADEMIC MOTIVATION OF U.S. STUDENTS

B. Bradford Brown

Over the past two decades a steady stream of reports has provided a pessimistic portrait of American high schools and their students. Boyer (1983) points to a steady decline between 1960 and 1980 in students' average scores on a variety of standardized measures of achievement—for example, scores have declined 30 points on the mathematics portion and 60 points on the verbal portion of the Scholastic Aptitude Test. Ravitch and Finn (1987) despair over students' shockingly low knowledge of American history. Lerner (1982) acknowledges that in mathematics and science American students are routinely outperformed by students of the same age in Europe and the Far East.

To be sure, educators must shoulder some of the blame for the poor performance of American high school students. Teachers often rely on "drill and lecture" rather than challenge students to higher-

---

Preparation of this chapter was supported in part by the Office of Educational Research and Improvement, Washington, D.C., by the Spencer Foundation, Chicago, Ill., and by the Wisconsin Center for Education Research, University of Wisconsin—Madison. The opinions expressed are those of the author and do not necessarily reflect the views of the sponsoring organizations. For further information, write to B. Bradford Brown, Dept. of Educational Psychology, 1025 W. Johnson St., Madison, Wis., 53706.

order thinking (Newmann, 1988); systems of tracking or ability grouping often serve the needs of high achievers better than those of low achievers (Gamoran and Mare, 1989). Yet, such factors cannot explain students' remarkable absence of academic discipline and intellectual curiosity. On average, American teenagers devote less time to homework each *week*—three and one-half hours or so (see Chapter 6 in this volume)—than they spend watching television each *day*. Little of their out-of-school time is devoted to reading, hobbies, or other academic pursuits (Csikszentmihalyi and Larson, 1984).

What factors, beyond school itself (instructional strategies, school structure), might account for the apparent anti-intellectual orientation of American youth? The peer group is one possibility. Many educators and social scientists have argued that peer groups distract teenagers from academic achievement by focusing their attention on more frivolous matters: popularity or social status, athletic prowess, and so on (Coleman, 1961; Fordham and Ogbu, 1986). Others, however, contend this is much too generic and too pessimistic a portrait of teenage peer culture (Brown, 1990). How is the peer culture organized in high schools? What contributions do peer-group norms and peer pressures make to students' achievement patterns? What can educators do in response? We will address these questions in the remainder of this chapter.

TEENAGE PEER CULTURES: THE EMERGENCE OF SCHOOL CROWDS

To understand the role that peer groups play in students' motivation to learn, it is best to begin with an understanding of the peer-group system. To accomplish this, one must approach the school from an adolescent's, rather than an adult's, perspective. Adults often view the high school simply as an institution for learning, a place in which students march from classroom to classroom in pursuit of knowledge about a variety of academic disciplines. Yet, at least one-third of teenagers' time at school is spent in *nonacademic* environments (the lunchroom, extracurricular activities, etc.). In fact, most students experience high school as a series of constantly shifting landscapes: from structured to semistructured to unstructured activities, from teacher-dominated to peer-oriented environments. What is more, when asked to specify the *best* thing about high school, far more students respond "being with my friends" than something about teachers, classes, learning, or achievement (Everhart, 1983).

From the student's perspective school is not just a place to master the English vocabulary or unravel the mysteries of science. It is a place to work on the broader "developmental agenda" of adolescence, which in twentieth-century America involves adjusting to bodily changes precipitated by puberty, becoming more autonomous and self-directed, acquiring a sense of identity, making initial decisions about an occupation or career, committing to a set of values, and mastering new social skills—especially those related to romantic relationships. All these demands are on teenagers' minds while they are, ostensibly, busy learning in high school classrooms. And all these demands figure into a teenager's behavior at school—in and outside the classroom.

Because teenagers share the same basic developmental agenda, one might suspect that they exhibit similar attitudes, activities, and behaviors. Indeed, one of the strongest stereotypes of adolescents is that they are fastidious conformists, all listening to the same music, wearing the same type of clothing, endorsing the same values, and so on. Such an assumption underlies many portraits of the "youth subculture" and generational conflict (see Brown, 1990). In reality, however, there are a variety of ways to respond to the developmental demands of adolescence: different occupations to pursue, different values to espouse, different identities to internalize, and so on. As a result, even in rather homogeneous communities adolescents display a wide range of lifestyles or patterns of adaptation.

Some of the lifestyles are reified into what are commonly referred to as "crowds." They represent prototypic responses to the developmental demands of adolescence. Some crowd labels are timeless. Groups such as the jocks, brains, populars, and nerds emerge in descriptions of the social world of high school that have been written decades apart. Other crowd labels are time-bound—prototypic lifestyles that respond to the historical moment: greasers, rappers, skinheads, and the like. The crowd label reflects an especially salient characteristic of the prototypic lifestyle: intellectual competence (brains, "speds"), ethnic background (Asians, blacks, Mexicans), family socioeconomic status (richies, west-siders), a prominent activity or extracurricular pursuit (jocks, druggies, thrashers, "band fags"), social status or social skill (populars, nerds, snobs). Behind the label, however, is a much more extensive set of stereotypes that describes the group's hangout at school, academic orientation, typical weekend activities, involvement in illegal activities, orientation toward others (cliquish, friendly, combative), and so on (Brown, Lohr, and Trujillo, 1990; Eckert, 1989; Kinney, 1990; Larkin, 1979). Adolescents seem well aware of the crowds in their school. They can identify the stereotypic norms of each group and specify which of their peers belongs to each crowd (Brown, Lohr, and Trujillo, 1990).

In other words, crowds are a prominent feature of the social fabric of adolescence. They are not only the subject of social scientific (especially ethnographic) studies of teenagers, but also the focus of classic novels (e.g., the work of S. E. Hinton) and films about teenagers (e.g., *Grease, The Breakfast Club, Revenge of the Nerds*). Further, they are essentially an adolescent institution. Fully articulated crowd labels are not apparent until adolescence and they are rarely used by adults to describe or categorize a set of individuals. To be sure, children often label peers with crowd-like terms: "she's good at sports," "he's a brain," "she's such a nerd!" But these labels point out one characteristic of the peer, not a whole set of stereotypic attitudes and activities as adolescent crowd labels do. Adults also shy away from the global descriptions that crowd labels provide in favor of more specific statements about others: "she's quite ambitious," "he's too aggressive," "they're a loving family."

Why are crowds so prominent during adolescence? Because, some social scientists respond (Newman and Newman, 1976), becoming affiliated with a crowd is the preeminent developmental task of early adolescence, a necessary precursor to developing an autonomous sense of identity. After all, coming to terms with who one is and committing to an occupation and a set of values are formidable tasks, especially when one is struggling to adjust to a new body and master new social roles (boyfriend/girlfriend, part-time worker). Individuals who feel uncertain or overwhelmed by the demands of adolescence may find great comfort in "latching on" to a crowd because it offers a well-defined provisional identity (in its stereotypic activities and values) and a base from which to develop a social network or support system. Technically, crowds are not groups in the traditional sense of the term: a set of people who interact with each other. Instead, crowds define and "group" adolescents according to their most obvious abilities, interests, or activities (Brown, 1990). But since "birds of a feather flock together," it is not uncommon for members of a particular crowd to coalesce into a circle of friends. Thus, a teenager who is good at sports may consciously strive to become part of the jock crowd not only because the norms of this crowd seem to fit well with her or his own budding interests and values but also because it will bring the teen into contact with like-minded peers who can become friends or partners in social activities. Other teenagers who act in "jockish" ways may be consistently labeled as jocks by peers; they will be expected to conform to jock crowd norms and endorse the stereotypic attitudes and behaviors of this crowd.

In sum, crowds emerge in adolescence to help individuals master the developmental tasks of this stage of life, especially in developing an autonomous sense of identity. They do not simply identify one prominent characteristic of a teenager but define in more comprehensive terms a lifestyle and value orientation. The diversity of teenage crowds underscores the fact that adolescents are not a homogeneous group. They confront the developmental tasks of adolescence in diverse ways, which are recognized as disparate lifestyles. The tendency of teenagers to routinely separate each other into crowds affirms the existence and importance of these disparate lifestyles and strategies of adaptation.

There are two important lessons to be learned from these insights about the social system of the high school. First, it is foolhardy to speak of teenagers in generic terms, as if they were all alike. One can speak of the *average* level of achievement or motivation to learn, but such statistics fail to capture the important diversity within the student body of most high schools. Second, attempts to treat high school students strictly as individuals are also misleading because they ignore the social pressures that teenagers face to align themselves with a crowd. In other words, understanding the dynamics of high school crowds can provide important insights into the nature of students' motivation (or lack of it) to excel academically.

THE CONNECTION OF CROWDS TO SCHOOL AND ACHIEVEMENT

For this to be true, however, it must be the case that crowds have some bearing on students' lives in high school, particularly their level of academic motivation and academic achievement. In other words, one must demonstrate that crowds are an important component of school and that schooling (or learning) is an important component of crowds.

School as the Locus of Crowd Interactions

As has been noted, teenagers spend a good number of their waking hours at school and come to regard it as a place for peer socializing and personal development as well as a place for academic instruction and learning. Crowds figure heavily in these components of teenagers' lives, so it is not surprising that crowds are readily apparent at school. In fact, crowds often become institutionalized, formally or informally, into the structure of the school. Members of one crowd often lay claim to a specific table in the lunchroom or to one of the entrances or hallways in the school as their hangout (Cusick, 1973; Eckert, 1989; Larkin, 1979). Crowds often develop an implicit "ownership" of particular school-sponsored activities. Larkin (1979), for example, described how the "socies" were placed in charge of selecting acts for the talent show in one school, and how student government officers routinely came from the ranks of the "politicos." What is more, school rules or policies may be altered to accommodate the needs or interest of a particular crowd, as, for example, when the administration establishes a "smoking lounge" that quickly becomes a hangout for the druggie crowd.

In sum, crowds routinely "stake out turf" at school, locating a place and a set of activities that can accommodate their interests and activities. The school serves as the social institution in which crowds originate, coalesce into distinctive groups, socialize members into how to act, and forge alliances or enmities with other crowds. But this fails to establish the link between peer crowds and student achievement patterns. It is possible that teenagers divide their time at school into two distinct spheres—informal interaction with peers under the guidance of peer crowds and peer norms, and formal academic instruction and extracurricular participation, which are controlled and supervised by adults. Many social scientists choose to portray teenage peer culture in just this fashion—as a world apart from academic achievement and other pursuits that prepare an adolescent for adulthood (Coleman, 1961). Thus, they tend to dismiss peer culture as an essentially anti-intellectual component of teenagers' lives.

This perspective, however, fails to recognize that to a large extent crowds are identified and organized by the ways in which members respond to the formal mission of the high school. Academic performance levels, commitment to learning, and extracurricular participation are major dimensions by which all crowds are routinely stereotyped (Brown, Lohr, and Trujillo, 1990). In many cases, crowds derive their label from one of the high school's two major formal programs: academic instruction (e.g., brains) or extracurricular activities (e.g., jocks, politicos). In fact, according to one recent study (Clasen and Brown, 1985), school involvement (whether or not to try for good grades, get along with teachers, go out for school activities) is one of five major domains in which adolescents perceive peer pressure to be operating; the others are peer involvement, family involvement, peer conformity, and misconduct.

Peer Pressure and Academic Achievement

Like peer culture, peer pressure is not a straightforward phenomenon. Not only do adolescents perceive peer pressure in a variety of domains, but they disagree about its direction. That is, some adolescents report that friends exert pressure to engage in a certain activity while other adolescents assert that their friends pressure them to refrain from the activity (Clasen and Brown, 1985). In some cases, the degree and direction of peer pressure varies considerably by adolescents' age or crowd affiliation; in other cases, perceptions of peer pressure appear to be uniform across age groups or crowds.

In view of the limited attention that most American students give to academics, one might expect to find *academically* related peer pressures to be uniformly low or even negative (friends discourage adolescents from studying or getting good grades). Surprisingly, however, of the fifty-five items on Clasen and Brown's peer-pressure inventory, pressure to "finish high school" was the highest-scoring item in all four schools in their study; pressure to "get good grades" also was in the top five items in two of the schools. As a group, school-involvement pressures were clearly overshadowed by peer-involvement pressures, but were just as strong as peer-conformity pressures and significantly stronger than peer pressures to be involved with family or in misconduct (see Figure 4.1). Of course, the strength of school-involvement pressures varied considerably among crowds. The

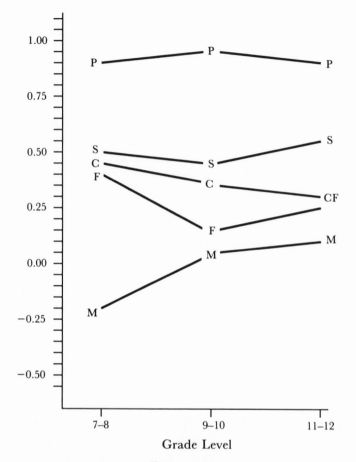

Grade Level

Figure 4.1

Grade Differences in Mean Levels of Perceived Peer Pressures

P = peer involvement
S = school involvement
C = peer conformity
F = family involvement
M = misconduct.

Scores above 0.00 indicate mean pressure is *toward* the activity; scores below 0.00 indicate mean pressure is *against* the activity.

fact remains, however, that most teenagers reported that their friends encourage them to do well in school and put considerable pressure on them to get a high school diploma. It would be premature to generalize these findings beyond Clasen and Brown's (1985) predominantly white, middle-class, Midwestern sample. Yet, the findings offer a puzzling contrast to the common image of middle-class, teenage peer culture as anti-intellectual.

ACADEMIC PRESSURES AMONG ADOLESCENT CROWDS

If adolescents are, indeed, devoted to their peers and intent on fitting into a crowd, and if crowds, in general, do encourage members to achieve in school, then why aren't teenagers dedicated to the task? Is this a plausible portrait of peer pressure? Is it possible that adolescents blithely ignore the press toward achievement that they receive from friends?

Unraveling this puzzle requires a more careful analysis of the nature of peer pressures that adolescents report. It is especially important to distinguish between academic *achievement* and academic *excellence* and to recognize the orientation of peer pressures toward academic *products* rather than *processes*.

Achieving Versus Excelling

Decades ago, Coleman (1961) asked students from several Chicago-area high schools what they would most like to be remembered for in high school: a brilliant student, an athletic star (among boys) or leader of activities (among girls), or the most popular person in the class. The relatively small number of students (31 percent of the boys and 28 percent of the girls) selecting brilliant student as their answer bolstered Coleman's case that the teenage peer culture was oriented toward social or extracurricular fame rather than serious scholarship. Although this is one reasonable interpretation of the findings, there are others. Coleman forced respondents to choose among three extreme types. The choice was not between being a dedicated student, an extracurricular performer, or a sociable person, but between being an academic, extracurricular, or social *standout* or star. Perhaps adolescents were disinclined to select "brilliant student" as their legacy not because of the focus on academics but because of the emphasis on brilliant, exceptional achievement. After all, students in his sample *did* acknowledge good grades as an important criterion for gaining membership in the leading crowd. In most schools it ranked fourth or fifth in importance among a list of nine criteria that Coleman presented to students.

Support for this interpretation can be found in Clasen and Brown's (1985) recent analysis of adolescents' perceptions of peer pressures. As noted already, academic peer pressures—especially pressure to finish high school—were perceived to be quite strong in their sample. On closer inspection, however, one realizes that adolescents were identifying pressures to *get by* academically more than to excel. The encouragement from peers was simply to *finish* high school or get *good* grades, not necessarily to graduate *cum laude* and head off to a first-rate college. In fact, another item on Clasen and Brown's inventory, peer pressure to "excel" (to stand out in academics or athletics or whatever), finished well down the list when items were rank ordered from most to least pressure. It is not surprising, then, that many adolescents are fearful that doing *too* well in school (academically) will lead to social sanctions (Ishiyama and Chabassol, 1985). These studies reveal that the general peer norm is neither to disparage academic achievement nor to exalt it, but to encourage adolescents to do moderately well, to strive for academic *adequacy* rather than academic *excellence*.

Product Versus Process

Furthermore, according to Clasen and Brown's (1985) work, adolescents focus more on product than process. The pressures students perceived from peers were oriented toward finishing high school and getting good grades rather than working hard or learning. The objective is not necessarily to master a body of knowledge and develop scholarly habits and skills but to fulfill a requirement or get a diploma. To be sure, one way of obtaining good grades is to work hard and learn the material, and some students will follow this formula. There are, however, other means of responding to the pressure: becoming "test-wise," cheating, or cajoling the teacher into lowering expectations—all of which allow students to make the grade and get the diploma without putting forth great effort to acquire knowledge.

Several observers of American high schools have reported that high school teachers routinely forge implicit treaties with their students in which academic demands are lowered in exchange for students' compliance with norms of conduct in the classroom (Boyer, 1983; Powell, Farrar, and Cohen, 1985). Teachers agree not to challenge students' intellect if students agree not to challenge teachers' authority. We know, as well, that the number of high school students who admit to cheating occasionally is quite high—55 percent of students in one recent survey (Norman and Harris, 1981). Practices such as copying homework are so commonplace that students often do not regard them as cheating (Greenberger and Steinberg, 1986).

The general point, however, is that peer pressures direct high school students toward moderate levels of achievement but stop well short of encouraging true devotion to scholarship. In some respects, then, it is inappropriate to point to peer pressure as the root cause of the lack of academic effort observed among high school students. Yet, peer pressure does seem to be a factor in that it imposes upper (as well as lower) limits on the intellectual effort that students can put forth without fearing some sanctions from their peers.

Again, however, I am guilty of speaking of peer influence in generic terms, as if peer pressures were roughly equivalent for all adolescents. I noted earlier that the magnitude of academic peer pressures varies substantially among crowds. Clasen and Brown (1987), for example, found that whereas "brains" reported strong peer pressure to do well in school, "druggies" and "dirtballs" perceived little if any academic pressure from friends, with other groups (jocks, normals, populars, and unpopulars) posed at various points between these two crowds (see Figure 4.2). Such differences in achievement norms and pressures can set adolescents on a "collision course" if, as is often the case in American high schools, members of different peer groups find themselves mixed together in the same classroom.

THE DYNAMICS OF ANTI-ACHIEVEMENT PEER PRESSURES

In conversations my colleagues and I conducted recently with high school students participating in a study of family and peer influences on school achievement patterns, we discovered that many

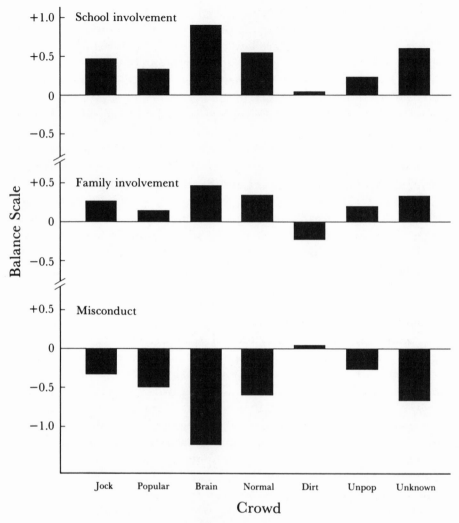

Figure 4.2
Crowd Differences in the Balance of Perceived Peer Pressures
Scores above the line indicate a balance of pressure toward the
domain; scores below the line indicate a balance of pressure against
the domain. (Adapted from Clasen and Brown, 1987.)

freshmen enter high school with a sense of foreboding. They perceive the academic requirements of high school to be much more difficult and demanding than what they experienced in middle school, forcing them to study harder and cope with test grades that are below their accustomed standard. They express great sympathy for classmates who cannot seem to meet teachers' demands or understand subject material well enough to get adequate grades. Often they will try to assist a struggling peer by studying with the student or allowing the student to copy their homework. But their sympathy and concern for those who are having difficulty are counterbalanced by the enmity and ridicule they direct at high-achieving peers. Rather than regarding these students with envy or esteem, the ninth graders tended to blame the high achievers for their own frustrations and endow the high achievers with undesirable characteristics. This was our first hint of the normative pressures and sanctions that are brought to bear on those who strive to excel academically in high school.

The "Brain-Nerd" Connection

Reports on American schools often focus on students' *disinclination* to apply themselves academically. Nevertheless, there have always been and, one hopes, will continue to be a good number of students in high school who are dedicated to the task of learning. In fact, this group constitutes one of the most frequently identified crowds in the peer-group system (Brown et al., 1990; Schwendinger and Schwendinger, 1985). With labels such as "grinds," "intellectuals," "straight-As," or "brains," this group is singled out for its emphasis on excelling academically. Yet, as I have argued earlier, there is more to a group than its label. There is more to being a brain than getting good grades, just as there is more to being a jock than doing well in athletics. Brown and colleagues (1990) asked a sample of adolescents to list the major crowds in their school, then indicate the stereotypic traits of each group. Not surprisingly, 99 percent of the respondents who mentioned a brain crowd described them as immersed in their studies; but there was also general consensus that brains were only moderately involved in extracurricular activities, given to conservative dress and grooming styles, and likely to hang out at school in the library or academic classrooms. What is more, 82 percent of the sample portrayed brains as prone to spending leisure time alone rather than with peers, and three-fourths of the respondents described brains as socially inept ("not with it"). Often, adolescents will put this stereotype more bluntly, equating the brain crowd with the group known as nobodies, losers, geeks, or nerds (Kinney, 1990). Lockwood (1989, p. 5) cites one teenager who confessed:

[High achievers] are definitely different, but I don't know how to say it without sounding really bad! I guess most high achievers would be labeled nerds or wouldn't have much of a social life. The popular kids are the ones who always go to dances and are on Homecoming Court and you don't see high achievers in those positions a lot of the time. . . . A lot of high achievers are really focused on school and don't even care about having a social life. And others—but not very many–do really well in school and are ambitious but still have a good time.

This is hardly a flattering portrait of the brain group's social interests and social skills. Yet, the stereotype of brains as a "nerdish" group is a common one. Socially inept intellectuals are common characters in television "sit-coms" (e.g., Frazier and Lilluth on "Cheers") and Hollywood movies (e.g., *Revenge of the Nerds*). Perhaps the association between brains and nerds in teenage peer culture is simply a reflection of a prejudicial view of intellectuals common to the larger culture. On the other hand, adolescents may be sending a message to high-achieving peers that there is a heavy price to be paid for academic excellence. In becoming scholarly a teenager risks inheriting the reputation as a brain and because of the social ineptitude expected of this crowd, being ostracized from peer social activities.

Why are teenagers so derisive of high-achieving peers? Two reasons spring to mind (Brown, 1989b). First, high achievers are "swimming against the developmental tide" of adolescence, in which one is expected to replace dependence on adults with an autonomous sense of identity and a capacity to make one's own decisions and chart one's own course in life. High achievers, on the other hand, reinforce a system of adult control that interferes with this developmental press toward autonomy and freedom from adult restrictions. Other than parents, the adults most likely to impose rules on teenagers are teachers, and school *is* a very rule-laden environment (Boyer, 1983; Hampel, 1986). High achievers not only accept this arrangement but seem to thrive on it, affirming the legitimacy of adult control at a time when many adolescents want to question it.

A second reason for peers to deride the brain crowd is that high achievers make other students work harder. Their academic diligence and academic success can incite teachers to raise expectations for the entire class and, correspondingly, raise requirements for C or B or A level work. Often, this process is made quite explicit by teachers, with comments such as "The assignment is not that hard; if you all just buckled down and studied like Maria does, you'd get good grades too!" Students who choose not to work harder or who cannot perform up to the higher standards even with additional effort can develop resentment for the high achievers who seem to be the source of their academic failings.

In short, high achievers reinforce a system of adult control and set standards of performance that increase the efforts that their peers have to put into schoolwork. Peers seem to express their dissatisfaction or resentment by turning academic winners into social losers, that is, by classifying high achievers as brains and emphasizing the "nerdish" character of this crowd's social interests and abilities. This process is not necessarily vengeful or even conscious. Nor is it necessarily a distortion of reality. In unpublished data from our most recent study, for example, we have discovered that students associated with the brain crowd do report spending less time with friends and less time "partying" than students associated with most other major crowds. Further, nerds outscore all other major crowds on our measure of "school engagement" (fascination with classes and learning). The process of linking brains to nerds is better understood as a rather unconscious effort to use peer-group stereotypes to vent anxiety and frustration over the academic demands of high school.

However accurate the association between brains and nerds really is, the social stigma attached to the brain crowd seems to be a powerful disincentive for associating with this crowd. In a recent study of three Midwestern high schools, Brown (1989b) discovered that less than 10 percent of the students with a straight-A average perceived themselves to be part of the brain crowd; the percentage was much lower among females (4 percent) than males (18 percent) but did not vary substantially by ethnic background. What is more, of the students who were consistently associated with the brain crowd by their peers, less than a third saw themselves as one of the brains. Kinney (1990) found a similar process of denial in his ethnographic study of a different Midwestern school. In his study, students tended to lump the brains and nerds ("dweebs") into the same crowd. Most members of this group, however, denied their peers' labels, preferring instead to be viewed as part of the "normals."

High achievers seem to be uncomfortable with the brain label. Many simply deny the association peers draw between themselves and the brain/nerd group, but there are other strategies for avoiding this derogatory peer-group classification. The most obvious one is simply to stop devoting oneself to classes and getting high marks—to become an underachiever. It is unclear how many high achievers adopt this strategy, but in mixed-ability classrooms it is an attractive solution to the threat that high achievers receive from peers to lower their devotion to studies or suffer a degree of social ostracism. Indeed, adolescents' efforts to cope with peer pressure against academic excellence deserve more attention than they have received from researchers.

The Burden of "Acting White"

Peer pressures against academic excellence, about which I have spoken in generic terms so far (as if they applied rather equally to different demographic groups of teenagers), display an intriguing "twist" when observed among minority adolescents. Fordham and Ogbu (1986) recently described the plight of high achievers whom they observed and interviewed in an inner-city high school serving a virtually all-black, lower-class population. As in studies of middle-class whites, the high achievers in this school were accorded the label of "brainiac," which was associated with a variety of undesirable characteristics (wimpishness, suspicion of homosexual tendencies). In addition, however, brainiacs were accused of "acting white"— disavowing their ethnic heritage in an effort to become accepted by the dominant group in the wider society. This, the authors argued, reflected the belief system of many black teens that academic achievement was not a reliable path to occupational success unless it was accompanied by renouncement of one's cultural background in favor of white, middle-class values. High achievers were not simply reinforcing a system of adult control but embracing a different cultural value system. By getting good grades and getting along well with teachers, they were acceding to the subtle but powerful racial prejudice that keeps oppressed minorities such as blacks in economically disadvantaged circumstances. Others have observed similar pressures operating in samples of black and Hispanic youth (Fuller, 1984; Matute-Bianchi, 1986). In Matute-Bianchi's study, however, the derisive comments about high achievers acting white were concentrated in one crowd, the Chicanos, rather than emanating from Hispanic students as a whole. Thus, there is some question about just how broadly based the sanctions against "acting white" are among minority youth. Survey studies, rather than the ethnographic methods on which researchers have relied to date, may be better suited to answer this question.

In Fordham and Ogbu's (1986) study the responses of black high achievers to anti-achievement peer pressures were similar to those that appear among white, middle-class high achievers. Some continued to work hard in their classes but also adopted a different image among peers so that they could escape the derogatory "brainiac" crowd label. For example, a high achiever would "cut up" in class when the teacher was not looking so that peers would regard him as a "regular guy." Leading such a double life—the serious student in the eyes of teachers and the "class clown" in the eyes of peers—without being caught in their deception by either group was clearly an emotional strain on many of these students. Some high achievers chose the simpler strategy of lowering their achievement levels to a point where they no longer risked any peer sanctions.

At present, however, we have little idea how frequently minority students suffer these ethnically based pressures against high achievement, or how frequently they employ various strategies to respond to the pressures. Matute-Bianchi (1986) did not comment on student reactions to accusations of "acting white," but because the accusations were confined largely to one crowd, it may have been easier for good students to ignore them—especially if the crowd of accusers did not enjoy very high status in the peer system. In other words, the power of these peer sanctions should depend on the dynamics of the peer system. The more generalized the association between high achievement and acting white, and the stronger the minority student's desire to maintain a sense of ethnic identity, the more it is likely to undermine students' achievement efforts. Researchers should press for a more systematic and comprehensive examination of the effort in minority culture to link academic achievement to renouncement of ethnic identity.

The Higher Priority of Nonacademic Pressures

The brain-nerd connection and the burden of acting white highlight the contributions that peer groups can make toward diminishing the academic efforts made by high achievers or intellectually gifted adolescents. But critiques of American schools and student achievement patterns suggest that these are not the only students who seem undevoted to academics. To understand the dynamics operating in other peer groups, we may again return to the portrait of group norms and peer pressures presented earlier. As was illustrated in Figure 4.1, for most adolescents peer pressure toward school involvement is modestly strong but is overshadowed by pressure toward *peer* involvement, that is, to be active socially, spend time with friends, and the like (Clasen and Brown, 1985). Also, I pointed out earlier that although academic achievement forms the cornerstone for the stereotypic image of some crowds (e.g., brains, speds), nonacademic activities are the most salient characteristic of other crowds (e.g., populars, jocks, thrashers). These factors indicate that for adolescents in a number of crowds, devotion to classes and schoolwork may be tempered not so much by a general lack of interest in learning and achievement but by the more pressing demands of other peer-group norms and expectations. A member of the popular crowd cannot study so hard that it interferes with the social schedule expected of populars. An aspiring member of the thrashers understandably may put homework on the back burner and devote hours to polishing the skateboarding skills that are key to gaining acceptance by the thrasher crowd.

Often, the competing priorities of crowds contribute to a decline in student achievement through the economic pressures that they place on crowd members. That is, students find that they need a source of income to keep pace with the crowd. Maintaining the popular crowd image requires one to dress in the latest fashions. The anchor of the jock image may be a pair of $100 athletic shoes. To achieve status as a low rider, one must have an appropriately souped-up car. Efforts to keep up with the crowd in these ways prompt many students to acquire part-time jobs. Part-time employment among youth is very widespread, and it is common for adolescents to spend the vast majority of their earnings on immediate "lifestyle" purchases (clothes, cars, food) rather than saving for college or contributing to the family income (Greenberger and Steinberg, 1986). As the economic demands of the teenager's lifestyle increase, hours per week spent working tends to rise. These hours are taken from other pursuits. Typically, extracurricular activities are the first to suffer, followed by time devoted to homework (Greenberger and Steinberg, 1986). There is a significant, inverse correlation between hours spent working and a student's grade-point average (Steinberg and Dornbusch, 1991). Educators are aware of this and, of course, concerned about it. Often, however, they fail to realize that adolescents' interest in working long hours is motivated in large measure by their commitment to keeping up with the crowd. The desire to have enough money to be in step with friends outweighs the desire to dedicate oneself to learning and achievement. Of course, many students make an effort to keep their grades up even as the hours they devote to working rise—especially if parents have stipulated a certain grade average as a prerequisite for keeping the job. However, the strategies often employed in this quest (taking easier courses, copying homework or assignments from friends, bargaining with teachers to lower requirements) belie the student's diminished commitment to learning and achievement (Greenberger and Steinberg, 1986). The root cause of this diminished sense of purpose is not so much greed or an addiction to conspicuous consumption, as some have proposed, as it is a response to the subtle, materialistic pressures of the peer group and the need adolescents feel to be accepted and part of the crowd.

In sum, in many adolescent crowds, peer pressures and peer-group norms work against academic achievement in a more indirect fashion—not by actively subverting students' devotion to learning but by distracting them to activities that are more central to the crowd's image and more significant in determining status among peers. Coleman (1961) argued that teenagers generally were not oriented toward getting good grades because academic success was not critical to membership in the leading crowd. This presumed that virtually all students were preoccupied with joining the elite crowd, a presumption that has been successfully challenged in subsequent work (Eckert, 1989; Kinney, 1990; Larkin, 1979). A more accurate statement might be that because academic success is not critical to membership or status in *many* adolescent crowds, one should expect members of these groups to focus on schoolwork only to the extent that it does not interfere with acquiring and maintaining characteristics that will keep them in good standing with their crowd. In essence, for students in many crowds, academic work is avoided not because it is disparaged by their crowd but because it interferes with activities they find more essential to maintaining status in the crowd.

Anti-Achievement Pressures in Academically Alienated Crowds

Although many adolescents may simply be distracted from school achievement by more pressing norms within their peer group, there are some crowds whose reputation is based, in part, on an active dislike of the academic portion of school (teachers, classes, learning). Brown, Lohr, and Trujillo (1990) reported that a majority of adolescents stereotyped the druggie and tough crowds as groups that not only do poorly academically but "hate" school and look forward to leaving it. These groups, artfully portrayed in many films about teenagers (e.g., the character of John Bender in *The Breakfast Club*; the "homeboys" gang in *Stand and Deliver*), seem to thrive on confrontations with school staff, on an attitude of boredom and defiance in the classroom. The norms of this crowd are such that members may be ostracized if they show a genuine interest in academics (Cusick, 1973; Eckert, 1989). The dynamics in these groups are strikingly similar to those observed in the brain-nerd connection: group members who are genuinely interested in achievement must either relinquish such aspirations or hide them from their peers in order to maintain status within the crowd. The challenges that high achievers must face in such a peer environment are poignantly portrayed in the film *Stand and Deliver*, in which one student, named Angel, struggles to balance his talent and interest in mathematics against his status among the homeboy crowd. He finagles an extra copy of the textbook from his mathematics teacher so that he can study at home without risking the derision of his peers for carrying a book home. With some ambivalence, he also occasionally sacrifices study time to join in the crowd's high jinks. Yet, the strain of maintaining a foothold in the very separate worlds of scholar and homeboy takes its toll on Angel; he struggles to retain his friendships and at the same time remain in good standing with a teacher whom he admires.

Crowds with a high proportion of dropouts and at-risk students also display a more direct normative press against school achievement, but often for a different reason. In these crowds the school no longer serves as the locus of crowd interaction. Because a number of crowd members are no longer attending school, the group must rely on out-of-school contexts (the street corner, the neighborhood, members' homes) to maintain the social ties within the group. Typically, students in such crowds have established a record of poor or marginal academic success, so that they experience classes as frustrating and punishing environments (Ekstrom, Goertz, Pollack, and Rock, 1986). With encouragement from friends who have already dropped out, they regularly cut classes or skip school. For these crowd members, classes and schoolwork interfere with their opportunities to socialize with group members and, thus, threaten the continued existence of the group. Such students may come to class only when it is "convenient" or only frequently enough for them to avoid failure or suspension.

Hating school or learning is not necessarily a feature of crowd norms. In fact, as Ball (1981) points out, members of these crowds do not so much dislike school as they find it (and the value system that underlies school as a social institution) utterly irrelevant to their current and future lives. Learning is regarded as neither appealing nor important. Further, attendance at school can be a relatively lonely, isolating experience because many (if not most) of their friends are literally not present. With neither classes nor peer social interactions to look forward to, members of such crowds have little motivation to attend school. Efforts to rescue these crowds must involve not only creating academic successes and a more positive orientation toward learning, but also moving them into a different social network for which school is a more salient social context.

Summary

This is by no means an exhaustive examination of peer influences on school achievement patterns. The intent, instead, is to illustrate how the effect that peers may be expected to have on student achievement and the mechanisms by which peer influences operate are contingent on the type of crowd with which the teenager is affiliated or wishes to be affiliated. High achievers must weigh the risk that their academic efforts may be resented by peers and that peers will associate them with a crowd that is routinely omitted from social activities. Minority students who strive to excel academically risk being ostracized by ethnic peers for appearing to "sell out" their own cultural heritage for a spot in the majority culture. Students in more activity-oriented (versus academically oriented) crowds must be careful that academic efforts do not distract from activities and interests that are more central to their status in the peer group. And members of crowds with an antischool or anti-achievement ethic run the risk of being disinherited by peers if they show too strong an interest in their classes. In each case the consequence is to depress student effort toward academic achievement, but the mechanisms and motivations are markedly different.

It is important to acknowledge that this is a one-sided portrayal of peer pressures and peer-group norms that bear on student achievement patterns in secondary school. The effort has been to accentuate ways in which peer influences discourage or depress academic achievement. In reality, of course, the opposite dynamics can be witnessed as well. The high-achievement norms of the brain crowd can inspire a healthy and vigorous academic competitiveness among crowd members, driving them to maintain a commitment to scholarship even in the face of anti-achievement pressures from other groups. The status accorded to athletes attracts many marginal students to the jock crowd (Coleman, 1961; Spady, 1971). They may redouble their efforts in classes in order to maintain academic eligibility for participating in sports and thus continue their image among peers as a sports hero. Most crowds hold positive attitudes toward school achievement, at least to a modest degree (Brown et al., 1990; Clasen and Brown, 1987). The argument, then, is not that peers are an anti-intellectual force in the lives of most secondary school students. Rather, I wish to suggest that achievement-oriented norms and pressures from peers vary dramatically among crowds, and that in a number of groups (and for a variety of reasons that seem particular to different crowds), peers seem to delimit students' devotion to academic achievement.

THE POLITICS OF EFFORT: HOW ADULTS CAN UNDERMINE STUDENT ACHIEVEMENT

To this point the discussion has focused on adolescent peer groups and peer pressures, with little consideration of how adults get "caught up" in the dynamics of peer influence. From one perspective, this is not a significant oversight. A common theme of treatises on the teenage "youth culture," mostly written several decades ago, was that it operates with little or no input from adults. In fact, the assumption was that the youth culture strives to be utterly independent from adults because of teenagers' rejection of adult values and their devotion to forming a "counterculture," an alternative social order (see Brown, 1990). In subsequent studies researchers discovered that this provocative thesis overstated the cultural gap between generations (Conger, 1977) and overlooked the diversity of crowds that operate within the social system of teenagers. What is more, it ignored the many ways in which adults contribute to crowd norms and student behaviors. Adult influence on teenage peer culture is substantial. In the academic sphere, adults contribute in several ways to what might be called the "politics of effort," that is, the reasoning adolescents employ to justify their degree of dedication to academic achievement. In this section I will illustrate how the actions of teachers and other adults help teenagers to rationalize the limited effort they put forth to learn and achieve academically. Obviously, I could highlight other teacher behaviors that enhance rather than delimit student achievement, but it seems more appropriate to first indicate how adults *undermine* achievement before, in the final section, considering strategies by which adults can encourage teenagers to dedicate more effort to scholarship.

To be sure, teenagers depend on crowds to help them manage the developmental agenda of adolescence. Crowds offer provisional identities, they facilitate the development and maintenance of social networks and social support systems, and they regulate interactions among the diverse array of peers that often greets students at the beginning of high school (Brown, 1990). Yet, as Newman and Newman (1976, p. 276) point out, crowds are equally vital for adults in the school: "School adults both passively accept and actively encourage the organization of students into peer groups." There is an implicit acceptance of the peer-group structure by teachers, Newman and Newman continue, to the point that teachers expect students who wear the badge of a particular crowd (in their dress and grooming or comportment) to behave according to the norms of that crowd. But teachers also actively encourage certain crowds whose leaders can be relied on to reinforce school norms of appropriate behavior.

Thus, both students and teachers or administrators have a vested interest in the peer-group system, an interest that motivates them to manipulate crowds to serve their own agenda. As school adults pursue this vested interest, however, they may provide members of various crowds with excuses for not applying themselves to their studies. Following are several illustrations.

The Glorification of Jocks

For well over half a century, American high schools routinely have supplemented the academic curriculum with a set of school-sponsored, organized extracurricular activities. Nowadays these activities are often regarded as a distraction from the academic mission of secondary schools, but proponents of the extracurriculum would argue that this perspective is very shortsighted. Several educators in the 1920s and 1930s reasoned that incorporating extracurricular activities into the school program was an excellent method of extending adult control over youth to the students' leisure time (Brenzel, Roberts-Gersch, and Wittner, 1985). The activities were designed to reinforce students' commitment to conventional adult norms, but it appears as if, over time, this emphasis on extracurricular activities has somewhat eroded a strong commitment to learning and achievement.

Interscholastic athletics compose the most prominent component of the extracurriculum. They also provide a social context for one of the most prominent and enduring adolescent crowds: the jocks. For decades, jocks have enjoyed the envy of their peers as members of the highest or nearly highest status crowd (Coleman, 1961; Eckert, 1989; Spady, 1971). The jocks, however, are also esteemed by school adults, so much so that students often complain about the special treatment that jocks are accorded by teachers and administrators (Boyer, 1983; Delgado-Gaitan, 1986). Essentially, the complaints are that jocks get more academic help from teachers than do other students, are graded with less stringent criteria, and often "get away with things" (violations of school rules) for which other students are disciplined. These might be regarded as the perquisites accorded to members of the jock crowd by teachers in exchange for their allegiance to conventional adult norms.

This may seem to be a functional and mutually beneficial contract between generations: jocks enjoy high prestige in exchange for helping to ensure that teachers will face a compliant student body. The "perks" that keep this system operating, however, may easily undermine jocks' devotion to academics. If a jock can earn good grades without much effort, then why should he or she bother to work hard in classes, especially in the face of an exhausting schedule of practices and games (not to mention post-game parties)? It is quite possible that this dynamic helps to explain why in our recent study, students out for "glory" sports (football, basketball, baseball) had the lowest levels of school engagement and highest rates of deviance in school (cheating, cutting class) of any major category of extracurricular participant (Brown, Kohrs, and Lazarro, 1991).

Peer-Group Isolation Through Ability Grouping

Some researchers argue that the effect school adults have on the achievement motivation of crowds is much more powerful and direct. In essence, they argue that a major component of school structure—tracks or ability groups—serves to create crowds (or create coalitions among certain groups) and distance those who are achievement oriented from those who are not. On the one hand, ability grouping might seem to be a clever means of dissipating the pressures not to achieve that result from the brain-nerd connection. If average- and low-ability students resent the academic pressures they suffer because of the "curve wreckers" in their midst, then why not remove high achievers to a separate track? As students in each track pursue scholarship at their own level of ability, effort, and motivation, they should feel no pressure from students in other tracks and, therefore, no need to harass high achievers by giving them unattractive labels.

In reality, however, tracking systems may drive a wedge between crowds that undermines the achievement motivation of lower-track students. According to Schwartz (1981), the erosion of achievement motivation in certain crowds begins before the crowds actually emerge, that is, during the elementary school years. Schwartz's observations of elementary and middle schools in the Northeast revealed that students in high- and low-ability groups have very different orientations toward school as well as toward their peers. High-ability students develop the capacity to attend to the academic requirements of the classroom (answering the teacher's questions, working on assignments) while at the same time engage in covert interactions with peers (passing notes, exchanging glances). They work cooperatively with peers on academic assignments and are effective at balancing social interactions with academic work during class time that is not directed by the teacher.

Lower-track students, on the other hand, display a more competitive, combative interaction style, not only in relationships with the teacher but also with each other. Class time that is not directed by the teacher tends to be wasted in efforts to derogate peers or in conversations with friends about life outside school. In other words, the two groups manifested dramatically different styles of classroom behavior. High-ability students developed interaction skills that enhanced their standing among teachers and peers, adding to their success at school and making their school experience quite enjoyable. Lower-track students developed styles that alienated them from teachers but also from peers. These differential behaviors served to exacerbate the academic differences between the two groups so that, to a certain extent, one's assignment to an ability group became a self-fulfilling prophecy.

Studies of ability groups in British secondary schools reveal similar social dynamics. Ball (1981), Hargreaves (1967), and Lacey (1970) all found that as high- and low-ability students become academically differentiated they become socially polarized as well. Each develops a separate subculture. Status in the high-track group is derived from academic achievement, whereas status in the low-track group is derived from defiance of school and teacher norms.

These authors implied that tracks actually create peer groups (that members of each ability group coalesce into a separate crowd). I would argue that ability groups in high schools are more likely to forge alliances between pre-existing crowds, if most members are assigned to the same track, or increase the "social distance" (Brown, 1989a) between crowds whose members are routinely assigned to separate tracks. The more widespread that tracking is in a school (the more courses in which students are divided among ability groups), the more students' opportunities for social interactions with peers are regulated by their academic achievement levels. Thus, widespread ability grouping underscores the academic dimension of peer-group norms or stereotypes. If high-ability crowds such as brains have little opportunity to interact with low-ability groups such as druggies, then they must rely more on crowd stereotypes to understand each other. This seems to increase the dislike or mistrust that the two crowds harbor for each other (Ball, 1981). This, in turn, may actually exacerbate the brain-nerd connection. Equally important, however, is that ability grouping isolates low achievers from peers who can model stronger achievement motivation and more effective strategies for balancing the academic and social agenda that peers confront in secondary schools.

In short, academic tracking systems underscore and exacerbate achievement-oriented differences among adolescent crowds. They isolate low achievers from peers who can model behaviors that lead to academic success and satisfaction in school. Although tracking reinforces the achievement norms of academically oriented peer groups, it also solidifies peer groups whose value systems oppose school norms and achievement efforts. The net effect may be to alienate and isolate high achievers from the preponderance of peer groups, in which academic achievement is not a central criterion for popularity or peer status.

Blaming the Victim and Excusing the Victim

Another danger of ability grouping is that it separates students into racial, ethnic, or socioeconomic groups (Hampel, 1986). Of course, such divisions may reflect the reality of significant class or ethnic differences in average levels of academic ability or achievement motivation. Yet, it may also heighten students' awareness of the class and ethnic background of peers and prompt adolescents to focus on these factors in identifying peer groups in the school. Thus, students will speak of Mexicans, rappers, Vietnamese, richies, and cholos, rather than jocks, brains, thrashers, and nerds (Brown and Mounts, 1989; Ianni, 1989; Matute-Bianchi, 1986). Such crowds provide fertile grounds for the proliferation of ethnic or class stereotypes. It has not been uncommon for educators to attribute the low academic achievement levels of economically disadvantaged and minority students to lack of effort. "If only they would try harder," the argument goes, "they might get decent grades." Matute-Bianchi (1986), for example, observed a high school in which the Hispanic student population was divided among several peer crowds, defined largely by their ethnic orientation and generation in the United States. According to Matute-Bianchi, teachers were prone to rationalize the limited academic success of recent immigrants as the result of poor academic preparation (in Mexico) or limited English proficiency. For the American-born students in the Chicano and cholos crowds, however, failure in school was attributed to ". . . lack of motivation, interest, and respect for schooling. They are perceived to fail in school because they reject what the school has to offer" (Matute-Bianchi, 1986, p. 241).

To other educators, this line of thinking is tantamount to "blaming the victim" (Ryan, 1976). They argue that the family background of these students provides relatively little to motivate them to do well in school. Such students are at risk for dropping out of school not because they fail to put forth effort but because the succession of academic failures they have experienced through the years, the lack of real intellectual stimulation at home, and the absence of encouragement from parents to do well in school have eroded their motivation to put forth any effort. Instead of "blaming the victim," they urge a response that amounts to "excusing the victim"—lowering expectations and minimizing academic demands so that students can experience academic successes that will rekindle their achievement motivation.

Ironically, however, the effort of teachers to help students in certain crowds surmount ethnic or class stereotypes may actually be subverted by crowd norms and peer pressures. In Matute-Bianchi's (1986) study, for example, the Chicano crowd often referred to themselves as "homeboys" and "homegirls"; they derided peers in the "schoolboy/schoolgirl" crowd for their tendency to attend class, study, and obey school rules. With these crowd labels the Chicanos underscored their disaffection from school and their contempt for Hispanic peers who put forth a genuine effort to achieve academically. In crowds such as the Chicanos, students may *embrace* the role of victims who, because of their environment, cannot be held accountable for their minimal efforts at academic achievement. They interpret reductions in academic demands as a major accomplishment in itself: they have duped the teacher into lowering their workload, and members of these crowds may be tempted to respond by reducing their effort even further.

A corollary to "excusing the victim" is to attribute racial or social-class differences in standardized test scores to the cultural biases of the test. However accurate this explanation is, it provides students with an excuse for not trying to do well on standardized tests. Of course, some students may respond by redoubling their efforts to obtain high scores and thereby demonstrate that they can overcome even these invidious racial or ethnic prejudices. But for students whose peer group places little value on academic achievement, emphasis on the cultural biases of standardized tests provides a superb justification for putting forth minimal academic effort at school.

Summary

In general, it is important to recognize that adults—especially educators—may have a profound effect on the academic motivation of high school students, but not necessarily in the way they intend. Unwittingly, educators may contribute to a decline in student motivation, either by creating a reward structure in the school that devalues academic achievement, by structuring learning opportunities in a way that isolates students with low achievement motivation from crowds of high achievers who model more effective academic behaviors, or by applying well-intentioned strategies to particular categories of students without regard to the achievement norms of these students' reference group. Again, I must emphasize that not all of educators' efforts go awry or lead students astray as I have illustrated here. These examples, however, underscore the need for adults to be more aware of the dynamics of peer groups as they attempt to combat the academic malaise that seems to be gripping a good number of students in American high schools.

STRATEGIES FOR REDIRECTING PEER INFLUENCES AND REKINDLING ACHIEVEMENT MOTIVATIONS

It is ironic, I think, that efforts to improve the quality of American high schools have focused on nearly every aspect of the school except its clientele—adolescent students. School-improvement and school-restructuring programs lay heavy emphasis on teaching strategies, curriculum reform, administrative organization (teacher empowerment, decentralized control), parent involvement, and community assistance. Somehow in this process, the role and responsibilities of students in educational reform have been misplaced. This is unfortunate because in disassociating students from reform strategies, educators and policymakers often design programs that fit imperfectly with the ways in which students commonly experience high school.

In this chapter I have attempted to assess the high school from the *students'* perspective, beginning with the recognition that to most students, school is more than a place to learn. It is a context for adolescent development—for physical, social, and psychological growth as well as academic learning. High school students are a diverse lot, manifesting different approaches to the developmental demands of adolescence, approaches that give rise and lend credibility to a social system that divides students into a set of peer groups, or crowds. In most cases, crowds derive a portion of their identity from the academic and extracurricular components of high school life, and they display peer pressures that direct members' attitudes and behaviors in these contexts. Although peer pressure is generally oriented toward rather than against school achievement, it does seem to discourage outstanding achievement and delimit the academic efforts of many students whose crowds accord more status to achievements outside the classroom. Thus, peer-group norms may undermine academic achievement for many students, but to a varying extent and for different reasons, according to the norms of the student's crowd. The efforts of teachers and administrators to maintain order in school and motivate students to achieve quite often go awry and serve, instead, to reinforce the anti-achievement orientations of certain peer cultures.

What then can educators do to enhance rather than undermine the academic motivations of American adolescents? Three important strategies should be emphasized.

1. *Increase awareness of adolescents' social system.*

First, *educators must become more aware of the peer-group system*: the division of students into crowds, the norms that operate within each crowd, the relationships of one crowd to the next, and the allegiance that students display to their own reference group. Too often, teachers are prone to group students into categories that make sense only to adults: high achievers versus low achievers, at-risk versus learning disabled versus normal-ability students, students whose parents are supportive and involved in school versus those whose parents are not, and so on. These categories describe important clusters of students in terms of the academic programs that the school offers, but they fail to capture the social reality that preoccupies students.

Greater awareness of the dynamics of peer groups can help teachers understand the peculiar patterns of behavior observable in the classroom. For example, recognizing the hostility that two crowds harbor for each other may help teachers understand why a work group composed of members of those two crowds is not as productive as a work group composed of students from a more amicable mix of crowds. Being sensitive to the anti-achievement norms of the druggie crowd may encourage teachers to refrain from public praise of druggies who perform well on an assignment; in such cases a private congratulation may allow the student to enjoy his or her success without risking embarrassment in front of peer-group members. Appreciating the dynamics of the brain-nerd connection, or the "burden of 'acting white'" among minority students, may dissuade a teacher from holding a high achiever up as the standard for other class members to emulate.

There is, of course, the danger that in trying to be sensitive to the dynamics of the peer-group system, teachers will respond to students in ways that simply reinforce crowd stereotypes. Teachers must bear in mind that jocks, burnouts, Mexicans, and so on, are simply *prototypes*, and that students' crowd affiliation only *approximates* their actual attitudes, interests, and activities. Like school norms and family norms, peer-group norms influence adolescents' attitudes and behaviors without overwhelming the person's individuality.

The objective, then, is to encourage teachers to *treat adolescents as individuals*, but with proper awareness of the norms and pressures that each student is facing as a function of his or her ties with particular peer groups. This approach will quickly lead to the recognition that there is *no generic solution* to the problems of achievement motivation among American high school students. Several strategies must be developed, and each must be adapted to the particular life situations (including peer-group norms and pressures) of each individual student.

2. Avoid making achievement a game of winners and losers.

One of the major factors delimiting adolescents' achievement motivation is that achievement is often a zero-sum game: for every academic "winner" there must be a "loser." Grading systems based on a curve place arbitrary and artificial limits on the number of high achievers that can emerge in a classroom. Because the importance of good grades is emphasized so heavily by adults, zero-sum grading systems create fierce competition among students and foster hostile relationships between the academically successful and unsuccessful students. The frustrations that result in the brain-nerd connection are based not on the fact that certain students obtain excellent grades but on the fact that their high achievement automatically devalues or delimits other students' achievement levels. The situation seems to be worsened by ability grouping, which differentiates in painfully visible terms the "smart" students, "average" students, and "dumb" students (Schwartz, 1981) and, in practice, locks low achievers into a pattern of low achievement, academic alienation, and isolation from other students in the school (Ball, 1981). There are, of course, alternative grading systems in which students compete against a standard of knowledge rather than against each other. Such systems encourage individualized attention and emphasize individual achievement. If adopted, these strategies would obviate the need for ability groups, which seem to breed much of the enmity and alienation that exist among adolescent crowds. The strategies also would diffuse the discouragement of academic excellence and permit high achievers to model more adaptive classroom behaviors for students whose crowds do not reward academic achievement as strongly.

3. Enhance the status of academic achievement.

Of course, becoming more sensitive to peer-group dynamics and removing the artificial barriers between crowds will not do nearly as much to motivate students to achieve as will raising the status of academic achievement within the peer system. In this effort educators must realize that they begin with an advantage, not a handicap. In general, peer pressures are oriented toward rather than against academic achievement (Clasen and Brown, 1985). Further, according to many researchers, there is a *positive* association between student achievement levels and popularity or peer status (Faunce, 1984; Schwartz, 1981). Even in Coleman's (1961) sample, the most popular students were those who were both good scholars and good athletes or activity leaders. Yet, schools can do much to increase the peer status that results from high achievement. The first step is to *give public recognition to high achievers*. Hawley and Rosenholtz (1984) point to this as one of the most prominent features of successful schools.

Second, schools should *avoid sending mixed messages* to students about the relative merit of academic and nonacademic achievement. When school is closed the day of the state athletic contest (ostensibly so that students can go cheer for their team in the playoff game), but school remains in session the day an academic team competes in a similar statewide tournament, it is easy for students to see that the jocks have more power and status in school than the brains do. One can easily determine the relative status of jocks and brains by how prominently academic and athletic trophies are displayed in the school.

Third, educators must strive to *recognize academic excellence in areas outside the core academic curriculum*. Trade fairs that feature the products of students in vocational classes are as important as awards assemblies for top mathematics and English scholars. By expanding public recognition in this fashion, schools give a variety of peer groups an opportunity to "shine" in front of peers, rather than forcing all crowds to play by the rules of the brain group.

CONCLUSION

In the 1950s researchers pointed out that at adolescence students become preoccupied with obtaining and retaining status within the peer culture (Coleman, 1961). That was correct. They further argued that academic achievement was not among the most salient determinants of peer status. That was less accurate because it falsely regarded the adolescent social system as a monolithic peer culture when, in fact, the system encompasses a variety of crowds with dramatically different and sometimes diametrically opposed value systems. Whereas some peer groups relish academic competition, others disdain any sense of bonding with the school, so that it is impossible for educators to apply any generic solution to the "problem" of student motivation and expect it to be effective. Instead, educators must become more aware of and sensitive to the dynamics of peer-group norms and pressures, to the ways in which such forces enhance or delimit students' academic interests in schools, and to the appropriate ways for school adults to engage this social system.

It is, of course, essential for educators to hold students accountable for their own success or failure at school. Cusick (1986, p. 148) cautions, "What school is like for students depends upon the way they enter or refuse to enter, take part or refuse to take part, engage or refuse to engage in the institution. . . . An education is available, but it is up to each student to wrest it out and find those good classes, appealing teachers, and rewarding relationships with teachers and peers." Yet, the student is not utterly alone in this struggle. He or she is joined by peers who, through the dynamics of crowd norms and pressures, reward or fail to reward the student's achievement efforts, direct or distract his or her efforts at becoming engaged in learning, and foster or inhibit the development of the student's academic potential. Peer-group influences are especially powerful at adolescence, though they do not necessarily guide all students in the same direction. For adolescents, high school is more than a series of classrooms and assignments, of relationships with a succession of teachers. As Boyer (1983) remarks:

High school *is* home for many students. It also is one institution in our culture where it is all right to be young. Here, teenagers meet each other, share hopes and fears, start love affairs, and experiment with growing up. This role will never appear on the report card of the American high school unless perhaps the old-fashioned category of "deportment" is added to the list; and unless we grade the school, not just on academic performance, but also on its sensitivity toward students. [P. 38]

REFERENCES

Ball, Samuel J. *Beachside Comprehensive*. Cambridge, Mass.: Cambridge University Press, 1981.

Boyer, Ernest L. *High School: A Report on Secondary Education in America*. New York: Harper and Row, 1983.

Brenzel, Barbara; Roberts-Gersch, Cathy; and Wittner, Judith. "Becoming Social: School Girls and Their Culture between the Two World Wars," *Journal of Early Adolescence* 5 (1985): 479–488.

Brown, B. Bradford. "Can Nerds and Druggies Be Friends?: Mapping 'Social Distance' between Adolescent Peer Groups." Paper presented at the Annual Meeting of the American Educational Research Association, San Francisco, 1989a.

Brown, B. Bradford. "Skirting the 'Brain-Nerd' Connection: How High Achievers Save Face among Peers." Paper presented at the Annual Meeting of the American Educational Research Association, San Francisco, 1989b.

Brown, B. Bradford. "Peer Groups and Peer Cultures." In *At the Threshold: The Developing Adolescent*, edited by S. Shirley Feldman and Glen R. Elliott, pp. 171–196. Cambridge, Mass.: Harvard University Press, 1990.

Brown, B. Bradford; Kohrs, Diane M.; and Lazarro, Cary. "What Price Sports Glory?: Academic Costs and Consequences of Extracurricular Participation in High School." Paper presented at the Annual Meeting of the American Educational Research Association, Chicago, 1991.

Brown, B. Bradford; Lohr, Mary Jane; and Trujillo, Carla. "Multiple Crowds and Multiple Life Styles: Adolescents' Perception of Peer Group Stereotypes." In *Adolescent Behavior and Society*, 4th ed., edited by Rolf E. Muuss, pp. 30–36. New York: McGraw-Hill, 1990.

Brown, B. Bradford, and Mounts, Nina. "Peer Group Structures in Single versus Multiethnic High Schools." Paper presented at the biennial meeting of the Society for Research in Child Development, Kansas City, 1989.

Clasen, Donna Rae, and Brown, B. Bradford. "The Multidimensionality of Peer Pressure in Adolescence," *Journal of Youth and Adolescence* 14 (1985): 451–468.

Clasen, Donna Rae, and Brown, B. Bradford. "Understanding Peer Pressure in Middle School." In *Middle School Research: Selected Studies*, edited by David B. Strahn, pp. 65–75. Columbus, Ohio: National Middle School Association, 1987.

Coleman, James S. *The Adolescent Society*. New York: Free Press, 1961.

Conger, John J. "Parent-Child Relationships, Social Change, and Adolescent Vulnerability," *Journal of Pediatric Psychology* 32 (1977): 513–531.

Csikszentmihalyi, Mihaly, and Larson, Reed. *Being Adolescent*. New York: Basic Books, 1984.

Cusick, Philip A. *Inside High School.* New York: Holt, Rinehart, and Winston, 1973.

Cusick, Philip A. "Public Secondary Schools in the United States." In *Academic Work and Educational Excellence,* edited by Tommy M. Tomlinson and Herbert J. Walberg, pp. 137–152. Berkeley, Calif.: McCutchan, 1986.

Delgado-Gaitan, Concha. "Adolescent Peer Influences and Differential School Performance," *Journal of Adolescent Research* 1 (1986): 449–462.

Eckert, Penelope. *Jocks and Burnouts: Social Categories and Identity in the High School.* New York: Teachers College Press, 1989.

Ekstrom, Ruth; Goertz, Margaret E.; Pollack, Judith M.; and Rock, Donald A. "Who Drops Out of High School and Why," *Teachers College Record* 87, no. 3 (1986): 356–373.

Everhart, Robert. *Reading, Writing, and Resistance: Adolescence and Labor in a Junior High School.* Boston: Routledge, 1983.

Faunce, William A. "School Achievement, Social Status, and Self-esteem," *Social Psychology Quarterly* 47 (1984): 3–14.

Fordham, Signithia, and Ogbu, John U. "Black Students' School Success: Coping with the Burden of 'Acting White'," *Urban Review* 18 (1986): 176–206.

Fuller, Mary. "Black Girls in a London Comprehensive School." In *Schooling for Women's Work,* edited by Rosemary Deem, pp. 52–65. London: Routledge and Kegan Paul, 1984.

Gamoran, Adam, and Mare, Robert D. "Secondary School Tracking and Educational Inequality: Compensation, Reinforcement, or Neutrality?" *American Journal of Sociology* 94 (1989): 1146–1183.

Greenberger, Ellen, and Steinberg, Laurence. *When Teenagers Work: The Psychological and Social Costs of Adolescent Employment.* New York: Basic Books, 1986.

Hampel, Robert L. *The Last Little Citadel: American High Schools Since 1940.* Boston: Houghton Mifflin, 1986.

Hargreaves, David H. *Social Relations in a Secondary School.* London: Routledge and Kegan Paul, 1967.

Hawley, Willis D., and Rosenholtz, Susan J. "Good Schools: What Research Says about Improving Student Achievement," *Peabody Journal of Education* 61, no. 4 (1984): 1–178.

Ianni, Francis. *The Search for Structure.* New York: Free Press, 1989.

Ishiyama, F. Ishu, and Chabassol, David J. "Adolescents' Fear of the Social Consequences of Academic Success as a Function of Age and Sex," *Journal of Youth and Adolescence* 14 (1985): 37–46.

Kinney, David. "'Dweebs', 'Headbangers', and 'Trendies': Adolescent Identity Formation and Change within Sociocultural Context." Doctoral dissertation, Department of Sociology, Indiana University, Bloomington, 1990.

Lacey, Colin. *Hightown Grammar.* Manchester, England: Manchester University Press, 1970.

Larkin, Ralph W. *Suburban Youth in Cultural Crisis.* New York: Oxford, 1979.

Lerner, Barbara. "American Education: How Are We Doing?" *Public Interest* 69 (Fall 1982): 59–82.

Lockwood, Anne T. "Peer Influences: High School Seniors Speak," *National Center on Effective Secondary Schools Newsletter* 4, no. 2 (1989): 5–8.

Matute-Bianchi, Maria E. "Ethnic Identities and Patterns of School Success and

Failure among Mexican-descent and Japanese-American Students in a California High School: An Ethnographic Analysis," *American Journal of Education* 95 (1986): 233–255.

Newman, Philip R., and Newman, Barbara M. "Early Adolescence and Its Conflict: Group Identity versus Alienation," *Adolescence* 11 (1976): 261–274.

Newmann, Fred M. "Higher-order Thinking in the High School Curriculum," *NASSP Bulletin* 72, no. 508 (1988): 58–64.

Norman, Jane, and Harris, Myron W. *The Private Life of the American Teenager.* New York: Rawson, Wade, 1981.

Powell, Arthur G.; Farrar, Eleanor; and Cohen, David K. *The Shopping Mall High School.* Boston: Houghton Mifflin, 1985.

Ravitch, Diane, and Finn, Chester E., Jr. *What Do Our 17-Year-Olds Know?: A Report on the First National Assessment of History and Literature.* New York: Harper and Row, 1987.

Ryan, William. *Blaming the Victim.* New York: Vintage Press, 1976.

Schwartz, Frances. "Supporting or Subverting Learning: Peer Group Patterns in Four Tracked Schools," *Anthropology and Education Quarterly* 12 (1981): 99–121.

Schwendinger, Herman, and Schwendinger, Julia S. *Adolescent Subcultures and Delinquency.* New York: Praeger, 1985.

Spady, William G. "Status, Achievement, and Motivation in the American High School," *School Review* 79 (1971): 379–403.

Steinberg, Laurence, and Dornbusch, Sanford M. "Negative Correlates of Part-time Employment during Adolescence: A Replication and Elaboration," *Developmental Psychology* 27 (1991): 304–313.

Chapter 5

CARROTS AND STICKS: CAN SCHOOL POLICY INFLUENCE STUDENT MOTIVATION?

Florence R. Webb, Martin V. Covington, and James W. Guthrie

INTRODUCTION

Donkeys are rumored to be obstinate beasts, rarely inclined to move unless tempted with a carrot at the front end or threatened with a stick at the rear. The predominant model of motivation policy in American education makes similar presumptions about schoolchildren. Most such policies can be distinguished only by which end of the donkey they aim for. We will argue that these policies are largely wrong-headed not only because of the choice of target but also because of the choice of paradigm. More specifically, in this chapter we will focus on a group of motivational strategies of relatively recent origin: statewide and districtwide policies designed to provide positive incentives for school achievement, such as college tuition guarantees, or disincentives, such as withholding driving licenses or curtailing extracurricular activities for those students who fail to maintain a minimal grade-point average.

What is unique about these strategies, and as a consequence of special interest, is that they are mandated as part of wider institutional policy, instituted through top-down administrative fiat and to be applied across entire groups of youngsters irrespective of an individual's circumstances. This wholesale approach differs markedly from the traditional teacher-based methods for arousing and sustaining student effort, which for all their limitations have the advantage of flexible, judicious, and individual applications. For example, there is

99

clear evidence that the actions of specific teachers can stimulate and direct the effort of individual students. But can blanket, districtwide and statewide policies also provide effective incentives for increased learning? This is the question we will examine by looking at current research and thinking about what works and what does not work when it comes to motivating youngsters.

In the first section we will identify the assumptions about learning and learners that historically have dominated motivational policy in schools. In the second section we will consider the blanket strategies being discussed and implemented in America's schools in an effort to improve student motivation. Each strategy will be examined within the framework of the motivational theory outlined in the first section of the chapter. We will argue that to one degree or another these proposals reflect the metaphor of student as "obstinate beast." In the third section we propose an alternative metaphor, that of the "distracted learner," which we believe is not only more in keeping with modern motivational theory and findings, but also promises greater payoffs with respect to student achievement and well-being. We will also present several recommendations in the form of specific classroom examples that follow from this alternative perspective. In the last section we will consider several of the broader policy issues raised by this transformation in thinking about the nature of children in learning situations and about the mission of schools.

EVOLVING PARADIGMS OF STUDENT MOTIVATION

Today, many proposals for motivating students seem driven by a belief that students are "obstinate beasts" who see learning as a neutral or possibly an unpleasant activity to be avoided if possible. Indeed, some youngsters seem to have adopted an almost studious disregard for learning. By this reckoning, learning will occur only as a consequence of the forceful imposition of positive and negative incentives that impel students to act against their natural inclinations. This view assumes that it is the student who must change in order to improve the shameful statistics that often place American schoolchildren dead last in mathematics and science achievement compared to students from other industrialized countries; and correlatively, the responsibility of society is simply to make it clear to our students how important it is that they succeed.

During the last half century this bleak perspective on human nature has been occasionally tempered by an alternative view of "student as Rousseau-Idyll." This model assumes that, at least in a benign state of nature, students want to learn and that intellectual curiosity is a natural phenomenon. The basic assumption of this paradigm is that since children naturally enjoy learning, providing learning opportunities without restraint will allow them to proceed successfully. Failure is assumed to occur because the learning process has been rendered either overly restrictive or inappropriate to students' needs. In other words, it is the school that is to blame if the child does not learn; it is further assumed that were the school to offer appropriate fare, the child would eagerly partake. During the 1970s popular books such as A. S. Neill's *Summerhill* (1960) convinced many educators and parents that the structures and discipline of schooling were crushing what would otherwise be youthful spirits eager for learning. Many schools switched from formal lecturing to what one teacher aptly described as "lying around on pillows and rapping." Unfortunately, the hope that students would respond to this new freedom by becoming self-directed, self-fulfilling young scholars was not realized. The philosophy of openness and individuality was admirable; but according to Jonathan Kozol (1972), one of the founders of the "free school" movement, no one there learned how to read and "nongraded" often became a euphemism for unsupervised learning.

In the 1980s, in response to declining national achievement scores, reformers prescribed a more rigid and circumscribed curriculum typically referred to as "back to basics." This approach, too, has largely passed from favor but left behind traces of its passing. The back-to-basics curricula eventually lost support among parents who wanted their children to develop complex "thinking skills" and to be exposed to the humanities, to the arts, and to foreign languages. Also, as the importance of integrated curricula and hands-on learning experiences for children gained acceptance, and as business and educational leaders alike decried the substitution of memorization for analysis and critical thinking, the attraction of the traditional-looking basic school waned.

Since the heyday of this movement many of the rigidities of the "basics" curricula have been abandoned, but for many the assumption that children must be *induced* to learn has not. The most recent manifestation of this position has been referred to elsewhere as a policy of intensification (Covington, 1992; Guthrie, 1988). This is the belief that there is nothing wrong with our schools that cannot be remedied by doing more of the same—increasing the number of days in school, lengthening the school day, invoking stiffer requirements for high school graduation and college admission, raising standards, and requiring more homework. Some of these specific proposals have real validity. For example, if we are ever to reverse achievement declines, students *will* have to try harder and standards *will* have to be maintained if not increased. But these proposals taken by themselves are insufficient, and if applied indiscriminately without a radical shift in our views of learning and learners, may ultimately prove to be no solution at all.

MOTIVATION ASSUMPTIONS

By and large, the wholesale top-down incentive systems to be reviewed here are driven by the implicit assumption of students as obstinate beasts. The implicit expectation is that if schools (or society) can provide the *right* rewards or punishments, they can then arouse otherwise dispirited, lazy students to higher levels of effort. There are several related corollaries: (1) That the greater the rewards offered (or the more noxious the consequences of not complying), the harder students will try; (2) That the meaning of these rewards and punishments is essentially the same for minority and for Anglo, for poor pupils and for middle-class pupils; and (3) That arousal is maximized when rewards are distributed on a competitive basis.

As a group, these assumptions form an essential part of the behaviorist approach to learning, and knowingly or not, the architects of these incentive policies embrace the principles of behavior modification. The goal of behavior modification is to manipulate the individual's environment in order to ensure that any increase in desired behaviors (such as staying in school) will be rewarded while undesirable behaviors (like dropping out) go unrewarded, or even punished. Our review and critique of the various current incentive policies is organized around two of the most powerful kinds of behavioral manipulators: positive reinforcers (carrots) and negative reinforcers (sticks).

CARROTS

In behavioral terms a positive reinforcer is any stimulus that, when presented after a response, increases the likelihood of that response being repeated later. For example, Mrs. Wiggins finds that Ralph begins turning in homework assignments promptly when he learns that on-time behavior earns five extra-credit points.

Student Recognition

These days, student recognition and award programs, along with rewards in the form of money, job opportunities, attractive curricular options, and scholarships, are the carrots most often suggested by advocates of schoolwide policy designed to improve classroom performance. Honor societies and honor rolls have a traditional place in most high schools and in some middle schools. Extensions of these programs to the elementary level would appear to be a less common but growing phenomenon, if we can judge from the recent appearance of automobile bumper stickers proclaiming that the driver is the proud parent of an elementary school valedictorian.

"Student of the year" and other special awards have proliferated over the years, and many high schools now have a separate awards night preceding the senior graduation ceremony. Extracurricular programs at the local school site, including music, speech, drama, and athletics, have also developed their own forms of recognition. Nationally syndicated awards have become popular. In instrumental music the John Philip Sousa plaque and *Downbeat Magazine* award, etched with individual names and year, are often visible in high school band rooms.

We have no quarrel with the promotion of academic and personal excellence; indeed, we embrace it. But we are concerned with certain aspects of extrinsic rewards that are distributed on a competitive basis, an arrangement true of virtually all the examples cited above. In the absence of absolute criteria or merit-based rewards, that is, rewards given to all students who meet specific standards or goals, competitive awards may actually discourage achievement, or at least the most important kinds of achievement that require considerable personal commitment and higher-order thinking. The large body of research concerning the effects of competitively based extrinsic rewards on school performance has been summarized by Condry (1977):

Subjects offered an extrinsic incentive choose easier tasks, are less efficient in using the information available to solve novel problems, and tend to be answer-oriented and more illogical in their problem-solving strategies. They seem to work harder and produce more activity, but the activity is of lower quality, contains more errors, and is more stereotyped and less creative than the work of comparable nonrewarded subjects working on the same problems. [Pp. 471–472]

The reason for these decrements has been neatly captured by Kohn (1986), who remarks: "How can we do our best when we are spending our energies trying to make others lose—in fear that they will make us lose?" (p. 9). To be sure, competitive incentives do encourage learning under some circumstances and for some individuals who believe they can win the prize, and for those tasks considered to be chores, that is, tedious, boring, or repetitive assignments. Ironically, then, competition motivates performance best on those tasks that are of least importance in the larger educational mission, and arouses those who are least likely to need arousing.

A scarcity of rewards turns learning into an "ability game." The fewer rewards available, the more ability becomes the factor in attaining them. Students quickly come to understand this, and tend to respond (or not) in light of their own *perceived* ability. Those who feel confident, and believe they are *able* enough to win, are positively affected by competitive awards. Those who feel less able, and are convinced that others will always win, will be less inclined to expend effort (Covington, 1992). In contrast, however, when rewards signal the mastery of an important task, a successful group effort, or the overcoming of substantial obstacles, students experience a sense of accomplishment no matter how many other students also succeed (Covington and Jacoby, 1973). When this is the case, effort rather than ability becomes the deciding factor. Even more important is that students see effort as the deciding factor—all students can win, and they all are likely to respond accordingly.

Incentives or disincentives that are distributed on a blanket basis irrespective of specific circumstances and the needs of individual learners can be problematic in another way. In a now classic study, Goldberg (1965) investigated the effects of several broad grading policies for motivating improved school performance. Students were either graded leniently, on the assumption that positive reinforcement would best motivate future achievement, or graded strictly, on the theory that punishment in the form of a low grade is the best motivation. For a third group, Goldberg created a discrepancy between the grade expected by students and what they actually received, on the assumption that those who unexpectedly received a high grade would work harder the next time, while those students who unexpectedly received poor grades would work harder to improve them. No single policy proved more effective than any other for stimulating subsequent academic performance, nor were any of these groups different from a fourth control group that was graded on the traditional "normal" curve. These null results occurred because the incentives and disincentives, which were administered on a blanket, indiscriminate basis, motivated different students differently, thus causing a cancellation of the effects of a given policy. Already successful students responded positively to the threat of failure (a poor grade) because it signaled the need for them to try harder, whereas failure-prone students tended to give up because they interpreted failure as the result of their inability, for which they believed there was no remedy. By the same token, rewards of unexpected high grades to failure-prone students are likely to be met with disbelief if not suspicion because these students did not expect success. In these cases students attributed their success either to the humanitarian impulses of a teacher or to good luck.

In short, blanket approaches to inducing greater effort are likely to motivate mainly those students who need motivating the least. In addition, such policies may further discourage those who need motivating the most. Little wonder that the effects of a single uniform incentive policy on a group of students is unpredictable and may be counterproductive for many.

College Scholarship Incentives

Eugene Lang's "I Have a Dream" Foundation, which promises financial assistance for college tuition, has become the impetus for a national movement to encourage students to stay in school. Lang's incentive plan was first offered to students at his own East Harlem alma mater, P.S. 121, when he proposed to give each student $2,000 over four years for college tuition if they would graduate from high school (Wycliff, 1990). In 1987 Lang launched a nationwide program supplemented by funding from the U.S. Department of Education. By 1988 more than eight thousand students in twenty-five cities were participating with the help of local sponsors. The states of Rhode Island, New York, and Louisiana have all since established scholarship programs for low-income pupils (Wycliff, 1990).

As yet, there is no hard evidence on the effectiveness of such monetary rewards, either for reducing the dropout rate from high school or for increasing college applications. Evidence aside, however, we endorse the notion of such scholarship programs. Whether or not these efforts do motivate students directly, they certainly help reduce financial barriers to higher education. Also, the availability of these rewards conveys an impression that the welfare and future of students is important, and that somebody does care.

Our concern with the promise of scholarships as a motivating device largely involves the issue of timing. The time delay between the desired response—studying adequately or turning in one's homework regularly—and the contingent reinforcement, such as a college scholarship or a guaranteed job on graduation, is simply too great for the promised rewards to be effective. This is especially true for disadvantaged students whose sense of future, psychologically speaking, is compressed and the prospects of immediate gratification more salient. Also, for many children the promise of a college education is simply too abstract. Most children do not see college as having any particular relevance to their lives prior to entering high school; and for far too many children too much ground has been lost by that time for them to catch up. The most successful of these programs have involved significant support systems for high school students in addition to the promised college money. Unfortunately, there are far too few of these support programs available. The problems are exacerbated for children of color, the poor and immigrants—those for whom scholarship programs are typically targeted. All too often these youngsters see school as increasingly irrelevant to their lives. As they grow older they are preoccupied with the hassles of daily survival that have little to do with the academic lessons of school. Also, those minority students who do look ahead may see school as useless unless they are able to get jobs on graduation, a prospect that seems more and more remote to these youngsters. Herein lies a major problem with jobs incentive plans. States may promise financial help in college, but they cannot guarantee jobs, especially when job markets are tight.

In summary, we see no harm in using college scholarships to encourage young people to prepare now for future goals. But the effectiveness of such rewards is likely to be limited by their being too remote and impersonal.

STICKS

Those incentive policies that depend primarily on the mechanism of negative reinforcements (sticks) are among the most controversial of recent school policies designed to reverse academic deterioration. Negative reinforcers, like positive ones, are meant to increase the likelihood of a given target behavior. In this case the technique involves withholding a negative consequence rather than providing a reward. For instance, after she announces that for each day homework is late the grade will be dropped one point, Mrs. Jenson finds that Sally begins to turn in homework assignments quite regularly. Here the target behavior is promptness in completing assignments and the negative consequence is the potential loss of points. Other common threats featured in sanction policies include depriving students of the opportunity to participate in athletic programs, denial of driver's licenses, and even withholding family welfare payments for poor school attendance or poor grades.

No Pass / No Play

At least ten states have no pass/no play regulations, including Texas and California. In addition, NCAA regulations adopted in 1986 after considerable debate place academic requirements on college students to be eligible to play. For example, NCAA "Proposition 48" rules require that students have combined SAT scores of 700 or ACT scores of 15. Students must also maintain a GPA of at least 2.0 in eleven mandatory courses in college (Cotton, 1989).

As typically employed in schools, a no pass/no play policy requires students to pass a majority of their classes or become ineligible for school-sponsored athletic or extracurricular events. This general plan came to public attention in 1984 when Texas enacted a no pass/no play provision as part of a major reform effort. H. Ross Perot, flamboyant entrepreneur and chairman of the governor's educational task force, lobbied heavily in favor of the reform proposal. He pointed out that extracurricular activities, including football, were getting more attention than were academic subjects. He was particularly fond of drawing attention to the example of one Four-H student who had missed more than thirty days of school showing a pet rooster at fairs and stock shows. The Texas law calls for students to pass all subjects with an average grade of 70 percent. Failure to do so results in the loss of extracurricular eligibility for a period of six weeks. The Texas law has been tested in court and upheld, and legislators have resisted attempts to alter the requirement (Hansen, 1987; Kornacki, 1988). For additional information about no pass/no play policies, see Cotton (1989), Dorsey (1990), Laccetti (1987), and Slater (1988).

One worry that has led to support for this kind of sanction is that American children spend less time in school and on their studies than do children elsewhere. It does seem inappropriate to allow sports to distract students from an academic program already meager in terms of the time and commitment required of students. In addition, there is a reasonable concern that some adults—coaches and sometimes even parents—will occasionally lose perspective and take advantage of student athletes at the expense of their studies (Lapchick, 1989).

No pass/no play policies certainly do send a message that academics are meant to be taken seriously. Yet their effectiveness in actually causing concrete changes in those students who are at greater risk for academic failure is open to debate, and no hard data to our knowledge are available presently to test the proposition. In any event, as a motivational policy no pass/no play rules suffer from poor targeting. Those students most at risk for dropping out of school are generally not athletes; in fact, there is evidence that as a group student athletes are fairly good students already regardless of the presence or absence of sanction rules (Mathews, 1990). Moreover, denying some students the chance to participate in after-school sports may eliminate an effective way to reach out to them. High school athletes frequently identify with their coaches, and, thus, the latter can sometimes uniquely support and motivate these youngsters (Women's Sports Foundation, 1989).

No Pass/No Drive

In 1988 West Virginia enacted a provision for the State Department of Motor Vehicles to deny a driver's license to anyone under the age of eighteen who failed to prove either enrollment in or graduation from high school. The regulations approved by the State Board of Education also stipulated that ten consecutive days of unexcused absence from school or a total of fifteen unexcused absences in one semester were grounds for suspending a teenager's driver's license. Reinstatement of the driver's license could occur only after a successful semester in school with no more than five unexcused absences during that time (Ayres, 1989). By January of 1990 five states had enacted no pass/no drive laws, and twenty-four others were considering them. State legislators' acceptance of such policies seems to be growing and opposition is either not organized or nonexistent (Kelly, 1990). As yet, there is no convincing evidence on the effectiveness of these no-drive sanctions. State agencies in West Virginia have reported that 1,809 students who had dropped out returned to school in the first year of enactment, but there is no way to link no-drive sanctions to these actions. Also, 946 of these students dropped out again (Kelly, 1990).

The no pass/no drive policy also suffers from a matter of timing. In order for sanctions to make a real difference in the academic life of students, they would have to be introduced early enough to influence the child's formative academic development when critical study habits and reading skills are laid down—certainly no later than the early elementary years. But at age seven or eight driving sanctions are remote, if not meaningless. To be effective, these threats and the noxious consequences of not complying should be more or less contiguous; but here they are many years apart. By the time these threats become truly worrisome to targeted students, years of academic lethargy will have taken their toll in the form of deficient learning skills and negative attitudes toward school. Generally, those who advocate sanction programs assume that students can do better if they want to. But a high school student who is failing has usually been failing for some time, and may be many years behind in his or her studies. At this point even a meaningful threat may be of too little use in correcting the situation.

Welfare Reform

Wisconsin, Ohio, and Minnesota have been operating welfare or "learnfare" programs since the late 1980s. In Wisconsin, Aid for Dependent Children (AFDC) requires teenagers to be in school, or their families lose their AFDC benefits. The Wisconsin attendance procedures require tracking of students after they have logged in more than ten unexcused absences in a semester. Once in this category, students can have no more than two more unexcused absences before the sanctions kick in (Gerharz, 1990; *Milwaukee Journal*, 1990). In Ohio, the Learning, Earning, and Parenting Program (LEAP) requires all custodial parents under the age of nineteen on AFDC to attain a high school diploma or a general education diploma (GED). The LEAP Program includes a $62 bonus above the AFDC payment for those who attend school and a $62 sanction for those who are not in school. The bonus is tied to a rule permitting no more than four unexcused absences in a semester. Minnesota requires AFDC parents under the age of eighteen to attend school once their children are six weeks old. Their rules are less stringent than Wisconsin's and the state relies on local district attendance and enrollment data. Students are considered eligible for welfare payments as long as they are enrolled in school, and unexcused absences are not counted in the state formula.

Consider this opinion from the editorial pages of the *Christian Science Monitor* regarding the effectiveness of the Wisconsin Learnfare Program: "The program is based on two assumptions that are open to challenge. First, it assumes that poor parents can fully control the behavior of their 13-to-19-year-old children. Second, it assumes that poor kids are benefited simply by holding down a school desk, regardless of their interest, motivation, or ability to do the assigned work" (*Christian Science Monitor*, 1990). According to one evaluation study of the Wisconsin law conducted by the University of Wisconsin–Madison (*Los Angeles Times*, 1990), only 28 percent of sanctioned students were attending school regularly two months after being sanctioned. The study also indicated that an estimated 20 percent of the sanctioned children were believed to be abuse victims. When combining the children who have already been in trouble with the law and those with a documented need for protective services, over 41 percent of the children whose families had been sanctioned were in serious trouble outside school.

These data suggest that economic sanctions are unlikely to influence the behavior of many members of the underclass in positive ways, either inside or outside school. They also suggest that many students who fall under these sanctions are children whose absenteeism is associated with profoundly disturbed home lives. When a child is at war with his family, no matter who is at fault, sanctions such as these may prove more of a motivation to stay out of school than to attend. For some the ability to hurt family members may be used as a cry for help; for others the sanction can function as a weapon, handily provided by the state. For those children who are under the threat of sanctions but have returned to school, no evidence is currently available on how long they remain in school after reentry, whether their schoolwork improves, or what their prospects are for graduation from high school.

Whatever the results may be, other issues besides effectiveness are raised by "learnfare"-type programs. They include possible violation of due process rights in the case of automatic sanctions; the inherent unfairness of punishing an entire family for the behavior of one member; and the potential for providing delinquent youngsters with a powerful tool to use against their parents.

About Sanctions and the Need for Academic Support

To the extent that poor academic records are the result of inadequate preparation that may have gone unremediated over the years, a major shortcoming of sanction policies is that they are rarely linked to the resources that provide support services such as tutoring, mentor relationships, or individual and family counseling needed to remediate both motivational and academic deficiencies.

We do not suggest that these sanction policies will not work on occasion for specific children. Clearly there are some marginal students who want to play football badly enough or who simply must be able to drive to hold a job, and consequently will respond to sanctions by studying more or becoming more regular in their class attendance. However, these compliant students are probably few when compared to the vast majority of targeted youngsters who are likely to disregard these mandates.

Many students may believe they can get around the sanctions. This expectation is well justified by the numerous exceptions to the sanctions and by the special treatment given to some students, including athletes who are allowed to play in spite of not meeting the requirements. While we have recommended an individualized approach in dealing with school failure, it is not clear to us that *these* exceptions are always made with the student's academic success as the first priority. In the case of no pass/no drive sanctions, enforcement difficulties can render this policy meaningless. A majority of teenagers in some inner cities already drive without a license or are underage drivers. For them the no pass/no drive sanction holds no meaning.

ANALYSIS: WHY DON'T REWARDS AND PUNISHMENTS WORK?

We have considered the potential utility of various statewide and districtwide policies designed to ensure students' involvement in their studies and found many of these policies wanting—at best ineffectual and likely counterproductive for many students. Perhaps the most damning indictment of all is that these policies are simply too tame and unimaginative for dealing with the enormous problems that face American education today.

This verdict prompts an important prior question: Why are such piecemeal, desperate measures needed in the first place? What is it that makes schools and even learning itself seem so noxious that even the prospect of losing valued privileges is not likely enough to force compliance? The issue, as we see it, is not that the application of behavioral principles is an irrelevant or a weak solution to the lack of student effort and indifference in schools, but rather something quite different: that the effects of these normally powerful incentives are themselves opposed by equally strong peer-group, institutional, and societal influences that discourage learning, encourage aimlessness, and engender a hatred of school.

If the target behaviors we seek to enhance involve being orderly, energetic, planful, and studious, then by definition indifference, distractibility, and lack of effort are off-target behaviors. According to the principles of behavior modification, virtually any chronic behavior exists because of the presence of predictable reinforcers. What are the forces that encourage these off-target behaviors?

1. Too few rewards. Learning in schools is typically arranged as a zero-sum competitive game in which students compete among themselves for a fixed number of rewards that are distributed unequally. In effect, when one student wins (or gains rewards), other students must lose. This means that for many if not most students the goal of school is to avoid failure, not to approach success. From a behavioral perspective, this creates a highly noxious situation because the dominant reinforcers are negative—success is counted only in terms of avoiding something that is bad, not achieving something that is good.

2. *Failure to recognize motivational differences among cultures.* Educational policymakers frequently focus on K–12 education as if it were invariably preparation for college and professional careers. However, many students have different expectations for their own futures—early employment, motherhood, basic street survival, for example. Some researchers hold that members of various cultural groups may be more or less likely to hold these alternate expectations for themselves, and may prefer different means to reach their personal goals.

For example, Stack (1974) found that black youngsters tended to avoid competition within their own group of friends. A 1984 study concluded that different problem-solving styles in home and in school was a prominent factor in school failure, and thus there might be consistent culturally differentiated patterns of family problem-solving strategies (Hess and Holloway, 1984).

The notion of cultural capital as posited by Lareau (1987) suggests that children's exposure to a common set of linguistic patterns, literary and social referents, and rules of social behavior is necessary for school success. She proposes that both social-class and cultural influences can result in a child being disadvantaged in that the dominant culture of the classroom is unfamiliar to the child, and its expectations may be unfathomable.

It should be cautioned that each of these works, while presenting generalized evidence about interaction between homes, communities, and schools, fails to provide detailed evidence regarding how these interactions may differ among cultural groups (Graham, 1992). A more specific link is proposed by Ogbu in his study of what he calls "involuntary minorities"—that is, those whose original induction into a society was through force or conquest rather than voluntary immigration.

Ogbu confirms other researchers' thesis that the "white American cultural frame of reference upon which school values are based" is specifically threatening to the internal identities of involuntary minorities. He differentiates between voluntary and involuntary minorities' "folk theories" about achieving success, noting that "involuntary minorities stress collective effort" such as legal or legislative action or protest "as the best means of achieving upward mobility" because "historically (and in terms of jobs, wages, and social recognition) involuntary minorities have not been adequately rewarded for their educational achievement. . . . Involuntary minorities have not developed a widespread effort optimism or a strong cultural ethic of hard work and perseverance in pursuit of education" (Ogbu, 1990, p. 53).

Recognition by teachers that the social expectations of the classroom may be at odds with those of students' home and community lives, and that the problem-solving modes of children may differ along cultural lines, could motivate instructors to broaden their repertoires of teaching strategies. In a sense, even English-speaking minorities may be trying to learn a new "language" and may require, for a time, some degree of translation in order to become fully functional within classroom life.

3. Failure to recognize the ability versus effort dilemma. Teachers reason that although students are not all equally bright, at least everyone can try. As a result, students who are perceived as having tried hard are accorded more rewards in success and punished less in failure than those who do not try. Unfortunately, for many students effort is actually threatening. By not trying, students are attempting to protect a sense of worth, which in our society is often dependent on the ability to achieve competitively. To win is to be worthy, while to do poorly is evidence of inability and reason to despair one's worth. A student may not strive to feel competent through hard work because trying hard represents a specific threat to a sense of worth if the student is risking failure. In competitive incentive systems a combination of high effort and failure implies a lack of ability.

For this reason effort has been described as a "double-edged sword" (Covington and Omelich, 1979). Students value effort as a means to avoid feelings of guilt at having not tried. Yet, on the other hand, they fear the implication that arises from failing despite having tried hard—that they are incompetent and hence unworthy. Thus, lack of effort becomes protection against a kind of negative reinforcement—if one does not try, the negative consequences of unsuccessful effort (including seeing oneself as stupid) are unlikely to occur.

4. Failure to recognize individual differences. Teachers are faced with unavoidable differential effects when they attempt to motivate students through what seem to be obvious reward or punishment mechanisms. To some extent this is an almost inevitable result of the depersonalized atmosphere in a comprehensive high school. It is not unusual in some areas for such a school to house several thousand students, and for each teacher to see more than two hundred students every day. To expect anyone under these conditions to know each student well enough to predict what will motivate him or her best, is to expect a lot.

STUDENT MOTIVATION: AN ALTERNATE MODEL

In order to reverse the record of poor performance in schools, the distractions and obstacles to learning must be lifted. Specifically, schools must find ways to remove the prevailing disincentives for learning, reduce the fear associated with effort expenditure, and strengthen the perceived relevance of the lessons to be learned. The changes proposed by this analysis spring from an alternate metaphor to that of the obstinate beast: the "distracted learner."

The distracted learner model rests on the view that virtually all children are naturally curious and eager to learn from an early age, and remain so for their whole lives unless they become distracted. These distractions may be related to features of schooling as described earlier, or to factors outside school, including pregnancy, homelessness and hunger, child abuse, and urban violence. School is meaningless to the student whose energies are tied up in day-to-day emotional or physical survival.

We cannot overestimate the impact of these negative conditions on our nation's youth. Almost one child in four lives in poverty (Kirst, 1989); it is estimated that *at least* one in four girls and one in ten boys experience sexual abuse (Russell, 1984); reported cases of physical abuse are at an all-time high and rising (Barth and Berry, 1989); gang activity and general violent crime in most large cities are rising as well (*San Francisco Chronicle*, April 18, 1992). At the same time, resources needed to combat these conditions, such as child protective services, income support for families, and supervised recreation programs, are increasingly strained. In most areas of the country recession-ravaged budgets for these services are actually being cut back even as the need for them swells.

Nonschool causes of failure have long been a confounding factor in school improvement efforts. We believe that children's conditions of living and the school's expectations for those children are inextricably entwined and must be considered together in order to devise effective motivational strategies.

These, then, are the presumptions of our "distracted-mind" model: first, that learning basically is a pleasurable activity; second, that various conditions from inside and outside school distract students from learning; and third, that the impact of these distractions can be reduced so that more students will be motivated to remain in school and to work harder while there.

Now we turn to a series of specific recommendations aimed at reducing these distractions. Some are policy-related and others are directed at the profession of teaching. Where possible, we have included examples of specific, existing programs or practices we have observed that satisfy these recommendations.

RECOMMENDATIONS TO REDUCE DISTRACTIONS TO LEARNING

Suggestions for Educators

Every Child Should Be Known by at Least One Adult Authority. Since different children face different obstacles to educational success, it is necessary to understand each student as an individual. As was argued earlier, rewards and punishments do have the power to shape *individual* lives; but applied across the board, rewards and sanctions of the types reviewed here largely miss the mark. Those programs that provide students with individual mentorship—all too few, at this writing—hold the most promise for effecting real and lasting changes in student attitudes.

- At White Valley High School, a committee of students, teachers, and parents provides support to students in trouble. Any student whose history indicates academic or emotional problems and any student whose grades suddenly drop or whose behavior changes is referred to this group. Peers or adults may offer tutoring, referrals to support services for drug or emotional problems, or just a sympathetic ear to a student with difficulties. One measure of the success of the program is the high number of former recipients who volunteer to participate as mentors in later years.

- At Mill Stream Middle School, every incoming sixth grader is assigned to an older "big brother" or "big sister." From the day before school starts, when the "big siblings" guide the new children around the campus and introduce them to their teachers, these mentors are available to help with anything from school paperwork to peer conflicts. In each of the three years since the program began, the adjustment period for sixth graders has been shorter and less intense.
- Fieldstone Elementary School's teachers form impromptu "Contact Groups" when they encounter a student with whom they have chronic concerns. The group usually includes the principal, a current teacher, one or more of the child's previous teachers, and the parent(s). Together they work to find solutions to behavioral or academic problems.

Cultural Differences Should Be Understood and Honored. In addition to identifying the needs of individual students, school personnel must recognize the cultural dimensions that influence the impact of motivational policies. By using incentives that fail to acknowledge the values of ethnic minorities (such as cooperation and family cohesiveness), teachers and schools imply disrespect for community values. Students forced to choose between the teachings and living styles of the home and school are faced with an untenable conflict that cannot enhance their commitment to schooling activities. Furthermore, these conflicts are almost always resolved in favor of the nonschool influences.

- As part of its desegregation plan, Albey School District provided training for every teacher regarding the needs and cultural structures of the minority students in the district. Teachers learned about the family life, discipline patterns, priorities and values, and even dietary patterns and restrictions relating to different students' backgrounds.
- The counselors and teachers in Venice High School could not understand why their African-American girl students consistently refused to cooperate in P. E. swimming classes. Year after year, these girls stood in the pool and took failing grades for that part of the course. Finally, someone surveyed the mothers of the girls, and

discovered that the chlorine in the pool damaged the girls' brittle hair, causing it to break off. Alternate forms of exercise were offered to the girls, and performance in Physical Education improved.

Every Child Must Have a Chance to Succeed. We must arrange the rules of learning so that intrinsic payoffs (e.g., satisfying curiosity) as well as external rewards tied directly to learning become readily available to all who learn well. This means defining excellence in terms of making individual progress against absolute standards of excellence, not in terms of succeeding at the expense of others. This converts learning from being an ability game, with the value of rewards depending on their scarcity, to an effort game in which everyone can succeed.

- Mr. Gavin's fifth graders do most of their in-class work in cooperative groups. Individual children may be assigned to be resources to each other in areas in which that student is competent; groups that solve problems correctly are awarded points that can be converted into particularly desired learning activities. During discussions, one or two points are generally awarded for any correct or useful answer (or even a particularly astute observation) from any individual.

Learning Itself Should Be a Conditioned Reinforcer. While the dispensing of praise and other extrinsic rewards can be useful in moderation, the most important reward should be knowledge itself. Children who see the power in understanding, the usefulness of problem solving, and the beauty in knowledge will require fewer external rewards to learn. Wherever possible, classroom interactions should acknowledge and reinforce the view that learning is a gift in and of itself.

- Five-year-old Bobby has been weighing ceramic tiles on a scale. He has stacked them high, and found that his pile weighs seven pounds. His teacher comes over to him. "Seven pounds!" she exclaims. "Would you like to have a paper showing how much your tiles weigh?" When Bobby nods, she continues as she draws out a sheet of brightly colored paper and a marker. "I'll write '7 pounds' on this plain piece of paper and you can copy it on this yellow paper." When the child has written down the weight, the teacher helps him to add his own name and the date, and leaves him drawing a picture of himself weighing the tiles. The paper will be his to display during the day and to take home later. Bobby's reward is the mastery and display of new knowledge and skills.

Linkages Between Work and School, and Between the World and School, Should Be Made Explicit. Schools should teach children to think about problems relevant to their lives now and about the future. Knowledge acquisition should be arranged around projects, tasks, and the solution of real-life simulations. For example, in the process of determining which garbage products are biodegradable and which are not, students are introduced to principles of biology and ecology; by devising tests to assess the safety of cars, students learn applied physics; by role playing a guidance counselor, students incidentally learn about occupational choice.

In addition, we support efforts to make information about student work habits and performance available to and useful for employers. For those students who will not seek post-secondary education, the school should clearly convey the relationship between school performance and access to good jobs after high school.

- Mrs. Gordon assigns her sophomore English class a major paper in which they must identify a controversial issue in their community, interview parties involved in the issue, and discuss the conflict in relation to other conflicts they have studied through literature during the semester. This literature has included Farley Mowat's *Never Cry Wolf*, and the discussion of this work has included issues such as the government's attitude towards wolves, the government employee's responsibility for his job, and the way people respond when confronted with new information that conflicts with their beliefs.
- Mr. Bowman's fifth-grade math class does a series of "shop" projects during the year. Students must measure, draw up plans, compute how much material to buy, figure out costs, and apportion the construction tasks among working groups.

Cooperation Should Be Emphasized. Most adults must work in group situations where cooperation and coordination of responsibility are required for a successful outcome. Yet in many classrooms students work alone most of the time. Learning to function in a group, to resolve conflicts, to set common goals and to cooperate in meeting them, and to share responsibility are all important skills that additionally serve to enhance a commitment to learning. Because cooperative learning requires profound and fundamental changes in classroom management and teacher activities, staff training and ongoing assistance to teachers may be required to implement this type of reform.

- In Mrs. Jude's eighth-grade social studies class, the students prepare a project about a particular event in American history. Working in groups of four, the students take on roles of key participants in that event. Individually, each student researches the person they must represent and writes, in journal form, an account of the times. Jointly, they produce a narrative description of their event, a map of the region in which it occurred, and an oral presentation for the class describing the course of this bit of history.
- In Mr. Robert's fifth-grade class, each student at some time during the year is part of a four-member activity planning team. The team develops a half-day or full-day program for the class, with only two limitations: it must be centered around a learning activity and it must be something that can be done within the resources of the class. One year's activities included a linguistic treasure hunt at the local shopping mall and a lunchtime math carnival for the whole school, at which answers to math questions (developed for each grade level by the fifth graders manning the booths) earned treats made by the students.

Suggestions for Policymakers

We well understand the frustration among policymakers that has led to their desire to influence student motivation. Underachieving, seemingly indolent, listless, and unmotivated youth strike any reasonable person as tragic wastes of time and resources, their own and society's. However, as well intentioned as policymakers may be, it is our conclusion that most of the current genre of statewide or districtwide motivational policies will prove unproductive. They fail to take adequately into account the circumstances that contribute initially to students' motivational malaise, they are sometimes contrary to what is known about the nature of learning, and they often interfere with the practical options that should be left to the professional judgment of individual teachers.

We suggest three different approaches. No one of these by itself will immediately convert an alienated prospective dropout to a Nobel laureate. However, their cumulative effect may assist in elevating aspirations and in inspiring more students to stay in school and study. The three practical avenues available to policymakers are (1) better coordination of social and health services to at-risk students, (2) more effective teacher training, and (3) greater schoolwide cooperation in addressing questions of student motivation.

Coordinated Social Services. We have addressed this topic in the preceding section's advice to professional educators. We repeat it here, however, because there is much about this matter that resides outside the domain of teachers and administrators. Mental health, criminal justice, foster care, and health care services for youngsters are generally the result of state policy administered through county agencies. Education officials have little jurisdiction in many instances, and there are precious few incentives for social agencies to cooperate.

There are a variety of proposals for coordinating services for children. One is the use of "case workers" in schools who coordinate all agency services for the students assigned to them. Another proposal is to use schools as a center for service delivery by having clinics and other service personnel available in schools. This strategy is particularly attractive in secondary schools. Regardless of the particular approach, the intent is to identify means whereby the full spectrum of social services needed by children may effectively be brought to bear to dilute the personal, family, or neighborhood conditions that interfere with their ability to concentrate on and benefit from schooling.

Teacher Training. Eventually, it is classroom teachers and other school personnel who will prove most instrumental in motivating unconcerned youth. To become most effective in this task, teachers need to be informed about the psychosocial dynamics underlying learning; they also would benefit from having a wide variety of examples of appropriate instructional techniques provided to them.

Unfortunately, the current trend in teacher training is to downgrade training in the generic understanding of pedagogy, especially questions relating to motivation, human development, and individual differences among learners, and instead to emphasize specific instructional techniques related to a particular subject matter (e.g., science and mathematics). The result is that teachers may be underprepared to deal with those issues that touch on motivation. Problems of student motivation will always exist. However, the front line of defense for mitigating them is the preparation of teachers. Policymakers would do well to ensure that state requirements for teacher certification and recertification contain appropriate exposure to psychological tenets of motivation and pedagogical skills in addition to subject knowledge.

Schoolwide Cooperation. Individual teachers, counselors, school nurses, and vice-principals cannot singlehandedly address the problems of unmotivated students. Mechanisms are needed whereby the professional staff of a school, indeed the entire school community, understand that a collective effort is needed. Consequently, policymakers, including local school board members, should include measures of successful motivation (e.g., school persistence rates, students' absenteeism or attendance measures, and students' extracurricular participation measures) among the outputs they expect of schools and intend systematically to measure. Also, policymakers should emphasize required systems that induce schoolwide cooperation. Plans such as merit schools that require teamwork rather than intraschool competition may be particularly appropriate in this context.

SUMMARY

It is not our intention to minimize the importance to students' achievement of hard work and high expectations, the focal themes that inspired this volume. On the contrary, we are convinced that students and teachers as well as the larger community must redouble their efforts in order to reverse the crisis in American education. Students must study harder, teachers must upgrade their skills, and the community must provide the human and physical resources necessary to sustain excellence.

In the last analysis, the quality of student effort, whether it be directed into productive channels or subverted for the purposes of resistance, depends largely on the reasons for learning in the first place. The reasons reflected in many of the motivational policies reviewed here can for the most part arouse only negative responses. This is not to imply that those who advocate those policies are venal or insensitive. Like all of us, they are frustrated that our best efforts to make schools work often fail, and fail badly. On the surface, these policies are undeniably attractive in their simplicity, their straightforwardness, and their seeming common sense. We believe, however, that research findings in the laboratory and the field support our view that the very simplicity of these policies belies the complexity of what is not working in schools today.

By working directly with troubled students and improving the inherent attractiveness of class activities, schools and teachers can make learning more tempting to more students. Early in students' lives we must develop links between learning activities and practical, real-life problem solving. By recognizing the realities of students' lives, schools can participate in developing a collaborative, problem-solving relationship with schoolchildren and our communities. We predict that the development of such a relationship would make policy-level carrots and sticks unnecessary for the promotion of student learning.

REFERENCES

Ayres, B. D. "West Virginia Reduces Dropouts by Denying Them Driver's License," *New York Times*, 21 May 1989.

Barth, Richard P., and Berry, Marianne. "Child Abuse and Child Welfare Services." In *Conditions of Children in California*, edited by Michael W. Kirst, pp. 225–253. Berkeley, Calif.: Policy Analysis for California Education, 1989.

Christian Science Monitor. "Docking the Poor for Cutting Class," 3 January 1990.

Condry, John. "Enemies of Exploration: Self-Initiated versus Other-Initiated Learning," *Journal of Personality and Social Psychology* 35 (1977): 459–477.

Cotton, A. "Prop. 48 Costs More Than Season," *Washington Post*, 22 January 1989.

Covington, Martin V. *Making the Grade: A Self-worth Perspective on Motivation and School Reform*. New York: Cambridge University Press, 1992.

Covington, Martin V., and Jacoby, Keith E. "Productive Thinking and Course Satisfaction as a Function of an Independence-Conformity Dimension." Paper presented at the meeting of the American Psychological Association, Montreal, 1973.

Covington, Martin V., and Omelich, Carol L. "Are Causal Attributions Causal? A Path Analysis of the Cognitive Model of Achievement Motivation," *Journal of Personality and Social Psychology* 37 (1979): 1487–1504.

Dorsey, V. L. "High School Athletics Scrutinized," *USA Today*, 1 February, 1990.

Gerharz, G. "Wisconsin's Learnfare: A Bust," *New York Times*, 29 January 1990.

Goldberg, Louis R. "Grades as Motivants," *Psychology in the Schools* 2 (1965): 17–24.

Graham, Sandra. "'Most of the Subjects Were White and Middle Class': Trends in Published Research on African Americans in Selected APA Journals, 1970–1989," *American Psychologist* 47, no. 5 (1992): 629–639.

Guthrie, James W. "Editorial: Presidential Campaigns and Education Policy," *Educational Researcher* 17, no. 2 (1988): 4, 12.

Hansen, J. O. "Texas Students Passing, and Playing," *Atlanta Journal*, 8 February 1987.

Hess, Robert D., and Holloway, Susan D. "Family and School as Educational Institutions." In *Review of Child Development Research*, edited by R. D. Parke. Chicago: University of Chicago Press, 1984.

Kelly, D. "There's No License to Drop Out," *USA Today*, 2 January 1990.

Kirst, Michael W., ed. *Conditions of Children in California*. Berkeley, Calif.: Policy Analysis for California Education, 1989.

Kohn, Alfie. *No Contest: The Case Against Competition*. Boston: Houghton-Mifflin, 1986.

Kornacki, S. "Most 'Prop 48' Athletes Make Grade, Survey Shows," *Ann Arbor News*, 7 August 1988.

Kozol, Jonathan. *Free Schools*. Boston: Houghton-Mifflin, 1972.

Laccetti, S. "Rigid 'No-Pass, No-Play Rule' Is Being Called For," *Atlanta Journal*, 12 February 1987.

Lapchick, R. E. *Pass to Play: Student Athletes and Academics*, NEA Professional Library. Washington, D. C.: National Education Association, 1989.

Lareau, Annette. "Social Class Differences in Family-School Relationships: The Importance of Cultural Capital," *Sociology of Education* 60 (1987): 73–85.

Los Angeles Times, 1 July 1990.

Mathews, J. "Los Angeles Schools Drop No-Pass, No-Play Rule," *Washington Post*, 14 January 1990.

Milwaukee Journal. "Time to Give Up on Learnfare," 24 March 1990.

Neill, A. S. *Summerhill: A Radical Approach to Child Rearing*. New York: Hart Publishing Co., 1960.

Ogbu, John. "Minority Education in Comparative Perspective," *Journal of Negro Education* 59, no. 1 (1990): 45–57.

Russell, Diana E. H. *Sexual Exploitation: Rape, Child Sexual Abuse, and Workplace Harassment*. Sage Library of Social Research, Vol. 155. Beverly Hills, Calif: Sage Publications, 1984.

San Francisco Chronicle, 18 April 1992.

Slater, Jana K. "Pass to Play Legislation in California: Vegetables before Dessert!" *Educational Evaluation and Policy Analysis* 10, no. 2 (1988): 151–160.

Stack, Carol B. *All Our Kin: Strategies for Survival in a Black Community*. New York: Harper and Row, 1974.

Women's Sports Foundation. *High School Athletics Prove Boon*. New York: Women's Sports Foundation, 1989.

Wycliff, D. "Help Is Given in the Pursuit of Education Dreams," *New York Times*, 18 June 1990.

Chapter 6

CREATING PRESCRIPTIONS FOR SUCCESS IN URBAN SCHOOLS: TURNING THE CORNER ON PATHOLOGICAL EXPLANATIONS FOR ACADEMIC FAILURE

Antoine M. Garibaldi

Improving the quality of education in this country's many schools continues to be a high priority among parents, citizens, political leaders, and educators as we near the turn of the century. Numerous reform efforts have been initiated to restructure schools, to enhance the participation of parents in school affairs, and to change and upgrade the training of preservice teachers. But since these efforts are still in embryonic and experimental stages in some school districts and universities, it is still too early to determine if they are resulting in any significant improvement in education. Nevertheless, the condition of many urban schools clearly demonstrates that there is still a great deal to do to improve the quality and quantity of education for many students.

The majority of schools in metropolitan areas today are populated by nonwhite youth, many of whom are African-American or Hispanic. Unfortunately, these two groups disproportionately account for the high rates of academic failure and also for disciplinary actions, such as nonpromotions, special education placements, suspensions, and expulsions, resulting from misbehavior in school.

Nationally, while African-American students, for example, represent 16 percent of all students in school, they account for 25 percent of all suspensions and 35 percent of the students placed in classes for the educable mentally retarded but only 8 percent of the students in gifted and talented programs (Quality Education for Minorities Project, 1990). But even though the educational literature is replete with studies on the academic dysfunctions of students, particularly non-white youth, and on pathological explanations of underachievement, no single variable can explain the significant amount of failure in our schools.

Conventional wisdom and much research place a heavy burden on children for their lack of educational attainment and performance, but in this chapter I will attempt to show that reasonable prescriptions can be implemented to improve their educational situations. I will also focus heavily on the experiences of African-American students because they account for the largest number of nonwhite students in schools, because much educational research has focused on that group, and because I am most familiar with them.

SIGNS OF UNDERACHIEVEMENT

On almost every measure of educational achievement, the skills of our nation's youth have declined or remained stable over the last ten years. Scores on reading, mathematics, language arts, writing, and college aptitude tests indicate insignificant gains for students of all races. African-American students have made slight gains on some of these national tests, but their group average is still far from the national average. In a national assessment of reading comprehension, only about one thirteen-year-old in ten was considered an "adept" reader, that is, able to understand complicated written information (National Assessment of Educational Progress, 1985). And on similar national assessment tests requiring analytic or persuasive writing, fewer than one in five eighth graders wrote adequate or better essays (Applebee, Langer, and Mullis, 1986). These indicators of under-achievement in basic skills areas for all students are later magnified in high school and eventually in college, but the problem is much more grave for nonwhite students.

On the College Entrance Examination Board's Scholastic Aptitude Test, for example, the average scores for African-American students in 1990 were 352 on the verbal and 385 on the mathematical sections, compared to the national means of 424 and 476, respectively.

Similarly, student performance scores on the 1990 ACT, published by the American College Testing Program, indicate that African-American students increased their average score by four-tenths of a point to 17.0 over the previous year, but the national average for all test-takers was 20.6 (*Chronicle of Higher Education*, 1990). (White students' average score was 21.2, down one-tenth of a point from the previous year; Puerto Ricans and other Hispanics scored 19.3, the same as the year before; Asian-American students scored at 21.7, two-tenths lower than in the previous year; and American-Indian students had a mean score of 18, up from 17.5.) These scores of graduating high school students, which measure their competence in core academic subject matter, are signs that many students are not proficient in the basic skills after twelve years of education. But even more revealing is that many students are not even being exposed to rigorous subject matter and college preparatory courses (Maeroff, 1988, 1990). For example, of the students who took the ACT in 1990, just 45 percent took the recommended core high school curriculum that included four years of English and three or more years of mathematics, social studies, and natural sciences (compared to 36 percent in 1987). Taking college preparatory courses in high school does positively affect performance on these college entrance tests. This is best demonstrated by the statistic that the African-American students in the ACT sample who had taken college preparatory courses in high school (42 percent in 1990 compared to 30 percent in 1987) had a mean ACT of 18.2, while those African-American students who had not taken these courses scored an average of 16.1. Certainly all of the variance in improved ACT test performance by African-American students cannot be attributed solely to a higher percentage of them taking college preparatory courses, but it is reasonable to assume that more of them should do better on the tests if they have been exposed to the subjects on which the examinations are based. Two examples of African-American students' low participation in college preparatory courses in mathematics, for example, will be given later, but I want to point out here that these trends do exist and are widespread in school districts across this country.

While school reform efforts are indeed laudable at this point in our history, answers and solutions to the more fundamental questions and problems of underachievement and educational attainment of the masses of nonwhite students are needed now. We must ask, for example, what accounts for the fact that more than half of all African-American students score below the mean on standardized tests of basic skills? Is it because of their low abilities, their lack of effort and motivation to learn, their low academic and personal expectations, their low socioeconomic status, or the peer pressure that they receive to not do well in school? Or are low scores a function of the low expectations and self-fulfilling prophecies of teachers, less challenging curricula, or teachers' inability to reach students who come from cultural and socioeconomic backgrounds different from their own? There are no easy answers to these questions; all of these possibilities likely contribute in varied ways to students' underachievement.

LOCAL ATTEMPTS TO EXPLAIN EDUCATIONAL FAILURE, INEQUALITY, AND TREATMENT OF BLACK MALES

In 1987–88 I served as the study director and chairman of a committee of New Orleans educators and civic leaders who were asked to assess the educational status of African-American males in the local school system. In an urban school system where 87 percent of the 86,000 students are African-American and 43 percent are African-American males, we found that African-American males accounted for 58 percent of the nonpromotions, 65 percent of the suspensions, 80 percent of the expulsions, and 45 percent of the dropouts during the 1986–87 academic year (Garibaldi, 1988). While it is difficult to claim that these percentages of nonpromotions, suspensions, expulsions, and dropouts were racially disproportionate given the demographic composition of the school system, we were most concerned by their large absolute numbers in each of the above categories and the fact that the patterns of educational dysfunction started so early in these students' school years. But we also discovered that the situation for African-American females in the New Orleans public schools was also bleak, as they accounted for 34 percent of the nonpromotions, 29 percent of the suspensions, 20 percent of the expulsions, and 41 percent of the dropouts.

With respect to academic achievement, we also observed that one-third of African-American males and females scored in the lowest quartile on the reading and mathematics sections of the California

Test of Basic Skills. Only 18 percent of the males and 20 percent of the females scored in the highest quartile on the mathematics component of the test; and only 16 percent of the females and 13 percent of the males scored in the highest quartile on the reading test. These adverse trends in reading performance, particularly for black males and females, have been verified in analyses of national assessments by Winfield (1988) and by Winfield and Lee (1990), who note that minority females outscore their male counterparts to a greater degree than do white females on NAEP reading tests.

These findings have recently been replicated in a similar study on black males in the Prince Georges County (Maryland) school district (Simmons and Grady, 1990) and in Milwaukee (African-American Male Task Force, 1990). The results in Prince Georges County showed that the performance of black males and females on criterion-referenced tests in mathematics and reading was comparable to white students up to the third grade. But beginning in grade four, black males experienced a sharp decline on criterion-referenced tests in both mathematics and reading. Moreover, the percentage of black males in the top reading group among eighteen Prince Georges County elementary schools dropped significantly in grades four and six. In the first and fourth grades, 23 percent of the black males were in the top reading group, but by grade six only 12 percent were in that group.

In Milwaukee, the percentage of black males scoring at or above the national average on the norm-referenced test in reading in 1988–89 dropped from 28 percent in second grade to 24 percent in grades five and seven. On the mathematics norm-referenced test, 45 percent of the black males scored at or above the national average in second grade, but that proportion dropped to 33 percent in grade five and to 22 percent in grade seven. Black females in Milwaukee also unfortunately experienced the same declining score trends on norm-referenced tests in reading and mathematics. In reading, the percentage of black girls in Milwaukee scoring at or above the national average declined from 34 percent in grade two to 22 percent in grade five, but then surprisingly went up to 30 percent in grade seven. In mathematics, 45 percent of them scored at or above the national mean in the second grade, 37 percent in the fifth grade, and then down to 26 percent in seventh grade. Regressions in academic performance on mathematics and reading tests for African-American students around grade four are clearly evident, and further study is needed to identify those critical factors that are causing this phenomenon.

The only bright spot in the analysis of academic achievement in the New Orleans study was that roughly one-third of the African-American males scored at or above the mean on both sections of the test. But the disheartening fact that so many African-American males were not proceeding to the next grade level—800 of the 1,470 non-promotions in first grade and more than 1,600 of the close to 2,800 nonpromotions in the sixth through eighth grades—extinguished even the slightest bit of optimism. These high numbers of retentions and the poor academic performance of African-American males are being replicated in many other school systems, and it is clear that the academic failure begins early and eventually leads these youths to become disinterested in school and to drop out before they reach senior high school. Nevertheless, there are solutions to this malaise and they are applicable to *all* school children, male and female, who are not performing at or above grade level.

RAISING ACADEMIC EXPECTATIONS

One of the first ways to improve the low achievement of many African-American males is to raise their expectations for academic achievement. Many metropolitan communities are plagued by high homicide rates (black males are often the victims, and perpetrators, of such crime), by high unemployment and pervasive poverty, and by rampant drug cultures where the "reward" of earning money by selling illegal drugs, despite the risks involved, outweighs the value of attending and achieving in school. In such communities young non-white males see few positive role models and have little hope that a high school or college education will guarantee them a financially stable future as adults. These young men see negative images and stereotypes on television and in newspapers; their interest in immediate satisfaction, typical of many adolescents, is in direct opposition to delayed gratification; and their disproportionate number in the criminal justice system creates a self-fulfilling prophecy that they directly and indirectly internalize.

Despite the negative protrayals of this group in the press and the attitudes that many individuals have developed about their abilities, most African-American boys do want to finish school and many want to be challenged. In our survey of more than 2,250 African-American males in the New Orleans school district, 95 percent of them said they expected to graduate from high school. Moreover, 40 percent of them said that they believed their teachers did not set high enough goals for them and that their teachers should push them harder. Regardless of what the public and educators believe, the above results, which some might interpret as "cries for help," clearly indicate that schools must do more to motivate and encourage these young men, and realistic strategies must be implemented to acknowledge, promote, and reward their academic achievement in the same way that society and schools currently publicly recognize athletic prowess and musical talent.

REINFORCING ACADEMIC PERFORMANCE

When any individual receives reinforcement and positive feedback for doing well, positive changes do occur and goals are achieved. But young students, regardless of their race, gender, and socioeconomic status, need more intensive guidance and support to foster academic achievement. Acknowledging their successful experiences, no matter how small, gradually influences their self-concept, their academic confidence, and their awareness that society does reward intellectual accomplishments. This is critically important because the verbal and material reinforcement they might receive for academic pursuits can counterbalance the almost constant negative pressure from peers and negative models in their communities. Negative peer pressure, specifically against so-called "acting white" behavior, is a major deterrent to nonwhite students' academic performance and must be addressed by schools and teachers so that students who do perform at or above average are not ostracized, ridiculed, intimidated, physically assaulted, or belittled by their peers (Fordham and Ogbu, 1986). Such negative behaviors do exist and more must be done by parents, communities, the media, and educators to minimize the social and psychological stress that academically talented students must cope with each day.

REVERSING ACADEMIC TRACKING PATTERNS

While students must assume a large share of the burden for their academic failure and increase their motivation and desire to learn, educators and parents can help to improve their performance, increase the amount of time they spend on academic tasks, and reverse many of their negative academic trends. But teachers, administrators, and parents must take more initiative in determining what courses secondary school students should take rather than allow students to make by themselves those curriculum decisions that will affect their life chances and their ability to become productive citizens in the next century. Evidence abounds to demonstrate that many nonwhite youngsters are taking remedial courses that are watered down versions of the subject matter (Braddock, 1990). That many nonwhite students in urban schools are taking lower-level offerings in mathematics (e.g., Consumer or Business Mathematics rather than Algebra 2 or Calculus), natural sciences (Biology rather than Physics), and English (Grammar and Writing rather than Literature) is testament that there is an unequal treatment of students in our schools (Irvine, 1990; Maeroff, 1988, 1990; Ogbu, 1978; Oakes, 1985, 1986).

In the Prince Georges County study, Simmons and Grady (1990) reported that only 12 percent of the seniors taking Calculus were black males, even though this group of students represented 31 percent of the twelfth-grade class. However, 42 percent of the tenth-grade students taking Consumer Mathematics and 48 percent of the seniors taking Algebra 1, a course usually taken in ninth grade, were black males. Only about 514 of the 3,000 black males in ninth grade were taking Algebra in Prince Georges County in 1989. Moreover, only 26 percent of the 1,440 students taking Geometry were black males. Black females were also underrepresented in twelfth-grade Calculus (19 percent compared to their 32 percent share of the senior population) and they accounted for 31 percent of the eleventh graders in Consumer Mathematics and 31 percent of the twelfth graders taking Algebra 1. These disturbing patterns of participation in general and vocational track courses corroborate the research showing that the majority of nonwhite students are typically assigned to remedial, lower-level, and the least challenging courses (Braddock, 1990; Oakes, 1985, 1986). These students' chances of gaining access to, much less succeeding in, college are greatly diminished because they will be inadequately prepared to do well on college entrance examinations and in core college courses.

THE IMPACT OF NEGATIVE TEACHER PERCEPTIONS

Irvine (1990) asserts that African-American students are subject to school failure because of their race, social class, and culture, and she emphasizes that race is a "salient factor that contributes to unequal school treatment, participation and distribution of rewards for all black students." Like other researchers who have addressed this issue (e.g., Hilliard, 1989; Oakes, 1985; Ogbu, 1978), Irvine posits that there is a lack of "cultural synchronization" between students and teachers in many schools and this contributes to negative teacher expectations. Teachers' beliefs, attitudes, behaviors, and perceptions influence the level and type of communication and classroom interaction, the quality and rigor of instruction, and the affect the teacher shows toward her students (Irvine, 1990). In one of her own studies, Irvine (1985) found that a teacher's initial impression of a student was likely to remain stable, especially impressions of black males, which did not change throughout the school year. All teachers, regardless of race and gender, are influenced by the stereotypes held by the majority of the population, and they are prone to treat these young men consciously and unconsciously in the classroom as the "endangered species" characterized by the media and the public. However, positive teacher expectations are critical to raising students' self-concepts and their academic performance. But teachers must go one step further and help their students to appreciate and value learning and academic excellence.

If school reform is to succeed, curricula and teachers' expectations of students' abilities must be addressed first. Social promotions do not help students who are struggling to learn, but they do confirm some teachers' usually unsubstantiated perceptions that children from racially different and lower socioeconomic backgrounds cannot achieve more than the minimum. As Maeroff (1988) states:

Teachers in urban schools are confronted by a dilemma, especially in the upper grades, where the lack of earlier preparation leaves a mark of destruction on young people who are academically ill-prepared. A teacher who asks much of students who have not been equipped to meet the demands may not only be unrealistic, but may also be setting students up for frustration and failure. On the other hand, not having high expectations for students implies that minority students are incapable of doing the work and dooms them to the ranks of the underclass. [P. 636]

Earlier in this chapter I noted that African-American males in the New Orleans study said they expected to graduate from high school. About half of them said that their teachers did not set high enough goals for them and that they wanted their teachers to push them harder. But when we surveyed a random sample of 500 teachers (318 of whom responded), asking if they believed that their black male students would go to college, almost six in ten said they did not believe this would occur. This result was more troubling because 60 percent of our sample taught in elementary schools, 70 percent of them had ten or more years of experience, and 65 percent of them were black!

This discomforting response lends added support to the literature on the impact of teachers' expectations of children and confirms that nonwhite teachers too can hold negative self-fulfilling prophecies about the children whom they teach, even teachers whose racial backgrounds are the same as their pupils. I believe that class, more than racial, differences between students and teachers may be partially responsible for these low perceptions of students' ability and aspirations and that this "social distance" must be narrowed. Nonwhite teachers are also obviously influenced by public stereotypes and must deal with, perhaps even more than white teachers, their subjective beliefs and attitudes about the ability of young African-American males to succeed.

That many African-American males do succeed in school makes this issue even more important because any teacher who holds negative perceptions can inadvertently "turn off" male students who have high abilities, positive self-concepts and personal expectations, and achievable aspirations. All teachers, therefore, must challenge these young men and, when possible, provide them with immediate, continuous, and appropriate reinforcement and with positive feedback. These external means of encouragement by teachers can significantly enhance the importance and value of education to the long-term financial and personal success of all youth.

PARENTAL AND COMMUNITY RESPONSIBILITY

Teachers alone cannot change students' desire to learn and to succeed. Equally important are parents, who spend more time with their children and want them to succeed. In the New Orleans study, eight in ten of the 3,523 parents we surveyed indicated that they believed their sons expected to go to college. But one-fourth of them also responded that they had never gone to their child's school for parental conferences. This parental perception of African-American males' postsecondary interests obviously is not matched by parents' own interest in or contribution to the motivation, encouragement, and reinforcement of their sons. Therefore, parents must acknowledge and reward their sons' academic accomplishments; they must encourage them to do homework; they must emphasize the value of learning; and they must meet and consult with their sons' teachers to find out how they are performing and where they need assistance. Even more important, parents must monitor what courses their sons are taking and support their aspirations to go to college in the same way that they encourage their daughters.

But many parents, especially those who have little education, will need help from schools, teachers, and the community to accomplish all this. Just as some students are ostracized by their peers for doing well in school, so too are some parents intimidated by teachers and are reluctant to ask questions about their child's performance or behavior in the classroom. Teachers, therefore, must be prepared to communicate with the parents of their students. They must learn how to convey, in layman's language, the results of their pupils' performance on standardized tests. They must further learn to offer helpful suggestions to parents that can enhance their child's academic performance and participation in school activities.

At the same time, teachers must also inform parents about their children's academic strengths as well as their weaknesses. These types of balanced evaluations give teachers the opportunity to suggest to parents ways in which their children might develop better study skills and more constructively use their time after school. Emphasizing the positive characteristics of children, even when their abilities are below average, is a very constructive way of demonstrating to parents their role in encouraging, assisting, and monitoring more closely the academic performance of their children (Garibaldi, forthcoming). The differences among teachers, parents, and students in their perceptions of students' abilities must be corrected. This can be achieved only through cooperation, communication, and understanding among all three groups.

CONCLUSION

This chapter offers support to those who believe that success in urban schools is indeed possible and within reach. Children who come from culturally diverse backgrounds do exhibit learning differences. Yet, other factors such as parental support, encouragement, and motivation, and the teacher's ability to distinguish cultural differences from cultural deficits, can improve these youths' motivation, aspirations, and achievement (Boykin, 1979; Banks, McQuater, and Hubbard, 1979; Clark, 1983; Oakes, 1985; Irvine, 1990).

Identifying pathological explanations of academic failure without offering reasonable prescriptions to combat those negative indicators will not improve the schooling process for the masses of students in our urban schools. The following recommendations are offered for students, teachers, parents, and those who are chiefly responsible for the quality of education in the nation.

1. All students must be taught the value of education and the role it will play in their adult years.
2. Students' academic achievement must be acknowledged and rewarded in the school and at home.
3. Students' should receive consistent reinforcement and positive feedback from their teachers when they succeed.
4. Schools should work intensively to identify the factors contributing to regressions, which begin in the fourth grade, in the academic performance of all nonwhite students, especially African-American males.
5. The curriculum in schools must be challenging to all students, and patterns of tracking in senior high courses must be eliminated immediately.
6. Teachers must set high goals for all their pupils and avoid making stereotypical judgments about students' abilities, regardless of their race, gender, and social class. Furthermore, they should encourage all students to consider and prepare for postsecondary opportunities.
7. Teachers must be better prepared to communicate with and relate to parents so that they will clearly understand how their children are performing.
8. Parents must motivate their children to do well in school to

augment the reinforcement teachers give them. They must ensure that their children do homework. They must communicate regularly with their children's teachers.

9. Parents must hold their children accountable for low performance and socially inappropriate behavior at school and at home.

10. Community groups and businesses must find ways to support the aspirations and achievement of youth. Businesses can be particularly helpful by allowing their employees who are parents, through flexible scheduling or released-time arrangements, to attend report card conferences at the school.

11. The media and those in responsible positions of leadership must accentuate the good that is occurring in schools along with the negative.

No one doubts that schools are imperfect places today. But if more time is spent focusing on the possibilities of success rather than on the pathologies of failure, urban schools can become oases of achievement instead of the wastelands of desolation as they are so often characterized today.

REFERENCES

African-American Male Task Force. *Educating African-American Males: A Dream Deferred*. Milwaukee, Wis.: Milwaukee Public Schools, 1990.

Applebee, Arthur N.; Langer, Judith A.; and Mullis, Ina V. *Writing: Trends across the Decade, 1974–1984*. National Assessment of Educational Progress. Princeton, N. J.: Educational Testing Service, 1986.

Banks, W. Curtis; McQuater, Gregory V.; and Hubbard, Janet L. "Toward a Reconceptualization of the Social-Cognitive Bases of Achievement Orientations in Blacks." In *Research Directions of Black Psychologists*, edited by A. Wade Boykin, Anderson J. Franklin, and J. Frank Yates. New York: Russell Sage Foundation, 1979.

Boykin, A. Wade. "Psychological/Behavioral Verve: Some Theoretical Explorations and Empirical Manifestations." In *Research Directions of Black Psychologists*, edited by A. Wade Boykin, Anderson J. Franklin, and J. Frank Yates. New York: Russell Sage Foundation, 1979.

Braddock, Jomills H. *Tracking: Implications for Black Youth*. Report No. 1. Baltimore, Johns Hopkins University Center for Research on Effective Schooling for Disadvantaged Students, February 1990.

Chronicle of Higher Education, 5, 19 September 1990.

Clark, Reginald. *Family Life and School Achievement: Why Black Children Succeed or Fail*. Chicago: University of Chicago Press, 1983.

Fordham, Signithia, and Ogbu, John. "Black Students' School Success: Coping with the 'Burden of Acting White'," *Urban Review* 18 (1986): 176–206.

Garibaldi, Antoine M. *Educating Black Male Youth: A Moral and Civic Imperative*. New Orleans: New Orleans Public Schools, 1988.

Garibaldi, Antoine M. "Preparing Teachers for Culturally Diverse Classrooms." In *Restructuring Schools, Colleges, and Departments of Education to Accommodate Diverse Students in Schools*, edited by Mary E. Dilworth, forthcoming.

Hilliard, Asa. "Teachers and Cultural Styles in a Pluralistic Society," *NEA Today*, January, 1989.

Irvine, Jacqueline J. "The Accuracy and Stability of Teachers' Achievement Expectations as Related to Students' Race and Sex." Paper presented at the Annual Meeting of the American Educational Research Association, Chicago, 1985.

Irvine, Jacqueline J. *Black Students and School Failure*. Westport, Conn.: Greenwood Press, 1990.

Maeroff, Gene I. "Withered Hopes, Stillborn Dreams: The Dismal Panorama of Urban Schools," *Phi Delta Kappan* 70 (May 1988): 633–638.

Maeroff, Gene I. "Three Missing Keys to Public-School Reform." *Wall Street Journal*, 21 May 1990.

National Assessment of Educational Progress. *The Reading Report Card*. Princeton, N. J.: Educational Testing Service, 1985.

Oakes, Jeannie. *Keeping Track: How Schools Structure Inequality*. New Haven: Yale University Press, 1985.

Oakes, Jeannie. "Keeping Track, Part 2: Curriculum Inequality and School Reform," *Phi Delta Kappan* 68 (October 1986): 148–154.

Ogbu, John. *Minority Education and Caste: The American System in Cross-Cultural Perspective*. New York: Academic Press, 1978.

Quality Education for Minorities Project. *Education That Works: An Action Plan for the Education of Minorities*. Cambridge: Massachusetts Institute of Technology, 1990.

Simmons, Warren, and Grady, Michael. *Black Male Achievement: From Peril to Promise*, Report of the Superintendent's Advisory Committee on Black Male Achievement. Prince Georges County, Md: Prince Georges County Schools, 1990.

Winfield, Linda F. *An Investigation of Characteristics of High Versus Low Literacy Proficient Black Young Adults*. Final Report to the Rockefeller Foundation. Philadelphia: Temple University, Center for Research in Human Development and Education, 1988.

Winfield, Linda F., and Lee, Valerie E. *Gender Differences in Reading Proficiency: Are They Constant across Racial Groups?* Baltimore, Md.: Johns Hopkins University Center for Research on Effective Schooling for Disadvantaged Students, 1990.

Chapter 7

EXPECTATIONS AND EFFORT: COURSE DEMANDS, STUDENTS' STUDY PRACTICES, AND ACADEMIC ACHIEVEMENT

John W. Thomas

Researchers who are interested in gathering information about the learning proficiency of adolescents may arrive at very different conclusions, depending on the literature they consult. At least two characterizations of adolescents' learning capabilities and habits are discussed in the literature. The first such characterization can be found in extant models of metacognitive proficiency, in the literature on expert versus novice learners, and in analyses of studies in which adolescents are trained successfully to carry out complex learning strategies. Descriptions of the autonomous nature of academic studying have included characterizations of some adolescents as detective-like problem solvers in their studying, capable of deducing course requirements and developing cognitive and volitional plans of action appropriate to these requirements (Bransford, Nitsch, and Franks, 1977; Corno, 1987). Research on study-strategy training has shown adolescents to be proficient at using fairly complex study methods following only brief instruction (Anderson, 1978; Pressley, Snyder, and Cariglia-Bull, 1986). Even adolescents with a history of poor reading performance have demonstrated their ability to use and to train others to use planful, multiple-step, metacognitive strategies on school-like tasks (Brown, Palincsar, and Armbruster, 1984; Campione and Armbruster, 1984).

The second characterization of adolescents can be found in the literature on schooling. Recent commissioned reports and essays about the state of learning and instruction in the United States have presented a picture of the typical adolescent learner as relatively disengaged from learning, unmotivated, less than proficient at carrying out learning tasks on his or her own, and disposed to invest only a minimum of effort on academic tasks (e.g., Carnegie Forum on Education and the Economy, 1986; College Board, 1985; National Commission on Excellence in Education, 1983). Surveys taken at institutions of higher education confirm this latter characterization; high school graduates are described as having desultory study practices, low-level, repetitive study strategies, and poor time and effort management habits (e.g., Bossone, 1970). Further, virtually every college and university has instituted some type of program for entering students designed to provide remedial assistance in the area of learning and study skills (Roueche, Baker, and Roueche, 1983).

The analysis presented in this chapter proceeds from two propositions. First, the characterization available from laboratory research and training studies suggests that there is nothing about adolescents that renders them inherently incapable or unmotivated. Second, the characterization of learners in school settings suggests that we have more to learn about the influence of school factors and course features on students' study activities.

In order to explore this anomaly between what adolescents are capable of, on the one hand, and what they do autonomously, on the other, I present here a three-part analysis. First, the problem that has been characterized as the "academic effort" problem is examined by elaborating on what we know about its symptoms. Second, a brief review of research on the relationship between course features and students' study practices is presented. Third, a model is presented that has been used to guide research on the interrelationships among student characteristics, features of courses, students' study practices and academic achievement. Data from recent investigations of this kind provide examples of how teachers' course demands and instructional provisions affect the quality and quantity of students' study practices in high school science courses. The chapter focuses on adolescents and on aspects of the "academic effort" problem typically classified as students' deficiencies in study skills and work habits.

SYMPTOMS OF THE "ACADEMIC EFFORT" PROBLEM

The "academic effort" problem has been described in several ways: students spend a minimum amount of time studying and doing schoolwork; the activities they engage in during autonomous studying tend to be shallow, repetitive, and unproductive; they exhibit little of the metacognitive proficiency thought to be necessary for mature information processing and problem solving; and they do not seem to engage in planful, self-management activities in academic contexts (e.g., Brown, Armbruster, and Baker, 1986; Paris, Lipson, and Wixson, 1983).

Time Spent Studying

High school students report investing a relatively small amount of time in out-of-class work. A nationwide survey of high school seniors conducted by the National Center for Education Statistics (Fetters, Brown, and Owings, 1984) reported that in 1979 the average high school senior devoted 3.9 hours per week to doing homework assignments. More than three-fourths of these seniors reported devoting five hours or less to doing homework each week. Keith's (1982) analysis revealed that high school seniors studied less than three hours per week on the average, an allocation that was considerably smaller than the three hours per day these students spent watching television (Keith, Reimers, Fehrmann, Pottebaum, and Aubey, 1986).

Although Keith (1982) found a relatively strong positive correlation ($r = .32$) between time spent doing homework and students' grades in high school, this effect has not been duplicated in other studies. Schuman, Walsh, Olson, and Etheridge (1985) examined the relationship between college students' study time and achievements, using a number of specific indices including time spent studying during particular time periods and grades on particular tests. Finding correlations between study time and achievement to range between .06 and .11, they concluded that at least in college settings, the relationship between study time and achievement is negligible. In our research, conducted in junior high school, high school, and college-level social studies courses (Jensen Delucchi, Rohwer, and Thomas, 1987), the relationship between study time and course grade, whether indexed by routine or test-preparation study time, was not significantly greater than zero, although there was some indication that the magnitude of the relationship depends on the course.

Students' Autonomous, Cognitive-Processing Activities

Autonomous learning situations are those in which students are responsible for carrying out some or all of a learning episode on their own. Autonomous learning contexts include both in-school (e.g., attending a lecture) and out-of-school (e.g., studying for a test at home) situations. At the high school level, it has been rare, in our experience, to find schools or courses in which some form of autonomous learning is not explicitly expected or assigned. In this setting, autonomous learning typically takes the form of doing assigned reading, doing homework assignments, taking notes in class, and studying for quizzes and tests.

Central to these tasks are processing activities that act to encode (e.g., reading), select (e.g., taking notes), and integrate (e.g., making outlines) information. Elsewhere, we have described a model by which students' cognitive-processing activities (or their "study methods") can be classified hierarchically (Thomas, Strage, and Rohwer, 1991). According to these hierarchies, for example, students reporting that they take notes in class and trying to construct summaries from these notes (selective and integrative processing) would be engaged in higher-level processing than students who just take notes (selective processing), who, in turn, would be engaged in higher-level processing than students who just listen in class. A great deal of research has been devoted to describing the benefits associated with engaging in particular cognitive-processing activities while carrying out autonomous learning tasks. In a typical study, students might be asked to read a passage from a science text in preparation for taking a test on the passage. Students who engage in reading and study activities that involve selecting the most important information and generating integrative relationships between these central ideas have demonstrated superior comprehension, retention, and problem-solving performance compared to students who do not engage in these activities (e.g., Brown, Bransford, Ferrara, and Campione, 1983; Mayer, 1987).

However, despite attempts to pattern research studies on classroom tasks and to use school-like materials, we have not learned very much about the factors that affect student engagement in selective, generative-processing activities in naturalistic settings. Consider what we know about students' disposition to engage in simple selection activities such as notetaking and underlining, activities found to significantly enhance students' recall (Einstein, Morris, and Smith 1985; Kiewra, 1985) and comprehension of school-like material (Bretzing, Kulhavy, and Caterino, 1987). Schallert and Tierney (1980) surveyed the study practices of high school students enrolled in social studies and biology courses. Among the study activities reported by these students, the most popular activities consisted of reading the chapter once (66 percent), rereading the chapter (48 percent), and memorizing portions of the chapter (67 percent). In comparison, relatively few students reported engaging in more selective activities such as taking notes while reading (34 percent) or constructing an outline (16 percent). These results are consistent with those reported by Annis and Annis (1982) and those obtained in our investigation of high school biology courses (Warkentin, Wilson, and Rohwer, 1991).

Results from surveys such as these can be used to support a variety of inferences about educational needs. One such inference is that students of this age level are not able to take effective notes. A study by Bracewell (1983) provides some support for this view. In this study, only 15 percent of ninth graders and 50 percent of twelfth graders were able to select the most important ideas from passages, in comparison to a college sample, which found 93 percent of the students able to select the ideas successfully.

Yet, whatever their notetaking ability, it does not seem reasonable that students refrain from taking notes because they don't know how to do it effectively. Indeed, even low-achieving high school students and recent high school graduates report proficiency at finding the main ideas and taking notes (Bossone, 1970; Green and Rankin, 1985). Perhaps a more supportable explanation for the low incidence of notetaking among high school students is that these students do not see the value of taking notes.

In our investigation of social studies courses, we found a significant difference between high school and college students' reported engagement in selective notetaking while reading. Moreover, we found significant and matching differences between these grade levels both in information load and in instructors' dispositions to provide students with a selection of the most important information in the text. That is, at the postsecondary level, the amount of material that must be covered in preparation for a test was significantly greater than at the high school level. More important perhaps, whereas all high school teachers provided their students with selective handouts just prior to the test (e.g., lists of terms or facts), these handouts were universally absent at the college level (Strage, Tyler, Rohwer, and Thomas, 1987). The inference from these findings, though less than conclusive at this stage, is that students may decline to take notes in a course when the workload is so low that notetaking is viewed as unnecessary or when they expect to receive complete, neatly typed "notes" from a very informed source, that is, the author of the upcoming tests in their courses.

Similar results have emerged from a more recent survey of students enrolled in high school biology courses. We asked these students to indicate what they did to prepare for a particular unit test in their courses. Fewer than one student in four reported constructing study materials to help prepare for the unit test in the course. Moreover, only 17 percent of the total study time of all students was devoted to "preparing study materials (notes, outlines, charts)." Almost half the total test preparation study time (44 percent) was devoted to doing homework or reading assignments (Warkentin, Wilson, and Rohwer, 1991).

Thus, although it is clear from laboratory research that constructing study aids such as summaries and outlines significantly improves adolescents' comprehension (Anderson, 1979), memory (Mayer, 1987), and problem-solving performance (Peper and Mayer, 1986), the spontaneous use of such techniques is the exception rather than the rule in secondary-level courses.

Students' Metacognitive and Task-Monitoring Strategies

Proficiency at academic studying demands something more than possession of a repertoire of appropriate skills. Good studiers have what is sometimes referred to as "metacognitive knowledge"—awareness of the demands of the task and an understanding of when and where to put strategies to use (Pressley, Snyder, and Cariglia-Bull, 1986). But again, investigations of the spontaneous strategies used by students while reading or studying sometimes provide a picture of students as being surprisingly unaware and nonstrategic. For example, high school and college students have been observed to exhibit fairly low levels of comprehension monitoring while reading. Students who are given passages to read that contain difficult paragraphs tend to read through the difficult sections of the passage without slowing down (Brown et al., 1983). In similar tasks, a substantial percentage of adolescent students given passages containing anomalies or inconsistencies fail to notice them or to question their meaning while reading (Baker, 1979).

A second example concerns students' awareness and appreciation of the demands of the task. Brown, Smiley, and Lawton (1978) asked students in grades five through twelve to study a passage in anticipation of a recall test. On each of several trials, students were allowed to hold on to some but not all of the idea units from the passage for review before receiving the test. ("Idea units" refers to ideas of varying degrees of importance encountered in the passage. About fifty idea units were typed out on cards and given to the students, who then selected twelve that they thought would be most helpful to them in recalling the passage.) Whereas college students began, over trials, to select idea units to study that they had not yet committed to memory, younger students, including high school seniors, continued to select the most important material to study even though they had demonstrated perfect recall of this material in previous trials.

This failure to adapt one's study strategies to specific task demands is also apparent in studies in which the experimenter manipulates the structure of the passage to be studied or the type of test anticipated. Higginson (1986) asked eleventh-grade students to study passages about either history or chemistry in preparation for a test. He also asked them to describe, in open-ended fashion, how they went about their studying. Some passages were familiar to students, some were not. The results revealed no differentiation in study activities based either on familiarity or on content. Other investigations have failed to detect differences between students' information-processing strategies based on differences in the type of test (essay vs. multiple-choice) expected (Kumar, Rabinsky, and Pandey, 1979) or on the presence or absence of orienting questions embedded in the text (Snyder and Pressley, 1989).

Students' Effort-Management Activities

The phrase "effort-management activities" is used to denote an assortment of study activities, referred to elsewhere as "study habits" and "self-regulated learning" activities. These activities have also been referred to as "support," (as opposed to "primary") activities (Dansereau, 1985), and "learner- versus task-focused" activities (Thomas and Rohwer, 1986). Effort-management activities include activities that serve to maintain and enhance attention, time, and effort devoted to learning. Thus these activities can be viewed as relevant for all students, but they are presumed to be especially relevant for students who, for one reason or another, are distracted from learning by internal or external factors (Covington, 1984). Effort-management activities may be especially important in any setting in which students are given appreciable responsibility for their own learning, where they have to manage tasks over a period of time, or where the learning environment is particularly stressful (Thomas, 1988). Effort-management activities appear to be especially important in college settings (Weissberg et al., 1982). College students rank "studying efficiently" and "budgeting time" as the most difficult tasks in adjusting to college (Leong and Sedlacek, 1981).

In contrast, despite the fact that tests seem no less important at the high school level than the college level for determining grades, and that academic performance at the high school level determines to a great degree one's opportunities at subsequent levels, high school students do not seem to be much concerned with studying efficiently or with time management. In a survey conducted by Green and Rankin (1985), students were asked if they "have a study schedule or plan in which they set aside time each day for homework." Only 25 percent of high school seniors indicated that they "usually" or "always" have such a schedule or plan. Moreover, in this same survey, 53 percent of ninth graders and 49 percent of twelfth graders indicated that they "usually" or "always" study while listening to a radio or watching TV.

Similarly, in our survey of high school students enrolled in biology courses, we asked students if they had trouble concentrating while they were studying for a particular unit test in their courses. Most students (55 percent) reported having difficulty. But, when asked how they solved this problem, the most popular response among seven corrective strategies was to take a study break (46 percent of all responses). Again, the inference might be that students are not very diligent about their studies. Yet, the seriousness of this apparent lack of effort-management strategies on the part of high school students cannot be weighed without knowing something about the benefits and consequences of students' effort-management practices. At the moment, this remains a gap in our knowledge.

THE RELATIONSHIP BETWEEN STUDENTS' STUDY PRACTICES AND FEATURES OF COURSES

Over the past few years, there has been an important shift in our understanding of the relationship between so-called "process" variables such as classroom factors and "product" variables such as learning and achievement. Until recently, classroom variables have largely been described in terms of people's perceptions of the psychosocial climate (e.g., cohesiveness, involvement) in the classroom (Boocock, 1978) or in terms of gross classroom arrangement factors (e.g., class size). Researchers have recently begun to examine the influence on learning of more concrete and functional factors (e.g., amount of homework), to measure such factors directly rather than via people's perceptions and, most important, to assess the effect these factors have, not only on learning outcomes but on the intervening variables (i.e., students' autonomous learning activities) that affect learning directly (Brown et al., 1983; Rohwer, 1984). According to Doyle (1981), in order to answer the question of how teaching effects occur, "it is necessary to trace the process that connects classroom events to outcomes—to analyze, that is, the student processes that mediate teaching effects" (p. 3).

A Framework for Understanding the Effect of Course Features on Students' Study Practices

In our research conducted in classroom settings, we not only found students' study activities to vary from course to course, but also found particular characteristics of courses associated with variations in students' study practices (Christopoulos, Rohwer, and Thomas, 1987). In this study, we distinguished between "constructive," "interpretive," and "duplicative" processing. We defined constructive-processing activities as activities that act to relate ideas to one another. Generating a summary or outline are common examples of constructive processing. Interpretive-processing activities are activities that give meaning to information, for example, trying to figure out the meaning of information from contextual cues. Duplicative-processing activities consist of techniques that involved the repetition of information. Common examples of duplicative processing include rereading, copying notes, and repeating information over and over while studying. We found that students engaged to a greater extent in constructive processing in courses in which instructors required students to put together integrative responses on tests. We also observed variation in the extent to which instructors helped students to engage in integrative processing by means of the questions they posed in class, homework assignments, and quiz items. Among the findings from this investigation was an indication that students were more apt to engage in constructive and interpretive processing and less likely to engage in duplicative processing in courses in which the instructor (1) regularly required students to demonstrate their competence at integrating the ideas they had read about, (2) provided integrative-processing aids on a routine basis, and (3) refrained from rehearsing with students the precise criterion items prior to the test.

The framework that emerged from this study includes a threefold distinction among course features (Strage et al., 1987). First, courses can impose differential *demands* on students' study activities. Demands are standards, tasks, or criterion performance events that students must meet or accomplish in order to fulfill the requirements of the course. Overall, demands usually prompt students to engage in autonomous learning activities to cope with those demands. Raising standards, increasing homework, and constructing more frequent and more challenging tests are all ways of increasing the demands placed on students' study activities. For some students and in some contexts, these kinds of demands have been found to be associated with increases in both studying and achievement (Light, 1990).

Supports are course features that serve to prompt or sustain students' engagement in particular demand-responsive study activities. Supports are often teacher-provided aids that help students carry out demand-appropriate study activities. These aids can take the form of information, training, rewards, or psychological support. For example, increasing students' workload is presumed to increase the demand placed on students' time- and effort-management activities. Routinely providing guidance for students in setting and working toward proximate goals for completing their workload may serve to support students' engagement in demand-appropriate study activities.

Finally, some course features act to reduce demands. These features, which we have called *compensations*, serve to abrogate the need for students to engage in demand-responsive study activities. Compensatory practices are, on the surface, similar to supports in that both consist of provisions, typically from the instructor, designed to help students cope with course demands. However, whereas supports prompt students to cope with demands on their own, compensations reduce the effect of demands, thus reducing the need for students to engage in the appropriate study behavior. In our previous research, we found compensatory practices to be nearly universal at the secondary level (Strage et al., 1987). For example, whereas college instructors either did not give in-class reviews prior to tests in their courses or used the last class before the test to answer students' questions (a support), secondary-level teachers were observed to rehearse the topics, and sometimes the very questions and answers to be covered on upcoming tests, in teacher-led reviews held on the day before the test. This teaching practice, we believe, acts to reduce students' need to select important information and to engage in interpretive and integrative study activities on their own.

Demand Features That Affect Students' Routine Study Activities

Workload. Workload refers to the amount of coursework (assigned reading, homework, lecture material, etc.) that must be completed and processed in the course, the relative difficulty of that coursework, and the pace at which the coursework is administered. The relative absence of workload at the secondary school level has been suggested as a contributing factor in explaining why some high school graduates exhibit study skill deficiencies when they reach college (Losak, Schwartz, and Morris, 1982). Increasing students' workload has been suggested as a means of improving students' academic effort and achievement at the elementary and secondary school levels (Bennett, 1986; National Commission on Excellence in Education, 1983).

However, the relationship between workload and student effort seems less than straightforward. On the one hand, the presence of homework (Keith et al., 1986) and the amount of homework (Wolf, 1979) show a moderately positive relationship to academic achievement at the secondary school level. On the other hand, research conducted at the college level suggests that high levels of workload, indexed by students' perceptions of that workload, are associated with student engagement in lower-level, "shallow" processing as opposed to higher-level, integrative or "deep" processing (Entwistle and Ramsden, 1983). Indeed, in our research conducted in high school science courses, we found a negative relationship between workload (i.e., number of pages of reading) and engagement in self-initiated, diligent study activities (Bol and Thomas, 1991). For example, the correlation between workload and student engagement in diligent, effort- and time-management activities was −.54.

It is not clear from the available evidence whether the relationship between workload and study practices is direct or curvilinear, as has been suggested for the effect of high standards at the secondary level (Natriello, 1987). Given a curvilinear relationship between workload and student effort, there may be some threshold above which raising the workload might result in decrements in achievement. The data from college students must also be interpreted with caution because research relied on students' perceptions. Additionally, it is conceivable that workload interacts with ability or with students' self-concept of their ability. Clark (1982) reports that lower-ability students tend to achieve better with low information (work) load and high-ability students do better with high information load.

Frequency of Test Events. Frequent testing would seem to place demands on students to keep pace with the coursework and to distribute review and other test-preparation activities throughout the course. The former effect would seem to place particular demands on students' time and on their routine reading- and homework-completion habits. The latter effect may act to facilitate students' memory for course content by means of memory-augmentation activities. Some support that frequent testing has a positive effect on students' motivation, learning strategies, and achievement is offered in recent reviews (Crooks, 1988; Natriello, 1987) and in a study of college courses (Light, 1990) popularized in the press (Fiske, 1990). Moreover, there is evidence that the very act of taking a test facilitates retention for tested content better than equivalent time spent reviewing (Nungester and Duchastel, 1982).

Teachers concur with the assertion that testing prompts students to be more diligent about doing homework and to study harder (Gullickson, 1984; Haertel, 1986). Frequent use of quizzes and tests is the rule rather than the exception at the secondary level (Haertel,

1986). In our survey of high school biology instructors, all teachers administered unit tests, approximately every three to four weeks on the average. Most teachers (80 percent) gave quizzes, and the average number of such quizzes was just short of two per unit.

Demand Features That Affect Students' Test-Preparation Activities

Testing Practices. Teacher-made tests play a major role in students' decisions about what and how much to learn from a given course. Students have been described as being disposed to plan their study activities with the primary goal of doing well on classroom tests (Crooks, 1988) and to focus their effort on what they expect to be on the test (Laurillard, 1979; Miller and Parlett, 1974). Yet, there remain some important gaps in our knowledge concerning the relationship between testing practices and students' test preparation study activities. At least three components of testing practices might be linked to students' study activities: the format of the items on the test, the degree of cognitive challenge associated with these items, and the overall importance of the test to the students' course grades.

Production Demand of the Test Items. In our survey of high school biology courses (Thomas, Strage, Bol, and Warkentin, 1990), we found that, on the average, 68 percent of the items teachers construct for their tests were objective items, primarily multiple-choice in format. The remaining items were mostly short-answer items, with very few of the teachers administering extended production (e.g., essay) items. These results are similar to those of other surveys. Fleming and Chambers (1983) reviewed 342 tests developed by teachers throughout the Cleveland, Ohio, school district (all grades). They found that essay questions accounted for less than 1 percent of all test items. This survey found matching items the most common item format.

The important point of a teacher's test construction practices with respect to item format is presumed to be the effect that students' expectations about item format has on the kinds of cognitive-processing activities they engage in when they study for tests in these courses. In a study by d'Ydewalle, Swerts, and DeCorte (1983), students who prepared for a recall test allocated more study time, used more study time, and performed better than students who prepared for a recognition test, regardless of the test they received. In other studies, students who expected an essay rather than a multiple-choice test were observed to take notes on ideas of higher structural importance (Rickards and Friedman, 1978) and to pay more attention to the relationship among ideas to be remembered (Connor, 1977). In a survey administered to college students, Entwistle and Tait (1990) found that students who expected multiple-choice tests reported engaging in "shallow" (low-level, duplicative) processing strategies when studying for these tests to a greater extent than students who expected essay items.

The significance of these findings for secondary school settings remains undetermined however. Other studies demonstrate that secondary-level students (Kumar, Rabinsky, and Pandey, 1979) and even college students (Hakstian, 1971) do not change their study practices on the basis of what kinds of test items they expect. Although the inference remains to be determined, students' failure to adapt their study strategies to information they receive about the format of the test may reflect their insensitivity to the cognitive-processing requirements of different item formats, or it may stem from the tendency, in their experience, for instructors to develop questions, regardless of format, that require reproduction of facts and details rather than integration of information (Haertel, 1986).

Cognitive-Processing Demand of the Test Items. Fleming and Chambers (1983), in their survey of classroom tests, classified teacher-developed test items on the basis of Bloom's taxonomy of instructional objectives. They found that over all grades, 80 percent of the items on teachers' tests were constructed to tap the lowest of the taxonomic categories—knowledge (of terms, facts, or principles). At the high school level, the percentage of knowledge items on teachers' tests dropped to 69 percent. However, the percentage of application items was just 2 percent of all items of this level. Fleming and Chambers observed significant variation between disciplines. Application items, for example, were found most often in mathematics and least often in social studies courses. In high school social studies courses, 99 percent of the test items tapped knowledge-level capabilities.

Similarly, in our survey of American history courses, we collected the teacher-developed tests administered in a sample of junior high school, high school, and college courses. Items were classified on the basis of whether they called on students to reproduce or recognize items of information, to interpret information, or to integrate information (relate two or more ideas). A comparison of the items administered at the three levels of schooling revealed that the percentage of items that called on students to integrate information in constructing their answers did not increase by grade level from junior high (18 percent) to high school (14 percent), but the difference between the secondary and college levels was particularly remarkable. At the college level, fully 99 percent of the items on instructor-developed tests required the integration of ideas; only 1 percent of the items we collected required memory or comprehension of items of information (Rohwer and Thomas, 1987). We hypothesized that this discontinuity in the level of processing required by test items might account for some of the difficulties college students experience in their ability to cope with the demands of college courses (Thomas, Strage, and Rohwer, 1991).

In fairness, it should be noted that results from our survey of high school biology courses represents a departure from the Fleming and Chamber survey as well as from our survey of social studies courses. Teachers in these biology courses developed unit tests that contained a comparatively large percentage (40 percent) of items that required students to engage in higher-level integrative processing. Moreover, on the average, a relatively large percentage of the items from these tests focused on principles (42 percent) versus concepts (35 percent) and factual information (21 percent). Yet, there is reason to believe that our data were unrepresentative of high school science courses. First, the biology unit on genetics we selected as the focus of our study was replete with the application of principles. Second, several teachers volunteered that their treatment of this unit was quite different from that of other units, particularly in their focus on problem solving. Yet, there was substantial variation among instructors in the demands posed by items on their unit tests. For example, one teacher administered a unit test consisting mostly (91 percent) of items calling for knowledge of facts or details.

To reiterate, the significance of these data on the processing demands posed by test items is that students' expectations concerning the kinds of cognitive demands that test items are likely to pose should affect the type of cognitive processing students engage in during autonomous learning activities. In turn, students' processing activities should affect how well they master the material to be learned and how well they are able to apply what they have learned (Anderson, 1980; Marton and Saljo, 1976; Thomas, Strage, and Rohwer, 1991). Given the widespread belief that academic achievement can be increased by augmenting the importance and rigor of curriculum-embedded tests (Carnegie Forum on Education and the Economy, 1986; College Board, 1985; National Commission on Excellence in Education, 1983), these inferences need to be substantiated by experimental studies.

Although our research to date must be termed preliminary, the evidence we have collected does not support the idea that there is a direct, linear relationship between the processing demand of test items, on the one hand, and students' study practices in preparing for tests and achievement, on the other hand. In our investigations of high school American history courses (Christopoulos, Rohwer, and Thomas, 1987), we found that the likelihood that students engage in higher-level cognitive processing activities while studying was higher in courses that included a larger number of integrative and problem-solving items on teacher-developed tests and lowest in courses in which the majority of test items tapped knowledge of facts and details. Yet, requiring integrative processing on test items was no guarantee that students would engage in appropriate integrative-processing activities while studying. In fact, overall, students at the high school level were more apt to engage in duplicative-processing activities (reading, rereading, copying notes) than in integrative-processing activities (making summaries, constructing charts, taking integrative notes) regardless of their instructor's test-construction practices. Moreover, the tendency for integrative tests to prompt integrative study practices, at least for some students, seems to depend on the presence of instructor-provided supports such as practice questions and integrative frameworks (Bol and Thomas, 1991; Thomas, Strage, and Rohwer, 1991).

An additional qualification of the proposition that increasing the rigor of tests will prompt better learning and achievement concerns the mediating role of student characteristics. From available research, there is reason to believe that increasing the cognitive demands associated with test items may promote better study practices and learning on the part of only a segment of the student population, while depressing the performance of other less able or less self-efficacious students (Clark, 1982; Covington, 1984).

Importance of the Test. The weight of a particular test in a course is expected to relate to the quality and quantity of students' study activities. According to an expectancy theory of work performance (Natriello, 1987), study effort should be based on the benefits that students expect will be obtained from studying. Thus, insignificant tests should engender little effort, whereas important tests should prompt increased effort, providing that students believe that such effort will result in rewards.

Classroom testing is of considerable significance to most teachers and students at the secondary level. Data from the Study of Stanford and the Schools (Haertel, 1986) reveal that, on the average, classroom testing takes up 10 to 15 percent of class time. In our survey of high school biology instructors, the average weight of tests was 45 percent of the term grade, with a range across courses from 13 percent to 81 percent (Thomas et al., 1990). This finding is consistent with that of Haertel, who found the average weight given to all tests to be 50 to 75 percent in all subject areas except English.

Again, however, there is not evidence that increasing the weight of tests is a productive method of prompting effective learning or boosting academic achievement. In our investigation of high school biology courses, we found no relationship between test weight and either students' academic achievement (Strage and Thomas, 1991) or students' engagement in proficient study activities (Bol and Thomas, 1991). In fact, the correlations between the weight of tests in determining course grade and students' engagement in proactive, diligent, and generative study activities in these courses were all moderately negative.

It is often difficult to establish how important tests are in particular classrooms. Some instructors establish practices, referred to by Sanford (1987) as "safety nets," that act to sabotage the effect of tests. For example, in our study of high school biology courses, we found that in some courses characterized by nominally important tests, instructors allowed students to compensate for poor test grades by doing extra credit work. In these instances, the demandingness of tests may be significantly reduced, at least for some students. We found that in courses in which instructors provided extra-credit options to make up for low test grades, students were less likely to construct test-preparation study material on their own and more apt to use their study time engaged in superficial reading and rereading activities than students in courses in which the instructors did not provide such options (Bol and Thomas, 1991).

Supports for Routine Study Activities

Provision of Clear, Obtainable Goals. Studying is an isolated activity often conducted by students without advice or a clear understanding of what constitutes being prepared for an upcoming test. The provision of teacher-established goals can convert study tasks from arbitrary to meaningful for students; knowledge of the performances and performance levels on which grades will be based can act to focus and sustain student effort in the course (Anderson and Armbruster, 1984; Natriello, 1987; Thomas and Rohwer, 1986). In a study by Duckworth, Fielding, and Shaughnessey (1986), the relationship between teachers' testing practices and the quality of students' study efforts was examined in sixty-nine high school courses in biology, English, and history. Teachers were asked to indicate the extent to which they established standards that students must meet before moving to a new unit. This measure of goal "clarity" was found to correlate .32 with students' self-reported effort in the course.

In addition to the importance of establishing clear goals and standards and communicating them to students in advance of coursework, the specificity of goal statements may also affect students' study activities and achievement. Types of specificity that have been found to facilitate learning and achievement include establishing specific levels of attainment on learning tasks (La Porte and Nath, 1976), emphasizing, with examples, particular kinds of competencies over others (Mayer, 1987; Muth, Glynn, Britton, and Graves, 1988), and stressing mastery and intraindividual achievement over competition and normative standing in the classroom (Ames and Felker, 1979; Covington, 1984; Kurtz and Borkowski, 1984). Unfortunately, instructors' goal statements are usually specific about what needs to be processed (e.g., text pages), rather than about how such processing should be carried out or about what students should be able to do after they study (Anderson and Armbruster, 1984).

Finally, there is some evidence that high standards and difficult goals, as opposed to low standards and easy goals, prompt greater student effort and higher achievement. In his review of the impact of evaluation processes on students, Natriello (1987) claims that high classroom standards yield better student performance, including greater student effort on school tasks, greater effort on homework, and better class attendance. These standards, however, must be perceived by students as obtainable, according to Natriello, otherwise students become disengaged from learning. In the La Porte and Nath (1976) study, students who were given difficult but obtainable goals outperformed students who received easier goals on a prose learning task.

Provision of Guided Practice. Students who are called on to read texts and listen to lectures in the courses that they take are expected to carry out a sequence of complex selective processing, memory augmentation, and integration activities on their own. Often they receive inadequate instruction on techniques and rarely do they receive feedback concerning the effectiveness of their self-generated methods. Whereas elementary school students often receive information and guidance from their teachers to complete their coursework assignments, high school students are routinely expected to complete assignments and study for tests on their own, and it is rare that courses or schools provide training in study techniques (Thomas and Rohwer, 1986). Thus, studying can become sophisticated detective work for a small number of "cue seekers," but it can constitute guesswork or blind, routinized behavior for the majority (Bransford, Nitsch, and Franks, 1977).

Although we did not encounter courses in which the instructor gave guidance on study techniques, in the course of our investigation of high school biology courses we did observe instructors who (1) routinely gave homework exercises that required students to engage in high-level integrative processing and the application of biological principles and (2) reviewed in class the process of arriving at correct answers to these assigned exercises. The benefits associated with these support practices were assessed by measuring the relationship between the extent to which instructors gave higher-level processing items in practice exercises and the tendency for students to engage in higher-level processing during test preparation study episodes. The correlation between the provision of guided practice and students' level of cognitive processing during studying was .74. In addition, guided practice was found to be positively associated ($r = .55$) with time spent studying outside class (Bol and Thomas, 1991).

Supports for Test-Preparation Study Activities

Correspondence Between Coursework and Test Items. The term "correspondence" refers to the similarity (i.e., articulation) in goals, content, and performance requirements between coursework and test items. Noncorrespondence can refer to situations in which (a) a significant number of test items involves content that had not been covered in practice exercises or quizzes; (b) a significant percentage of homework or classwork is not covered on unit tests; or (c) the treatment of material on unit tests is significantly different from the treatment of that material in coursework. High correspondence is expected to support students' engagement during test preparation in the kinds of processing activities that should result in proficient performance on curriculum-embedded mastery tests; low correspondence might be expected to lead to inappropriate processing, low effort, and desultory study practices.

Evidence that students' perceptions of correspondence is related to students' study practices is provided in the study by Duckworth, Fielding, and Shaughnessey (1986). Students were asked to rate the degree to which tests in their courses cover what they expect them to cover. This measure correlated .46 with students' ratings of how thoroughly they studied for the course and .57 with students' ratings of their efficacy in the course. ("Efficacy" was indexed by students' ratings of (a) whether they believed that effort would be followed by rewards and (b) how well they could predict their test performance.)

In our investigation of high school science courses, we measured the relative correspondence between items on practice material (homework exercise sheets and quizzes) and items on the unit test. One such measure of correspondence was the extent to which the format of test and practice items was similar. For example, noncorrespondence would be a course in which practice items call for matching responses while the tests consist of problems requiring constructed responses. Our results demonstrated that high correspondence in format between practice and test items is associated with student engagement in both high-level processing activities ($r = .59$) and high effort expenditure ($r = .71$) during studying (Bol and Thomas, 1991).

Given the vagaries of teachers' test-development practices (Anderson, 1972), a reasonable match between what was studied and what was tested may be rare in academic settings. According to Haertel (1986), the assessment practices of many teachers are not well articulated with the curriculum. In his review of classroom tests developed by ninth- through twelfth-grade teachers, Haertel found that "problems were included to see if students had done the required reading or had paid attention in class but not whether they were assimilating an organized body of knowledge" (p. 16).

Clarity of Criterion Performance Expectations. As described above, information concerning the nature of the criterion performances by which students' proficiency will be judged in a course tends to support students' engagement in criterion-appropriate study activities (Anderson and Armbruster, 1984; Rohwer, 1984). Explicit information about the criterion is expected to be especially supportive of students' study activities in preparing for tests. Duckworth, Fielding, and Shaughnessey (1986) asked students to rate the degree to which they knew what they were expected to be learning in the course. This measure, which the researchers called "clarity," correlated .40 with students' ratings of effort and .61 with their ratings of efficacy in the course. Likewise, students' ratings of "communication" (the extent to which they think that teachers gave advance notice about tests) correlated positively with effort and efficacy—.44 and .65, respectively.

More specifically, in our investigation of high school biology courses, students enrolled in courses in which instructors provided sample (but nonidentical) test questions during review sessions prior to the test engaged to a greater extent in self-initiated study activities ($r = .62$) during test preparation than did students enrolled in other courses (Bol and Thomas, 1991). Sample test questions seem to be a good way for an instructor to communicate precisely what students are expected to be able to do at test time.

Feedback. The effectiveness of feedback on learning and on subsequent test performance is generally acknowledged (Crooks, 1988; Kulhavy, 1977) and has been suggested as a key ingredient in college-level courses that facilitate more effective study practices (Light, 1990). The effect of feedback on high school students' study practices and effort is not as well known. Again, there is some indication that the provision of feedback supports students' engagement in productive study activities. Duckworth, Fielding, and Shaughnessey (1986) asked students to rate the extent to which they agreed with the statement, "The results from the test let me see easily what I need to review to get a good grade." This index of feedback correlated .29 with teachers' indications that they usually discuss test items following test events. Students' perceptions that their teacher provided feedback was found to correlate .30 with students' ratings of effort expended in the course and .53 with their ratings of efficacy in the course. Similarly, in our investigation of high school biology courses, the provision of extended feedback (written comments, grades for each item) correlated significantly with students' engagement in self-initiated study activities ($r = .70$) and in diligent effort-management activities ($r = .50$) while preparing for unit tests in the course (Bol and Thomas, 1991).

Although the importance of feedback is generally acknowledged by teachers (Thomas et al., 1990), teachers' routine feedback practices have been criticized for emphasizing social comparison rather than some measure of mastery (Crooks, 1988), and for failing to praise student effort as opposed to normative performance (Natriello, 1987). More important perhaps, typical feedback practices do not often extend down to the level of student performance on individual concepts or principles. In the survey we conducted with high school biology teachers, we found that although the majority of these teachers collected and graded homework assignments, only 33 percent returned homework with written comments. Similar results were obtained for quizzes; 75 percent of teachers graded quizzes, but only 25 percent provided written comments (Thomas et al., 1990). Although giving grades on quizzes and homework may be informative with respect to a student's standing in the course, it does not help students to know how to alter their study practices.

Compensatory Practices That Inhibit Students' Study Practices

Provision of Compensatory Review Sheets. Advance information about the content to be covered on the test tends to orient students and place them on the right track in their test-preparation activities. Such information may act to convince some students, who otherwise might be at risk of withholding effort in test-preparation activities, that their study efforts might have some payoff (Duckworth, Fielding, and Shaughnessey 1986). However, depending on the kind of information provided, advance information about the test can have a dysfunctional effect on students' study activities. Instead of providing orienting information (e.g., a list of content areas to be responsible for or examples of test-item formats), some teachers provide students with the products of studying (e.g., a selection of the items of knowledge that students should commit to memory, summaries of the main ideas of the course, or the very questions or answers that will appear on the test).

Providing students with the products of studying acts to reduce the need for students to engage in the appropriate study activity on their own. For example, lists of specific information to be responsible for act to reduce the need for students to engage in selective processing on their own. Summaries of main ideas may act to reduce students' engagement in autonomous integrative processing. In our observations at the secondary level, this kind of compensatory information is conveyed largely by means of review sheets provided a day or two prior to the test. In most instances, review sheets are reviewed orally by the instructor on the day before the test. Furthermore, these review sessions sometimes include drill or practice events that may further reduce the need for students to engage in memory-augmentation activities on their own.

Identity Between Test Items and Review/Practice Items. We have referred to a second compensatory feature as test item "identity." Identity refers to the degree of similarity between test items and items that students have been given in advance of the test in homework or in-class review exercises. In his examination of tests developed by high school teachers, Haertel (1986) concluded that "these tests sometimes fall short of measuring attainment of teachers' instructional objectives, often calling for little more than repetition of material presented in the textbook or in class or solution of problems almost exactly like those encountered during instruction" (pp. 4–5). "Students were not asked to apply their knowledge or understanding and even items that appeared to call for analysis or supported argumentation proved in fact to require no more than reproduction of what had been said in class." (p. 16).

Clearly, the demand posed by classroom tests can be reduced substantially when students come to expect that the items that make up the tests will include many items they know or are able to do as a result of prior reviews. The teaching practice of building tests from extant items, although it tends to ensure a modicum of student achievement on the tests, seems to sabotage the goal of prompting students to engage in higher-level processing activities when preparing for a test. When students do put in time preparing for such tests, they may tend to engage in verbatim memorization rather than more integrative-processing activities.

The tendency for test items to match items administered prior to the test appears to be pervasive in secondary schools. In our study of junior high school, high school, and college social studies courses, we had originally intended to collect teacher-developed unit tests and rate each item on the basis of the demand that item seemed to make on students' cognitive-processing activities (e.g., comprehension, integration). However, when we tried to improve our classification system by searching through source documents in order to describe differences in cues, wording, or treatment between source information (such as handouts or text) and the test, we discovered that a substantial portion of the items on the tests administered to junior high and high school students were identical or virtually identical to course documents (Thomas, Strage, and Rohwer, 1991). This pattern was no less true of essay items than it was of multiple-choice or matching items. In our study of biology courses, the degree of overlap and identity that we observed between course documents and test items was considerably less striking. According to our analyses of the tests of twelve high school biology instructors, the average percentage of items drawn verbatim from course documents was 22 percent, with a range of 0 percent to 64 percent (Thomas et al., 1990).

The effect of this kind of compensatory test development practice was to significantly reduce the quality and quantity of students' test-preparation practices. Students in courses in which the tests included a large proportion of previously administered items tended to engage in less diligent effort-management activities ($r = -.49$), were less prone to construct their own study material when preparing for the test ($r = -.60$), and reported spending less total time studying ($r = -.72$) than students in other courses (Bol and Thomas, 1991).

In our investigation of biology courses, we constructed a criterion test of our own design and administered it to all participating students. All the items on the criterion test were based on course material covered by all instructors, no matter what text was used in a particular course. None of the items on our criterion test had been seen or practiced by students prior to the administration of the test. The correlation between the number of test items drawn verbatim from teacher-developed tests and students' achievement on this experimenter-developed criterion test was r = −.54. Thus, although the practice of developing items for unit tests that are drawn verbatim from previously reviewed items may well facilitate performance on teacher-developed tests, it is associated with a significant decrement in achievement as measured by an independent test.

These results suggest that when students expect to be tested on a substantial number of items that they have seen before, they are less apt to engage in generative, effortful study activities and more apt to engage in duplicative activities such as reading and rehearsing. Furthermore, students enrolled in courses in which many test items were routinely drawn from teachers' handouts were less likely to master the material, as indexed by performance on the experimenter-developed criterion test, than were students enrolled in courses in which a low percentage of test items was drawn verbatim from previous coursework.

Undertesting: Setting the Test Demands Lower than the Practice Demands. An additional compensatory practice, which we have labeled "undertesting," is defined as the situation in which the average demand characteristic of items given as homework exercises or on quizzes is greater than the average demand characteristic of items on the test administered at the close of a unit (or term). In our study of biology courses, we assumed that tests can be rated on the basis of the degree of cognitive challenge posed by the items on the test. Items that require students to go beyond the information given and apply a rule are more challenging than items that call for the reproduction of information. Likewise, items that focus on principles are more challenging than items that focus on facts, and items that require students to construct an answer are more challenging than items that require recognition alone. Accordingly, we indexed the degree to which there was a discrepancy in demand (degree of challenge) between coursework exercises and test items in these three ways. Contrary to our hypotheses, we did not find undertesting associated with a decrement in students' diligence or level of cognitive processing during studying (Bol and Thomas, 1991). In our future research on the effect of undertesting, we will likely use units of instruction that are less peculiar than the unit on genetics.

Other Compensatory Practices. Additional compensatory practices common at the high school level are described in an article by Sanford (1987). These practices include assignments of group work, peer assistance, balancing difficult or unfamiliar content on tests with overlearned familiar content, allowing students to revise products, providing less exacting grading standards for low-achieving students, grading on completion of tasks rather than on performance, and using flexible grading systems that can be altered when the class does poorly on a particular test.

A MODEL FOR INVESTIGATING THE INTERRELATIONSHIP AMONG CHARACTERISTICS OF STUDENTS, FEATURES OF COURSES, STUDENTS' STUDY ACTIVITIES, AND ACADEMIC ACHIEVEMENT

Figure 7.1 presents the overall model that has guided our investigations of students' study practices. In this conceptualization, academic achievement is expected to be influenced by students' characteristics, course features, and students' study practices. These study practices are themselves influenced by students and course characteristics as well as by interactions between these characteristics. For example, the quality of students' study effort is influenced not only by students' feelings of self-efficacy (Thomas, Iventosch, and Rohwer, 1987) and by the relative rigor of the achievement standards set by instructors (Natriello, 1987), but also by the interaction between these

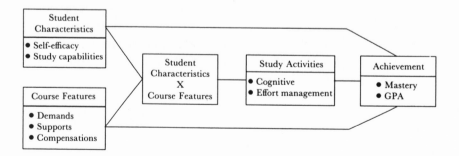

Figure 7.1
Guiding Conceptualization of Students' Study Practices

two classes of factors (Covington, 1984). Relationships between students' characteristics and study activities and those between study activities and achievement are described elsewhere (Rohwer and Thomas, 1987; Thomas, Iventosch, and Rohwer, 1987).

COURSE FEATURES HYPOTHESIZED TO INFLUENCE STUDENTS' ENGAGEMENT IN PRODUCTIVE STUDY ACTIVITIES DURING TEST-PREPARATION ACTIVITIES

Table 7.1 presents a list of certain demand features, support features, and compensatory practices that we focused on in our examination of high school biology courses. These features were selected for their possible influence on students' test-preparation activities. Other course features found to be important in other investigations, such as clarity of goals, standards, and criterion information, were excluded in this study because of our inability to observe all instructional days during the course of the unit and to collect all appropriate information from the beginning of the year. Still other course features such as "freedom in learning" (Entwistle and Tait, 1990) and classroom goal structure (Ames, 1984) were excluded from consideration because of the lack of variation in these factors at the high school level. Three categories of test-preparation demands are described in Table 7.1: (a) workload; (b) degree of challenge associated with items on teacher-developed tests, defined in terms of production, processing, and knowledge product demands; and (c) grading practices, defined simply as the importance of tests. Note that in this model "workload" does not include homework. Homework is expected to place demands on students' routine study activities, but it is hypothesized to provide a support for students' test-preparation activities.

Four categories of support features are listed: (a) presence of routine practice events, which refers to the number of practice opportunities provided during a particular unit; (b) correspondence between the demands of practice and test items, which refers to the extent to which the tests resemble practice material in their production, processing, and knowledge product demands, as well as their content focus; (c) presence and extensiveness of feedback; and (d) presence of checks on students' progress.

Finally, our study of high school science courses included attention to three classes of compensatory practices: (a) the degree of

Table 7.1
Demands, Supports, and Compensatory Practices Presumed to Affect Adolescents' Test-Preparation Activities

I. Demands expected to prompt productive study activities (depending on the presence of appropriate supports)

A. Workload
1. Amount of reading covered on the test
2. Number of discrete content categories covered on the test
3. Retention interval (number of days between tests)

B. Cognitive challenge associated with test items on teacher-developed tests
1. Production demand (recognition and simple recall vs. complex production)
2. Processing demand (encoding/comprehension and integration vs. extension)
3. Knowledge product demand (facts and concepts vs. principles)

C. Grading practices
1. Importance of unit test/all tests for determining course grade

II. Instructional supports expected to prompt students' engagement in productive study activities

A. Presence of routine practice/performance tasks
1. Number and distribution of quizzes
2. Number of homework assignments (i.e., practice exercises)
3. Number of practice items assigned

B. Correspondence between the demands of practice and test items
1. Correspondence in production requirements
2. Correspondence in processing requirements
3. Correspondence in knowledge product focus
4. Correspondence in content focus

C. Feedback
   1. Presence of feedback (homework, quizzes, tests)
   2. Extensiveness of feedback (overall grade, item grades, corrective comments)

D. Presence of checks on students' progress
   1. Extensiveness of teacher-student conferences
   2. Time allocated for student-initiated questions in class and review sessions

III. Compensatory practices expected to inhibit students' engagement in productive study activities

A. Identity (i.e., verbatim wording) between practice and test items
   1. Percentage of test items identical to practice items or text

B. Compensatory review practices
   1. Provision of list of terms, facts, definitions to appear on the test

C. "Safety nets"
   1. Presence of alternative ways of achieving a passing grade (e.g., extracredit)
   2. Availability of make-up tests
   3. Open-book tests
   4. Undertesting (format, processing requirement, or knowledge product focus of test items are less rigorous than practice items)

identity (verbatim overlap) between practice material and test items, defined in terms of identity with coursework and with material rehearsed during review sessions; (b) provision of compensatory review practices, typically providing students with lists of information to commit to memory; and (c) "safety nets," which include open-book testing, the presence of makeup tests or extracredit opportunities to compensate for failing grades, and the presence of undertesting, that is, administering tests that are less challenging than coursework.

CONCLUSIONS

The research reported on here has some important implications for further research and for the improvement of educational practices. In both areas, these implications include opportunities as well as dilemmas.

With respect to implications for research, the primary opportunity is that of developing theories of studying in academic settings and improving existing theories of classroom learning and teaching effects. Although the research reported here represents only a few years of work, these studies, when taken together, may lay the groundwork for an understanding of the interactions among students' characteristics, course features, students' study efforts, and achievement useful for understanding some of the anomalous findings from previous research. Different from former theories of classroom learning and of studying, these new theories would include attention to the functional relationships between course characteristics and students' study practices, the specificity of learning outcomes and students' study practices, the effect of student expectations about course demands on study behavior, and the effect of particular combinations of course demands, supports, and compensations on the study-achievement relationship. Such theories may be beneficial for understanding why certain study and teaching strategies have been found to facilitate learning in some studies but not others and why certain characteristics of students show a strong relationship with achievement in one context but not another. Finally, the specification of interactive relationships between course features and students' characteristics may, because of the focus on students' learning activities in such analyses, fulfill the promise raised by early discussions of the research on aptitude-treatment interactions (Biggs, 1976).

The principal dilemma faced by researchers is that the investigations that will be necessary to build a psychology of academic studying are exceptionally difficult to carry out. First of all, studying in academic settings is a very private and isolated activity. Describing students' study habits and cognitive activities without relying on students' self-reports requires a great deal of ingenuity from experimenters and willing cooperation from participants. Second, focusing on classroom processes and their effect on the study-achievement relationship requires fairly extensive, naturalistic investigations. These investigations are very time-consuming to conduct and must be carried out with a great deal of care in order to avoid interfering with teachers' instructional responsibilities. Furthermore, the absence of manipulation and control characteristics in naturalistic (versus laboratory) studies requires large sample sizes in order to obtain valid and reliable findings. Finally, the difficulty of conducting naturalistic investigations is compounded because of the centrality of teachers' testing and grading practices, topics that can be exceedingly sensitive in some settings.

Research on studying in general and on the relationship between teaching practices and the study-achievement connection in particular has great potential for improving instruction and learning in the classroom. Three benefits are informing educational reform efforts, improving teaching strategies, and improving students' learning proficiency. With respect to educational reform efforts, research on the interaction of course features and study activities can be helpful in guiding policies on the nature and timing of homework assigned, establishing schoolwide standards for educational achievement and academic work, increasing the amount and quality of schoolwork, establishing innovative testing and grading practices, implementing cooperative work groups within and across courses, and instituting instruction in study skills (Carnegie Forum on Education and the Economy, 1986; Bennett, 1986). Similarly, the development of a theory of studying in academic settings could produce guidelines useful for helping teachers develop classroom tests, informing students of their expected criterion performance, providing practice material articulated to the demands of those tests, providing feedback designed to influence students' study practices, and giving students advice concerning what and how to study.

Research on studying can lead to both direct and indirect benefits for students. Indirect benefits consist of changes in teaching practices and course conditions that would allow students to engage in extensive autonomous study activities with clear goals and achievement standards in mind, with minimal fears and anxieties, and with a sense of personal efficacy based on prior experiences of success following engagement in study activities. Direct benefits to students might include the provision of training opportunities such that students could learn and evaluate alternative study methods for themselves as well as gather knowledge concerning the principles and tactics of effective studying.

Achieving these benefits may have to await the resolution of certain dilemmas, however. The research reported here suggests a number of ways that teachers' practices could be changed in order to facilitate more effective study activities and better student achievement. For example, it appears that giving students compensatory review sheets, easy tests, and alternative (other than tests) ways of achieving a passing grade reduces student effort and interferes with their engagement in effective study practices. However, it is not reasonable to expect that teachers will easily be able to change such practices. Compensatory practices may well have their own benefits for teachers. These practices may ensure that students succeed in a course to some degree. Removing these compensations carries with it a great risk of student failure and, by extension, teacher failure. Although we may be able to specify the kinds of concomitant changes in course demands and supports that would ensure success in the absence of a teacher's compensatory provisions, we are not yet at the stage where we know how to make individual diagnoses of a teacher's instructional needs or to implement such combinations of demands and supports with confidence. In the meantime, the dilemma presents a barrier to progress. We cannot expect teachers to do things (such as increasing homework, raising standards, and dropping compensations) that will increase the risk of student failure unless and until we are able to demonstrate to them that other provisions (such as feedback, articulated practice material, and study skills training) will offset the risks they anticipate.

This same proposition—that raising demands will not result in educational improvements until concomitant changes in instructional supports have been both instituted and acknowledged—applies equally to students. They too are unlikely to undertake the increased risk of failure under conditions of high standards, more coursework, and harder tests unless they feel confident in their efforts. Achieving such confidence will require that expectations about coursework become linked to effort by means of training, feedback opportunities, and students' attributions of success to effort.

REFERENCES

Ames, Carole. "Competitive, Cooperative, and Individualistic Goal Structures: A Cognitive Motivational Analysis." In *Motivation in Education*, Vol. 1, edited by

Russell E. Ames and Carole Ames, pp. 177–208. New York: Academic Press, 1984.

Ames, Carole, and Felker, Donald W. "An Examination of Children's Attributions and Achievement-Related Evaluations in Competitive, Cooperative, and Individualistic Reward Structures," *Journal of Educational Psychology* 71 (1979): 413–420.

Anderson, Richard C. "How to Construct Achievement Tests to Assess Comprehension," *Review of Educational Research* 42 (1972): 145–170.

Anderson, Thomas H. "Another Look at the Self-Questionnaire Study Technique," *Reading Education*, Report No. 6. Cambridge, Mass.: Bolt, Beranek, and Newman, 1978.

Anderson, Thomas H. "Study Skills and Learning Strategies." In *Cognitive and Affective Learning Strategies*, edited by Harry F. O'Neil, Jr., and Charles D. Spielberger, pp. 77–97. New York: Academic Press, 1979.

Anderson, Thomas H. "Study Strategies and Adjunct Aids." In *Theoretical Issues in Reading Comprehension*, edited by Rand J. Spiro, Bertram C. Bruce, and William F Brewer, pp. 483–502. Hillsdale, N.J.: Erlbaum, 1980.

Anderson, Thomas H., and Armbruster, Bonnie B. "Studying." In *Handbook of Reading Research*, edited by P. David Pearson, pp. 657–680. New York: Longman, 1984.

Annis, Linda, and Annis, D. "A Normative Study of Students' Preferred Study Techniques," *Reading World* 21 (1982): 201–207.

Baker, Linda. "Comprehension Monitoring: Identifying and Coping with Text Confusions," *Journal of Reading and Behavior* 11 (1979): 363–374.

Bennett, William J. *First Lessons: A Report on Elementary Education in America*. Washington, D.C.: U. S. Department of Education, 1986.

Biggs, John B. "Dimensions of Study Behavior: Another Look at ATI," *British Journal of Educational Psychology* 46 (1976): 68–80.

Bol, Linda, and Thomas, John W. "The Relationship between Classroom Practices and Students' Study Activities in High School Biology Courses." Paper presented at the Annual Meeting of the American Educational Research Association, Chicago, 1991.

Boocock, Sarah S. "The Social Organization of the Classroom," *Annual Review of Sociology* 4 (1978): 1–28.

Bossone, Richard M. *The Reading-Study Skills Problems of Students in Community Colleges of the City University of New York*. New York: City University of New York, 1970.

Bracewell, Robert J. "Investigating the Control of Writing Skills." In *Research on Writing*, edited by Peter M. Mosenthal, Lynne Tamor, and Sean J. Walmsley, pp. 177–203. New York: Longman, 1983.

Bransford, John D.; Nitsch, Kathleen E.; and Franks, Jeffrey J. "Schooling and the Facilitation of Knowing." In *Schooling and the Acquisition of Knowledge*, edited by Richard C. Anderson, Rand J. Spiro, and William E. Montague, pp. 31–56. Hillsdale, N.J.: Erlbaum, 1977.

Bretzing, Burke H.; Kulhavy, Raymond W.; and Caterino, Linda C. "Notetaking by Junior-High School Students," *Journal of Educational Research* 80 (1987): 359–362.

Brown, Ann L.; Armbruster, Bonnie B.; and Baker, Linda. "The Role of Metacognition in Reading and Studying." In *Reading Comprehension: From Research to Practice*, edited by Judith Orasanu, pp. 49–75. Hillsdale, N.J.: Erlbaum, 1986.

Brown, Ann L.; Bransford, John D.; Ferrara, Robert A.; and Campione, Joseph C. "Learning, Remembering, and Understanding." In *Handbook of Child Psychology: Cognitive Development*, Vol. 3, edited by John H. Flavell and Ellen H. Markham, pp. 77–176. New York: Wiley, 1983.

Brown, Ann L.; Palincsar, Annemarie S.; and Armbruster, Bonnie B. "Instructing Comprehension-Fostering Activities in Interactive Learning Situations." In *Learning and Comprehension of Text*, edited by Heinz Mandel, Nancy L. Stein, and Tom Trabasso, pp. 255–286. Hillsdale, N.J.: Erlbaum, 1984.

Brown, Ann L.; Smiley, Sandra S.; and Lawton, Sallie Q. C. "The Effects of Experience on the Selection of Suitable Retrieval Cues for Studying Texts," *Child Development* 49 (1978): 829–835.

Campione, Joseph C., and Armbruster, Bonnie B. "An Analysis of the Outcomes and Implications of Intervention Research." In *Learning and Comprehension of Text*, edited by Heinz Mandl, Nancy L. Stein, and Tom Trabasso, pp. 287–304. Hillsdale, N.J.: Erlbaum, 1984.

Carnegie Forum on Education and the Economy, Task Force on Teaching as a Profession. *A Nation Prepared: Teachers for the 21st Century.* Hyattsville, Md.: Carnegie Forum on Education and the Economy, 1986.

Christopoulos, James; Rohwer, William D., Jr.; and Thomas, John W. "Grade-level Differences in Students' Study Activities as a Function of Course Characteristics," *Contemporary Educational Psychology* 12 (1987): 303–323.

Clark, Richard E. "Antagonism between Achievement and Enjoyment in ATI Studies," *Educational Psychologist* 17 (1982): 92–101.

College Board. *Excellence in Our Schools: Making It Happen.* New York: College Board Publications, 1985.

Connor, Jane M. "Effects of Organization and Expectancy on Recall and Recognition," *Memory and Cognition* 5 (1977): 315–318.

Corno, Lyn. "Teaching and Self-Regulated Learning." In *Talks to Teachers*, edited by David Berliner and Barak Rosenshine, pp. 249–266. New York: Random House, 1987.

Covington, Martin V. "The Motive for Self-Worth." In *Motivation in Education*, Vol. 1, edited by Russell E. Ames and Carole Ames, pp. 78–113. New York: Academic Press, 1984.

Crooks, Terence J. "The Impact of Classroom Evaluation Practices on Students," *Review of Educational Research* 58 (1988): 438–481.

Dansereau, Donald F. "Learning Strategy Research." In *Thinking and Learning Skills*, edited by Judith W. Segal, Susan F. Chipman, and Robert Glaser. Hillsdale, N.J.: Erlbaum, 1985.

Doyle, Walter. "Research on Classroom Contexts," *Journal of Teacher Education* 32 (1981): 3–6.

Duckworth, Kenneth; Fielding, Glen; and Shaughnessey, Joan. *The Relationship of High School Teachers' Class Testing Practices to Students' Feelings of Efficacy and Efforts to Study.* Eugene: Center for Educational Policy and Management, University of Oregon, 1986.

d'Ydewalle, Gery; Swerts, Anne; and DeCorte, Erik. "Study Time and Test Performance as a Function of Test Expectations," *Contemporary Educational Psychology* 8 (1983): 55–67.

Einstein, Gilles O.; Morris, Joy; Smith, Susan. "Notetaking, Individual Differences, and Memory for Lecture Information," *Journal of Educational Psychology* 77 (1985): 522–532.

Entwistle, Noel J., and Ramsden, Paul. *Understanding Student Learning*. London: Croom Helm, 1983.

Entwistle, Noel J., and Tait, Hillary. "Approaches to Learning, Evaluations of Teaching, and Preferences for Contrasting Academic Environments," *Higher Education* 19 (1990): 168–194.

Fetters, William B.; Brown, G. H.; and Owings, Jeffrey A. *High School Seniors: A Comparison Study of the Classes of 1972 and 1980*. Washington, D.C.: National Center for Education Statistics, 1984.

Fiske, Edward B. "How to Learn in College: Group Study, Many Tests," *New York Times* 5 March 1990, pp. A1, A11.

Fleming, M., and Chambers, B. *Teacher-made Tests: Windows on the Classroom*. San Francisco: Jossey-Bass, 1983.

Green, Charles A., and Rankin, P. T. *Detroit High School Students' Perceptions Regarding Homework and Study Habits, 1985*. Detroit: Detroit Public Schools, Office of Instructional Improvement, 1985.

Gullickson, Arlen R. "Teacher Perspectives of Their Instructional Use of Tests," *Journal of Educational Research* 77 (1984): 244–248.

Haertel, Edward. "Choosing and Using Classroom Tests: Teachers' Perspectives on Assessment." Paper presented at the Annual Meeting of the American Educational Research Association, San Francisco, 1986.

Hakstian, A. Ralph. "The Effects of Type of Examination Anticipated on Test Preparation and Performance," *Journal of Educational Research* 64 (1971): 319–324.

Higginson, Bonnie C. "An Investigation into the Self-Selected Study Strategies Used by College Bound Secondary Students: Implications for the College Reading Specialist." Paper presented at the Annual Meeting of the National Reading Council, Austin, Texas, 1986.

Jensen Delucchi, Joanne; Rohwer, William D., Jr.; and Thomas, John W. "Study Time Allocation as a Function of Grade Level and Course Characteristics," *Contemporary Educational Psychology* 12 (1987): 365–380.

Keith, Timothy Z. "Time Spent on Homework and High School Grades: A Large-Sample Path Analysis," *Journal of Educational Psychology* 74 (1982): 248–253.

Keith, Timothy Z.; Reimers, Thomas M.; Fehrmann, Paul G.; Pottebaum, Sheila M.; and Aubey, Linda. "Parental Involvement, Homework, and TV Time: Direct and Indirect Effects on High School Achievement," *Journal of Educational Psychology* 78 (1986): 373–380.

Kiewra, Kenneth A. "Investigating Notetaking and Review: A Depth of Processing Alternative," *Educational Psychologist* 20 (1985): 23–32.

Kulhavy, Raymond W. "Feedback in Written Instruction," *Review of Educational Research* 47 (1977): 211–232.

Kumar, Vanshi Krishna; Rabinsky, Leatrice; and Pandey, Tej J. "Test Mode, Test

Instructions, and Retention," *Contemporary Educational Psychology* 4 (1979): 211–218.

Kurtz, Beth E., and Borkowski, John G. "Children's Metacognition: Exploring Relations among Knowledge, Process, and Motivational Variables," *Journal of Experimental Psychology* 37 (1984): 335–354.

La Porte, Ronald E., and Nath, Rashu. "The Role of Performance Goals in Prose Learning," *Journal of Educational Psychology* 68 (1976): 260–264.

Laurillard, Diana. "The Processes of Student Learning," *Higher Education* 8 (1979): 395–409.

Leong, F. T. L., and Sedlacek, William E. *A Profile of the Incoming Freshmen of the University of Maryland.* College Park: Counseling Center, University of Maryland, 1981.

Light, Richard J. *The Harvard Assessment Seminars: Explorations with Student and Faculty about Teaching, Learning, and Student Life, First Report.* Cambridge, Mass.: Harvard Graduate School of Education, 1990.

Losak, John; Schwartz, M. I.; and Morris, Cathy. "College Students in Remedial Courses: Report on Their High School Preparation," *College Board Review* 125 (1982): 21–22, 29–30.

Marton, Ference, and Saljo, R. "On Qualitative Differences in Learning: II. Outcome as a Function of the Learner's Conception of the Task," *British Journal of Educational Psychology* 46 (1976): 115–127.

Mayer, Richard E. "Instructional Variables That Influence Cognitive Processes during Reading." In *Executive Control Processes in Reading*, edited by Bruce Britton and Shawn Glynn, pp. 201–216. Hillsdale, N.J.: Erlbaum, 1987.

Miller, C. M. L., and Parlett, M. *Up to the Mark: A Study of the Examination Game.* London: Society for Research into Higher Education, 1974.

Muth, K. Denise; Glynn, Shawn M., Britton, Bruce K.; and Graves, Michael F. "Thinking Aloud While Studying Text: Rehearsing Key Ideas," *Journal of Educational Psychology* 80 (1988): 315–318.

National Commission on Excellence in Education. *A Nation At Risk: The Imperative for Educational Reform.* Washington, D.C.: U. S. Government Printing Office, 1983.

Natriello, Gary. "The Impact of Evaluation Processes on Students," *Educational Psychologist* 22 (1987): 155–175.

Nungester, Ronald J., and Duchastel, Philippe C. "Testing versus Review: Effects on Retention," *Journal of Educational Psychology* 74 (1982): 18–22.

Paris, Scott G.; Lipson, Marjorie Y.; and Wixson, Karen K. "Becoming a Strategic Reader," *Contemporary Educational Psychology* 8 (1983): 293–316.

Peper, Richard J., and Mayer, Richard E. "Generative Effects of Notetaking during Science Lectures," *Journal of Educational Psychology* 78 (1986): 34–38.

Pressley, Michael; Snyder, Barbara L.; and Cariglia-Bull, Teresa. "How Can Good Strategy Use Be Taught to Children: Evaluation of Six Alternative Approaches." In *Transfer of Learning: Contemporary Research and Applications*, edited by Stephan M. Cormier and Joseph D. Hagman, pp. 81–121. Orlando, Fla.: Academic Press, 1986.

Rickards, John P., and Friedman, Frank. "The Encoding versus the External Storage Hypothesis," *Contemporary Educational Psychology* 3 (1978): 136–143.

Rohwer, William, D., Jr. "An Invitation to a Developmental Psychology of Studying." In *Advances in Applied Developmental Psychology*, Vol. 1, edited by F. J. Morrison, C. A. Lord, and D. P. Keating. New York: Academic Press, 1984.

Rohwer, William D., Jr., and Thomas, John W. "Domain-Specific Knowledge, Cognitive Strategies, and Impediments to Educational Reform." In *Cognitive Strategy Research*, edited by Michael Pressley, pp. 428–450. New York: Springer-Verlag, 1987.

Roueche, John E.; Baker, G. A.; and Roueche, Sueanne D. *College Responses to Low-Achieving Students: A National Study*. Orlando, Fla.: HBJ Media Systems Co., 1983.

Sanford, Julie. "Management of Science Tasks and Effects on Students' Learning Opportunities," *Journal of Research in Science Teaching* 24 (1987): 249–265.

Schallert, Diane L., and Tierney, Robert J. *Learning from Expository Text: The Interaction of Text Structure with Reader Characteristics*. Austin: Department of Educational Psychology, University of Texas, 1980.

Schuman, Howard; Walsh, Edward; Olson, Camille; and Etheridge, Barbara. "Effort and Reward: The Assumption that College Grades Are Affected by Quantity of Study," *Social Forces* 63 (1985): 945–966.

Snyder, Barbara L., and Pressley, Michael. "How Do College Students Make Use of a Textbook Restudy Opportunity? They Start at the Beginning and Reread." Paper presented at the Annual Meeting of the American Educational Research Association, San Francisco, 1989.

Strage, Amy, and Thomas, John W. "The Relationship between Teachers' Classroom Practices and Achievement in High School Biology Courses." Paper presented at the Annual Meeting of the American Educational Research Association, Chicago, 1991.

Strage, Amy; Tyler, Ann B.; Rohwer, William D., Jr.; and Thomas, John W. "An Analytic Framework for Assessing Distinctive Course Features within and across Grade Levels," *Contemporary Educational Psychology* 12 (1987): 279–302.

Thomas, John W. "Proficiency at Academic Studying," *Contemporary Educational Psychology* 13 (1988): 265–275.

Thomas, John W.; Iventosch, Lorraine; and Rohwer, William D., Jr. "Relationships among Student Characteristics, Study Activities, and Achievement as a Function of Grade Level and Course Characteristics," *Contemporary Educational Psychology* 12 (1987): 344–364.

Thomas, John W., and Rohwer, William D., Jr. "Academic Studying: The Role of Learning Strategies," *Educational Psychologist* 21 (1986): 19–41.

Thomas, John W.; Strage, Amy; Bol, Linda; and Warkentin, Robert W. "Features of High School Science Courses Expected to Prompt Students' Study Activities." Paper presented at the Annual Meeting of the American Educational Research Association, Boston, 1990.

Thomas, John W.; Strage, Amy; and Rohwer, William D., Jr. "Studying across the Life Span." In *Reading across the Life Span*, edited by Stephen R. Yussen and M. Cecil Smith. New York: Springer-Verlag, 1991.

Warkentin, Robert W.; Wilson, Mark; and Rohwer, William D., Jr. "The Relationship between Students' Study Behaviors and Achievement in High School

Biology Courses." Paper presented at the Annual Meeting of the American Educational Research Association, Chicago, 1991.

Weissberg, Michael; Berentsen, Mele; Cote, Angela; Cravey, Benjie; and Heath, Kathryn. "An Assessment of the Personal, Career, and Academic Needs of Undergraduate Students," *Journal of College Student Personnel* 23 (1982): 115–122.

Wolf, Richard M. "Achievement in the United States." In *Educational Environments and Effects*, edited by Herbert J. Walberg, pp. 313–330. Berkeley, Calif.: McCutchan, 1979.

Part III
Motivating Students in Elementary Schools

Chapter 8

ATTRIBUTIONAL APPLICATIONS IN THE CLASSROOM

Sandra Graham and Bernard Weiner

In this chapter, we focus on one particular theory of motivation: attribution theory. Although it is a general theory of motivation with broad applications, we will consider here what this conception tells us about motivation in the classroom.

CAUSAL ASCRIPTIONS

Attribution theory deals primarily with beliefs about causality, or what are known as causal attributions. Causal attributions answer "why" questions, such as "Why did I fail this exam?" or "Why don't any of my classmates like me?" These examples intentionally describe situations of failure because we are more likely to want to know "why" when we experience negative, unexpected, or atypical outcomes (Weiner, 1985b; Wong and Weiner, 1981). Thus we do not usually ask, "Why did I get an 'A' on the exam?" or "Why am I the most popular kid in my class?" Causal search is therefore functional because it may impose order on a sometimes uncertain environment.

In achievement contexts, success and failure typically are ascribed to an ability factor that includes both aptitude and acquired skills, an exertion factor such as temporary or sustained effort, the difficulty (ease) of a task, personality, mood, and help or hindrance from others. In the United States, ability and effort are the most dominant perceived causes of success and failure. When explaining achievement outcomes, individuals attach the most importance to their perceived competencies and how hard they try. That is, when students succeed, they probably say, "I worked hard" or "I am smart"; and if they do

179

not succeed, they are likely to conclude that "I didn't work very hard" or "I am not very smart."

CAUSAL ANTECEDENTS

But how do students arrive at these attributions about, for example, ability and effort? That is, how do we come to understand ourselves and others? Teachers probably often ask themselves, "Did the student fail because she didn't try hard enough or because she is not able?" And students probably ask themselves this same question, which implies that one learns more in the classroom than just subject matter. Equally important, one learns about oneself when one asks such questions as "Am I smart? Am I willing to do what it takes? *Can* I succeed?"

Ability Attributions

How do we know whether we have high or low ability? Because the conclusion one reaches is subjective, we consider here only what the student thinks about himself or herself and what the teacher thinks about the student. We also assume that believing that one has low ability is maladaptive and will impede motivation.

How do students know that they do or do not have high ability? Attributional research has identified a number of informational cues, such as prior performance history and social norm information, that influence causal attributions (Kelley and Michela, 1980). Furthermore, the information conveyed by these antecedents is rather direct. There is nothing at all subtle about the self-ascription implied by the knowledge that one has failed a test on which all others have succeeded. Thus when I fail and everyone else gets an 'A', that is very salient information I might use to infer that I am low in ability.

In contrast to these more straightforward causal cues, other sources of ability information may be more subtle and indirect. This appears to be particularly the case when the source of the information is the teacher. While teachers typically do not intentionally tell their students that they are low in ability, this attributional information may be subtly, indirectly, and even unknowingly conveyed. We believe that the unintended communication of low-ability information appears to be particularly likely when the teacher wishes to protect the self-esteem of the failure-prone student. In the following sections, we review evidence regarding three prevalent and seemingly positive teacher behaviors that can indirectly function as low-ability cues. The operation of these messages has not been sufficiently recognized by educators. The particular behaviors included in this category are (1) communicating pity following a student's failure; (2) offering praise following a student's success, particularly at easy tasks; and (3) offering unsolicited help (see Graham, 1990).

Pity Versus Anger. Attribution research has documented that when teachers perceive that a student's failure is due to low ability, they respond with pity or sympathy, whereas when teachers perceive that failure is due to lack of effort, they become angry (Weiner, Graham, Stern, and Lawson, 1982). For example, a mainstreamed retarded child who fails will probably elicit sympathy, not anger, from the teacher. In contrast, a student who is apparently smart, but who rarely does his or her homework, probably will elicit anger, not sympathy, from his teachers.

Now suppose a teacher does respond with pity or anger toward a failing student. It might be the case that the student will then use this affective display to, first, infer the teacher's attribution and, second, to develop his or her own self-ascription for failure. In other words, failing students can gain information about the causes of their achievement outcomes from the affective displays of teachers.

A few years ago, the role of pity and anger as indirect attributional cues was documented in a laboratory study where sixth-grade participants were induced to fail at a novel puzzle-solving task (Graham, 1984). Following failure, a female experimenter posing as a teacher communicated either pity or anger or gave no affective reaction. Subjects then reported their causal attributions for failure. As Figure 8.1 shows, the findings revealed that children were most likely to attribute their puzzle-solving failure to low ability when pity was conveyed and most likely to report lack of effort as the cause of failure when anger was conveyed. That is, the students used the emotional communications of the teacher to infer why they themselves failed.

We think that these principles we derive from laboratory work *do* apply in the classroom. For example, in some instances, pity may be indirectly displayed in the classroom through certain gestures,

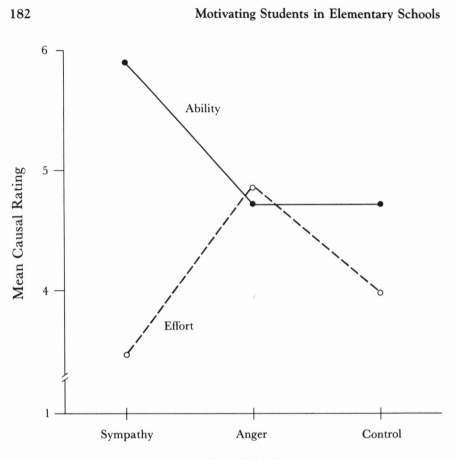

Affect Condition

Figure 8.1
Self-ascriptions for Failure as a Function of Affect Condition

(Data from Graham, 1984).

postures, or words. In other instances, this emotion, while privately experienced, may motivate particular behaviors in the classroom. For example, Brophy and Good (1974) suggest that well-documented teacher behaviors toward students for whom teachers have low expectations, such as teaching less difficult material, and setting lower mastery levels, may be determined, in part, by what the researchers call "excessive sympathy for the student" (p. 311). Of all the subtle attributional cues in classroom contexts, the emotional reactions of teachers may be among the most important antecedents of students' perceived personal competence.

Praise Versus Blame. Praise and the absence of blame from teachers can also function as indirect low-ability cues. This may seem somewhat counterintuitive, since traditional conceptions of praise suggest that this feedback should have positive motivational consequences. Why should such feedback serve as a cue to low ability?

According to attributional principles, praise and blame are related to perceived effort expenditure (Weiner and Kukla, 1970). The successful student who tries hard is praised or rewarded, whereas the failing student who puts forth little effort elicits blame or punishment. Indeed, the student with little ability who succeeds through hard work is maximally praised by the teacher. For example, the retarded pupil who works hard gets the most praise when he succeeds. The same kind of analysis applies in sports, which is a different kind of achievement domain. Think how we respond to the handicapped individual who competes in the Special Olympics and wins. Everyone praises her. In contrast, the high-ability student who fails because of low effort is maximally punished. Consider how negatively we react to the natural athlete who never practices. Thus, praise and blame from others can allow us to make inferences about effort as a cause for success and failure.

Although our focus here is on ability, ability and effort are related in a complex manner. They are perceived as "compensatory" (Kun and Weiner, 1973; Nicholls, 1978). That is, in both success and failure, the higher one's effort, the lower one's perceived ability, and vice versa. They are compensatory because as one increases, the other decreases. Thus if two students achieve the same outcome, the one who tried harder is often judged as lower in ability. Applied to the cue value of praise and blame, these attribution principles suggest that praise, relative to neutral feedback, leads to the inference of high effort, and the higher one's perceived effort, the lower one's perceived ability. In contrast, blame, relative to neutral feedback, leads to the inference of low effort, and the lower one's perceived effort, the higher one's perceived ability.

These ideas have been looked at in a laboratory study conducted by Barker and Graham (1987), in which children between the ages of four and twelve years watched videotaped teaching sessions depicting a pair of students solving a set of easy mathematics problems. In one videotape, both students successfully solved the easy problems. One student was praised by the teacher with such positive statements as "Good thinking!" or "Great job!" The other student received only neutral feedback such as "Correct." In the second videotape, both students failed the easy problems, but one student was criticized, whereas the other student merely received feedback that his answer was not correct. Research participants then rated the effort and ability of the two videotaped students.

The data revealed that the older the participant, the more the student praised for success and the student not blamed for failure were inferred to be *lower* in ability than their counterparts who received neutral feedback or were blamed. In other words, the presence of praise and the absence of blame functioned as low-ability cues for the older children in the study.

These ideas documented in the laboratory have been shown to be relevant to actual classroom settings. For example, Parsons and her colleagues recorded extensive classroom observations of feedback patterns between teachers and students in nearly twenty middle elementary-grade mathematics classrooms (Parsons, Kaczala, and Meece, 1982). These researchers found that frequent blame or criticism for the quality of one's work was positively related to high self-concept of mathematics ability and high future expectancies among students. Praise, on the other hand, was unrelated to self-concept regarding mathematics, although boys who were not praised believed their teachers held high expectations for them. Parsons and her colleagues (1982) concluded;

To suggest that teachers should avoid criticism or give praise more freely overlooks the power of the context in determining the meaning of any message. A well chosen criticism can convey as much positive information as a praise; abundant or indiscriminant praise can be meaningless; insincere praise which does not co-vary with teachers' expectations for the student can have detrimental effects on many students. [P. 336].

So far we have discussed the causes of success and failure, focusing particularly on effort and ability, and we have been asking what makes students think that they lack ability. We have described two apparently good teacher behaviors (pity and praise) that we ordinarily would not associate with negative ability perceptions, which shows that theoretical work can point out relationships we might not have considered. We will next describe another positive teacher behavior that might at the same time have adverse consequences.

Help Versus Neglect. Teacher help (versus neglect) is the third teacher variable that can indirectly function as a low-ability cue. As in the case of praise, simple reinforcement principles underscore the desirable consequences of help. Being the recipient of aid usually results in some tangible gain, at least when compared to undesirable alternatives such as failure. Why, then, might the offering of help have unintended effects on perceptions of ability?

The possibility that help can be a cue to low ability is based on an attributional analysis of helping behavior (Schmidt and Weiner, 1988; Weiner, 1986). According to this analysis, we are more likely to help others when the cause of their need is due to uncontrollable factors like low ability than when the need is perceived as due to controllable factors such as insufficient effort.

If a teacher's attributions determine likelihood of help, then we argue, as we did with pity and with praise, that these behaviors might function as a low-ability cue. In a recent study, Graham and Barker (1990) investigated the cue function of help versus neglect. Drawing on the videotape methodology used previously in the praise study, Graham and Barker filmed a classroom sequence depicting two male students solving a set of mathematics problems in the presence of their teacher. As the students worked, the teacher circulated around their desks, much as she might do in a regular classroom, stopping unobtrusively to gaze at their papers. With one of the problem solvers (the nonhelped student) the teacher casually looked over his shoulder and then moved on without comment. With the other problem solver (the helped student), the teacher also looked over his shoulder and then without apparent knowledge of the student's immediate performance, leaned down to offer help. Unsolicited help was administered when the teacher said, "Let me give you a hint. Don't forget to carry your tens." The help manipulation was therefore intended to coincide with the early stages of problem solving when the outcome was unknown and it was unclear whether the student would have solved the problems successfully on his own. After viewing the videotape, the research participants rated the two students' ability and effort.

One can see from Figure 8.2 that the results of this study were as

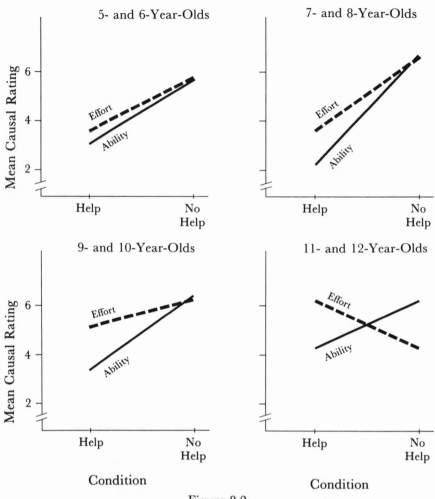

Figure 8.2
**Ratings of Ability and Effort as a Function of Help Condition,
Within Each Age Group**

(From Graham and Barker, 1990).

predicted. All age groups, including the youngest children, perceived the helped student to be lower in ability than his counterpart who received no such assistance. Thus unsolicited help, like pity and praise, can function as an antecedent to low ability, just as relative neglect, like communicated anger and blame, can be a cue to self-ascriptions of lack of effort.

Of course, we do not suggest that the teacher behaviors described here always function as low-ability cues. Sympathetic affect, generous praise, minimal criticism, and helping behavior are useful instructional strategies that often neutralize some of the immediate effects of failure, such as public embarrassment or frustration. Furthermore, it is important to distinguish what we might label "instrumental help," such as probing when appropriate, and "gratuitous help," such as supplying answers outright, for it is only this latter form of premature unsolicited help that is thought to be detrimental to self-perception of ability. Therefore, we are not advocating that teachers should never help their students or that they should always be angry rather than sympathetic, or critical as opposed to complimentary. The appropriateness of any of these feedbacks will depend on many factors, including the general classroom climate and the relationship between teacher and students. Rather, the general message we wish to convey is that attribution principles can facilitate our understanding of how some well-intentioned teacher behaviors may, at times, have unexpected or even negative effects on student motivation.

CAUSAL CONSEQUENCES

Thus far we have discussed some of the determinants of causal ascriptions such as low ability. Remember that low ability and lack of effort are the two most dominant perceived causes of success and failure. Now we want to turn to some of the consequences of these and other causal attributions. Therefore we ask, what does it mean if a student attributes failure to, for example, low ability, rather than to lack of effort, or success to extra help from others, rather than to high aptitude? Our intuitions tell us that if one fails because of low ability, this has a different meaning and connotation than if one fails because of lack of effort. But why should this be so? What do these causal beliefs mean in the context of an attributional theory of motivation?

Causal Dimensions

It appears that meaning, or what a cause connotes in a particular context, is conveyed by the underlying properties of that cause. We will use a nonsocial example to illustrate what we mean by properties. If we give individuals a variety of round objects that differ in ways such as color or size, and a variety of square objects that also differ in these ways, and we ask them to sort the objects, it is likely that the round objects will go in one pile and the square objects in another. Shape is therefore one of the perceived underlying properties of these objects. In the same way, causes have underlying properties, although these are psychological rather than physical representations. Three such properties, labeled "causal dimensions," have been identified with some certainty. They are called locus, stability, and controllability (Weiner, 1985a, 1986).

The *locus dimension* defines the location of a cause as internal or external to the individual. Among the dominant causes discussed earlier (such as aptitude, effort, difficulty or ease of the task) ability (aptitude) and effort are internal because they reflect characteristics of the person. Task difficulty and luck, on the other hand, are external or environmental determinants of outcomes. The causes we discussed previously can all be assigned a place on the locus dimension. The *stability dimension* designates causes as constant or varying over time. Ability is stable in that one's aptitude for a task is relatively fixed, whereas effort and mood are unstable because individuals may vary from one situation to the next in how hard they try and in how they feel. Finally, the *controllability dimension* refers to personal responsibility, or whether a cause is subject to one's own volitional influence. Effort is controllable because individuals are believed to be responsible for how hard they try. In contrast, aptitude and luck are generally perceived to be beyond one's personal control.

Causes therefore are classifiable within one of the eight cells of a locus × stability × controllability dimensional matrix. For illustrative purposes, Table 8.1 compares the dimensional placement of ability (aptitude) and effort ascriptions.

Ability, or aptitude, is an internal, stable, and uncontrollable cause. This means that failure due to low aptitude is perceived as a characteristic of the failing individual, enduring over time, and beyond one's personal control. The dimensional placement of effort, on the other hand, indicates that this cause is also internal, but unstable, and controllable. Ascribing failure to lack of effort thus indicates a personal characteristic that is modifiable by one's own behavior.

These properties determine the psychological consequences of causal attributions. In the next part of this chapter, we focus on some of these consequences.

Table 8.1
Ability and Effort Ascriptions Related to Causal Dimensions

	Causes	
Causal Dimensions	Ability	Effort
Locus	Internal	Internal
Stability	Stable	Unstable
Controllability	Uncontrollable	Controllable

Emotional Consequences of Causal Dimensions

The attributional consequences we address are emotional as well as behavioral because we think it is important to consider both how students feel and what they do. We will first relate dimensions or properties of causes to feeling states. Some of these relations are shown in Table 8.2 (those related to causal stability are not discussed here).

1. The locus dimension is primarily linked to pride and other esteem-related affects. We feel pride when we succeed because of our aptitudes, efforts, or other personal characteristics, whereas negative self-esteem is the consequence of attributing failure to these internal factors.

2. The controllability dimension is linked to a set of social emotions that includes guilt, shame, pity, and anger. Shame (humiliation) is more likely to be experienced when personal failures are due to uncontrollable causes such as low ability. One feels guilty, in contrast, when the causes of personal failure are due to controllable factors. This includes not only lack of effort but also any other causal ascription subject to one's own volitional influence.

Sympathy and anger are emotions directed toward others that follow perceptions of controllability. We already touched on these linkages in the earlier section on low-ability cues. We feel sympathy toward an individual whose failure we perceive is due to uncontrollable factors such as low ability. In contrast, anger is our dominant emotional reaction when we perceive that another's failure is due to controllable factors such as lack of effort.

How do these relations get played out in the classroom? We might

Table 8.2
Relations Between Causal Thinking, Emotions, and Action

Causal Antecedent	Emotion	Action Tendency
Success due to self	Pride	Self-reward; go toward task
Failure due to self is uncontrollable	Shame; humiliation	Recoil; go away from task
Failure due to self is controllable	Guilt	Reproof; go toward task
Failure of another is uncontrollable	Pity; sympathy	Restitution; go toward other
Failure of another is controllable	Anger	Retreat from other; neglect

imagine a learning-disabled child failing in a classroom of successful normal peers. These cues implicate low ability. The student feels ashamed or humiliated and the teacher communicates sympathy, which we already know feeds back into self-perceptions of low ability. This further exacerbates the student's feelings of shame or humiliation. On the other hand, one might imagine a situation where a student does poorly on an exam because of some intentional behavior on his part, like not paying attention. The teacher responds with anger and the student feels guilty. Thus, one strength of our theory-related perspective is that the psychology of emotion, or how we feel about ourselves, and the social psychology of emotion, or how we feel about others, both fit the conception and are intimately related.

BEHAVIORAL CONSEQUENCES OF EMOTIONS

We indicated we were going to relate causal dimensions back to feeling and behavior. We have considered feeling. Now what about behavior? How might achievement-related behavior be influenced by these feelings? Consider first the locus-pride relation. We know that pride follows an internal ascription of success. In addition, pride is a cue to approach achievement situations, perhaps to recapture a previously enjoyed emotion (see Graham, 1988; Weiner and Graham, 1989). In other words, internal attributions evoke pride, and pride, in turn, leads to further achievement strivings. Hence, we know that enabling students to attribute success to themselves rather than to, for example, help from others will promote achievement-related behavior.

How about failure? How might emotions influence reactions to nonattainment of goals? Shame leads to the intent to withdraw from the situation. When one feels ashamed, he or she wants to "curl up in a ball and disappear." And remember that feelings of shame come from a belief in low ability. But guilt, which is elicited by failure due to a personally controllable factor, often functions as a motivator of achievement strivings. For example, Covington and Omelich (1984) found that students who reported feeling guilty about their poor performance on a college midterm examination performed better on a make-up exam than did their nonguilty peers. Finally, pity and anger are directly related to the offering or withholding of help (see Schmidt and Weiner, 1988, for a review of this extensive literature). Pity instigates approach behavior and the desire to help a needy person, whereas anger begets avoidance, and the withholding of help. In sum, all of the emotions related to causal dimensions have motivational significance.

SUMMARY

To summarize all we have discussed here, we will convey how attribution theorists think about motivation as a complex thinking-feeling-acting sequence. A partial representation of this sequence is depicted in Figure 8.3, which serves as a useful framework to review briefly the material presented here.

The sequence begins with an achievement outcome such as success or failure. Success and failure instigate immediate affective reactions, like happiness and sadness, that we label outcome-dependent emotions. A causal search might then be initiated to determine why the outcome occurred. A number of antecedent cues guide particular self-ascriptions. We documented several attributional principles relating communicated sympathy, praise, and unsolicited offers of help to self-ascriptions of low ability. These were contrasted with principles relating communicated anger, blame, and the withholding of help to self-ascriptions of lack of effort.

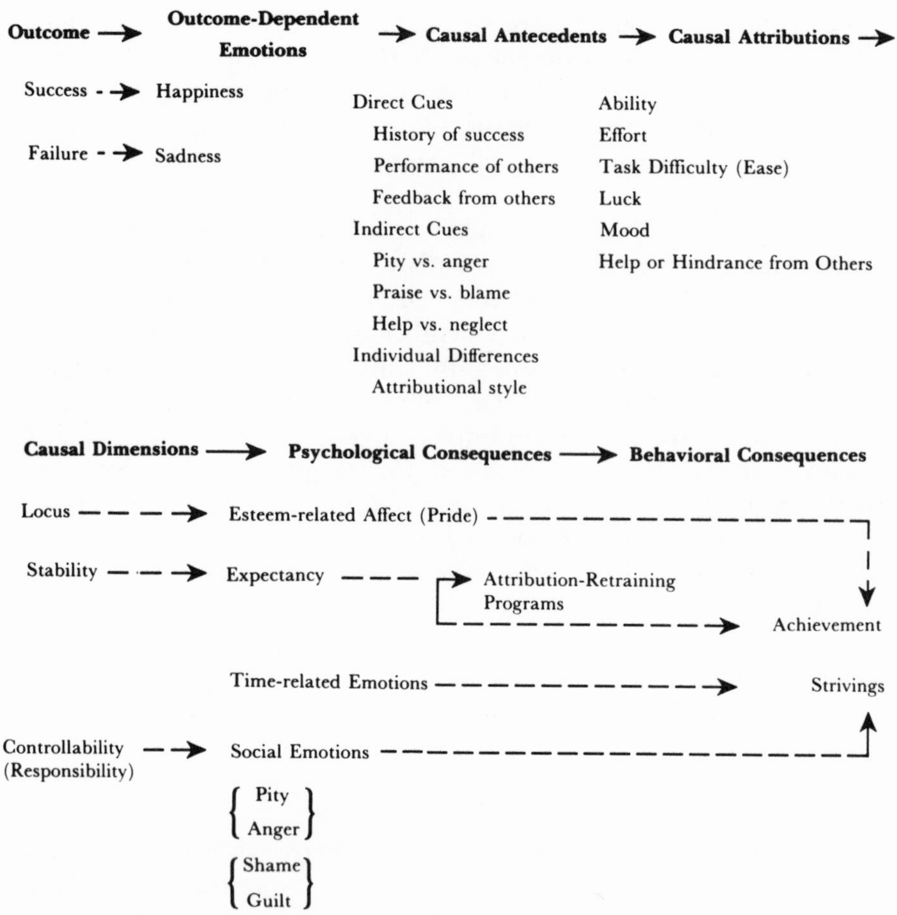

Outcome → Outcome-Dependent Emotions → Causal Antecedents → Causal Attributions →

Success → Happiness

Failure → Sadness

Direct Cues   Ability
    History of success   Effort
    Performance of others   Task Difficulty (Ease)
    Feedback from others   Luck
Indirect Cues   Mood
    Pity vs. anger   Help or Hindrance from Others
    Praise vs. blame
    Help vs. neglect
Individual Differences
    Attributional style

Causal Dimensions → Psychological Consequences → Behavioral Consequences

Locus − − − → Esteem-related Affect (Pride) − − − − − − − − − − − − − −

Stability − − → Expectancy − − − → Attribution-Retraining Programs

− − − − − − − − → Achievement

Time-related Emotions − − − − − − − − − → Strivings

Controllability (Responsibility) − → Social Emotions − − − − − − − − − − − − − −

{ Pity
  Anger }

{ Shame
  Guilt }

Figure 8.3

Partial Representation of an Attributional Theory of Motivation

Given a list of antecedents, the next linkage in Figure 8.3 shows the relatively small set of dominant perceived causes for success and failure and their underlying properties, labeled causal dimensions. Once a particular cause is endorsed, it theoretically is located in dimensional space (see Table 8.1) and these dimensions then have particular psychological and behavioral consequences. All of the dimensions are related to a complex set of achievement-related emotions including pride, shame, guilt, pity, and anger. Furthermore, the stability of causes determines expectations for future success, and this linkage has guided a body of application-oriented research on attribution retraining (which we have not considered in this chapter). Thus, at the very heart of this temporal sequence comprising an attributional theory of motivation is the specification of complex interrelationships between thinking, feeling, and acting.

Consider, for example, the following two achievement scenarios with quite different consequences, followed by their attributional interpretations:

1. Jane fails her mathematics exam and then seeks tutoring and increases her study time.
2. Susan fails her mathematics exam and decides to drop out of school.

In the first scenario, where following failure the student studies harder, the student has experienced a negative outcome. This should generate the outcome-related negative affects of frustration and sadness. Negative outcomes evoke a search to understand why the goal was not attained. Let us assume that Jane has performed well in the past, but on this particular test others do well and she performs poorly. Because the outcome is at variance with social norms, Jane attributes the failure to herself. And because the outcome is also at variance with her past behavior, the attribution is to an unstable factor—lack of adequate preparation and study time. As previously stated, these causes are perceived as internal and unstable, and also as controllable. Because the causes are unstable, Jane maintains a reasonable expectation of success in the future. Because the causes are internal and controllable by Jane, she experiences a loss of personal esteem and guilt, while her teacher and parents are angry and criticize her. High expectations of future success and guilt enable her to overcome her feelings of sadness and weakened self-esteem; they result in renewed goal strivings and increased motivation to perform better on the next exam.

In the second scenario, Susan has also failed her exam, but she, instead, drops out. This failure also elicits outcome-dependent emotions as well as causal search. Let us assume that Susan has failed exams in the past, while other students have performed well. Hence, Susan ascribes failure to herself. She attributes the poor performance to low ability, which is internal, stable, and uncontrollable. Because the cause is internal, Susan's self-esteem is lowered; because the cause is stable, Susan anticipates future failure; and because the cause is uncontrollable, Susan feels ashamed and humiliated. In addition, her parents and teacher feel sorry for her and communicate this without criticism, furthering her belief in her own incompetence. Thus in this achievement situation, Susan has a low expectation of future success and is feeling sad (outcome-related affect); she is low in self-worth (locus-related affect), and ashamed (controllability-related affect). These thoughts and affective states decrease achievement strivings and result in withdrawal from the setting.

If there is one message we want to communicate with this discussion, it is that motivational life is complex. No single word or principle such as reinforcement or intrinsic motivation can possibly capture this complexity.

A FINAL NOTE

The psychologist Kurt Lewin once reminded us that "there is nothing so practical as a good theory." Much of the practical significance of attribution theory lies in its applicability to real-world classroom motivational concerns—concerns that include emotional reactions to success and failure, perceived personal competence, persistence in the face of nonattainment of goals, and so on. We think that the study of these motivational mediators is a useful path if one's goal is to understand some of the complex determinants of academic performance.

REFERENCES

Barker, George, and Graham, Sandra. "Developmental Study of Praise and Blame as Attributional Cues," *Journal of Educational Psychology* 79 (1987): 62–66.

Brophy, Jere, and Good, Thomas. *Teacher-Student Relationships: Causes and Consequences.* New York: Holt, Rinehart, and Winston, 1974.

Covington, Martin, and Omelich, Carol. "An Empirical Examination of Weiner's Critique of Attribution Research," *Journal of Educational Psychology* 76 (1984): 1214–1225.

Graham, Sandra. "Communicating Sympathy and Anger to Black and White Students: The Cognitive (Attributional) Consequences of Affective Cues," *Journal of Personality and Social Psychology* 47 (1984): 40–54.

Graham, Sandra. "Children's Developing Understanding of the Motivational Role of Affect: An Attributional Analysis," *Cognitive Development* 3 (1988): 71–88.

Graham, Sandra "On Communicating Low Ability in the Classroom: Bad Things Good Teachers Sometime Do." In *Attribution Theory: Applications to Achievement, Mental Health, and Interpersonal Conflict*, edited by Sandra Graham and Valerie S. Folkes, pp. 17–36. Hillsdale, N.J.: Erlbaum, 1990.

Graham, Sandra, and Barker, George. "The Down Side of Help: An Attributional-Developmental Analysis of Helping Behavior as a Low Ability Cue," *Journal of Educational Psychology* 82 (1990): 7–14.

Kelley, Harold, H., and Michela, John. "Attribution Theory and Research." In *Annual Review of Psychology*, Vol. 31, edited by Mark R. Rosenzweig and Lyman W. Porter. Palo Alto, Calif.: Annual Reviews, 1980.

Kun, Anna, and Weiner, Bernard. "Necessary versus Sufficient Causal Schemata for Success and Failure," *Journal of Research in Personality* 7 (1973): 197–207.

Nicholls, John. "The Development of the Concepts of Effort and Ability, Perception of Own Attainment, and the Understanding that Difficult Tasks Demand More Ability," *Child Development* 49 (1978): 800–814.

Parsons, Jacqueline; Kaczala, Caroline; and Meece, Judith. "Socialization of Achievement Attitudes and Beliefs," *Child Development* 53 (1982): 322–339.

Schmidt, Greg, and Weiner, Bernard. "An Attribution-Affect-Action Theory of Motivated Behavior: Replications Examining Help Giving," *Personality and Social Psychology Bulletin* 14 (1988): 610–621.

Weiner, Bernard. "An Attributional Theory of Achievement Motivation and Emotion," *Psychological Review* 92 (1985a): 548–573.

Weiner, Bernard. "'Spontaneous' Causal Thinking," *Psychological Bulletin* 14 (1985b): 610–621.

Weiner, Bernard. *An Attributional Theory of Motivation and Emotion*. New York: Springer-Verlag, 1986.

Weiner, Bernard, and Graham, Sandra. "Understanding the Motivational Role of Affect: Lifespan Research from an Attributional Perspective," *Cognition and Emotion* 4 (1989): 401–419.

Weiner, Bernard; Graham, Sandra; Stern, Paula; and Lawson, Margaret. "Using Affective Cues to Infer Causal Thoughts," *Developmental Psychology* 18 (1982): 278–286.

Weiner, Bernard, and Kukla, Andy. "An Attributional Analysis of Achievement Motivation," *Journal of Personality and Social Psychology* 40 (1970): 1–20.

Wong, Paul, and Weiner, Bernard. "When People Ask 'Why' Questions and the Heuristics of Attributional Search," *Journal of Personality and Social Psychology* 40 (1981): 650–663.

Chapter 9

CHILDREN'S KNOWLEDGE OF DIFFERENTIAL TREATMENT IN SCHOOL: IMPLICATIONS FOR MOTIVATION

Rhona S. Weinstein

If you want one year of prosperity, grow grain.
If you want ten years of prosperity, grow trees.
If you want one hundred years of prosperity, grow people.
—Chinese Proverb

In this chapter I approach achievement motivation from the perspective of students and expectancy theory. I examine research on children's knowledge about differential treatment within schooling (as a reflection of "institutionalized" academic expectations) and the consequences of this knowledge for equality of motivational opportunity. Particular attention is given to how common practices such as instructional grouping, allocation of curricula, motivational strategies, assignment of responsibility for learning, evaluation of performance, and relationships among those in the educational environment are seen by students as informing their perceptions of ability and impacting their motivation. In the interests of enhancing motivation for all students, I also draw on theoretical advances and innovative programs that have implications for the redesign of schooling and its capacity to engage a diverse population of learners.

THE VOICES OF CHILDREN

It is surprising that in our research efforts to understand student motivation and in our policy initiatives to reform schooling, children's

197

views of their school experiences are virtually absent from the debate. We reflect a variety of perspectives—that of the researcher, theorist, teacher, administrator, parent, and government—yet the voice of the primary consumer of education remains silent.

This reality, however, easily matches the natural course of relationships within schooling: teacher talk dominating student talk in the classroom, teachers feeling powerless in the face of administrative mandates, and districts helplessly complying with federal statutes. Often those on the front lines are rarely asked for their input or their vision. This reality also reflects our uneasiness with the opinions of children. The context of predictable cognitive change that accompanies development undermines (as most see it) the value of children's views of schooling. Yet our perceptions and the meaning attributed to events, whatever their limitations, mediate the impact of environmental conditions on our beliefs and actions. We have much to learn from the perspectives of children when we seek to explain what motivates them to show interest in learning, to persist at difficult tasks, to try again after failure, and to love the subject matter.

CHILDREN'S MEDIATION OF THE EFFECTS OF TEACHERS' EXPECTATIONS IN THE CLASSROOM

One important risk factor that can enhance or diminish student motivation lies in the expectations that we in schools hold for children's academic performance and the potential that these expectations when expressed might become self-fulfilling prophecies. A burgeoning research literature provides supportive, albeit controversial, evidence (given methodological limitations of correlational research) that academic expectations when communicated in differential treatment can become confirmed in the achievement of students (for critical reviews, see Brophy, 1983; Dusek, 1985; Miller and Turnbull, 1986; Jussim, 1986; Wineburg, 1987).

Two phases characterized early teacher expectancy research: experimental studies seeking to document the effects of teachers' false beliefs on student outcomes and naturalistic correlational studies describing the conditions under which expectations are formed and communicated to children. The early models were largely behavioral in theory (with reinforcement seen as the key mechanism of change), narrowly focused on achievement or IQ as the only child outcome, and time-limited in the assessment of impact. Given the limitations of these models, the strength of such expectancy effects has been, if anything, largely underestimated.

In contrast, alternative models have emerged from anthropology and sociocognitive perspectives within psychology that provide a window on children's thinking about expectations and its links to motivation. This latter approach seeks to describe both the social context of expectancy processes and its meaning to participants by examining the thought processes that mediate self-fulfilling prophecies for students as well as teachers (Braun, 1973; Cooper, 1979; Cooper and Good, 1983; Darley and Fazio, 1980; Jussim, 1986; Weinstein and colleagues, 1979 to present). Here, motivated thoughts and actions are seen to occur within an *interpreted social context*. Children become engaged in subject matter in the context of their relationship with teachers, in comparison to and in full public view of their peers, and with the support or lack of it from both school and parents. Children's understanding of this context proves critical toward unraveling the relationship between expectations and motivation.

STUDENT KNOWLEDGE OF DIFFERENTIAL TREATMENT AND ITS CONSEQUENCES

Awareness of Differential Treatment by Teachers

There is now substantial evidence that children (even as young as first graders) are aware of differential treatment by teachers toward high and low achievers. These findings grow largely out of studies targeted toward a missing link in teacher expectancy research, that is, the extent to which such effects occur within children's awareness and are mediated by such perceptions. Differential treatment by teachers serves as a mechanism of communicating differential expectations to children. To what extent are children aware of such cues and how do such messages shape self-views and ultimately motivation and achievement?

The evidence for perceived differential treatment is clearest when children report on teachers' behavior toward the children's peers. In our research in Berkeley (summarized in Weinstein, 1989), we developed the Teacher Treatment Inventory (TTI) in order to assess children's perceptions of differential treatment. This measure consists of thirty teacher-student interaction items (grouped into three scales and administered in two independent forms) that ask children to rate the frequency of differential treatments toward an imaginary high or low achiever in their classroom. Across three separate studies of elementary school-age children at varying points in the school year (Weinstein and Middlestadt, 1979; Weinstein, Marshall, Brattesani, and Middlestadt, 1982; Weinstein, Marshall, Sharp, and Botkin, 1987), we have found that *in children's eyes* low achievers are likely to receive more negative feedback than do high achievers (e.g., "the teacher scolds him/her for not listening"), more rules and teacher direction (e.g., "the teacher watches him/her closely when he/she is working"), lower expectations (e.g., less frequently "the teacher trusts him/her"), and fewer opportunities or choices (e.g., less frequently "the teacher asks him/her to lead activities").

These results demonstrate remarkable consensus of perceptions within classrooms and across age groups. High and low achievers, boys and girls, and even children as young as first graders perceive these differences in teachers' treatment of others. Most important, the degree of differential teacher treatment that children report varies among classrooms. Consistent with the observational studies, children describe marked differential treatment in some classrooms and more equitable treatment in other classrooms. The influence of individual as well as developmental differences appears to surface in how children apply this knowledge toward an understanding of self.

Studies have also examined children's reports of their "own" treatment from the teacher. Brattesani, Weinstein, and Marshall (1984) found that fourth, fifth, and sixth graders in high differential treatment classes (where ability cues are accentuated) were more likely to report differences in treatment by teachers consistent with their expectancy status than were students in low differential treatment classes. Using frequency ratings with third graders, Mitman and Lash (1988) found perceived differential treatment of the high and low achievers for six of thirteen teacher behaviors, whereas Cooper and Good (1983), using comparative ratings ("more often," "the same," "less often than classmates") with fourth through sixth graders, documented perceived differential treatment for four of nine treatment items.

These studies also explored the "accuracy" of student perceptions as measured against teacher perceptions and observer ratings. In the Cooper and Good (1983) study, student estimates of teacher treatment matched observer frequency ratings on only one of the nine behaviors compared, although all the student means (under-estimates) were in the predicted direction. Student and teacher perceptions showed greater correspondence except in the case of praise. In the Mitman and Lash (1988) study, student and observer consensus about treatment of expectancy groups was greater for interactive than for feedback behaviors (the latter perhaps more difficult for students to interpret), and greater in classrooms where ability cues were accentuated.

These studies underscore that elementary school children are aware of differences in teacher treatment toward high and low achievers within the classroom. In children's eyes, different lives are lived within the very same classroom, as a function of expectations about ability. The spirit of these differences is best captured in the words of a fourth grader: "The teachers they work with them (high achievers), like, um, they don't even need help. And they work with them like 'ah, you could do that easily.' They just show them and they expect, um, they can do it."

Although similar studies have not been conducted at the high school level, anthropological investigations highlight student awareness of different treatment by teachers, such as this example from Eckert's *Jocks and Burnouts* (1989), an ethnographic description of student groups in high school. Here, Eckert argues that students who are seen as leaders have more credibility with the staff and hence more informal privileges to wander around the school, as exemplified by this student's description: "I can basically do whatever I want because they just figure I'm doing something for the school. And they know me, that I'm not going to get in any trouble" (p. 115).

The studies reviewed here also provide clear evidence that classrooms vary in *the extent and pattern of differential treatment* that children report. Agreement between student, teacher, and observer ratings of treatment appears greatest in classrooms where ability cues are more available, although "accuracy" relative to observer or teacher perspectives proves less important given our interest in the student experience and its consequences. Further, variations in what, when, and how children are asked about differential treat-ment (direct versus indirect methods, treatment of others versus treatment of self, frequency versus comparative ratings, time of year) all influence what children report about teacher behavior.

Areas of Differential Treatment: An Eight-Factor Interactive Model

The studies just described offer quantifiable instruments that can assess the degree of differential treatment that children perceive, with some concordance with teacher and observer perspectives. But the specific teaching behaviors depicted largely reflect the researcher perspective.

In contrast, open-ended interview studies with elementary school children have broadened and enriched our understanding of the processes that communicate expectations to students and the apparent institutionalization of these processes in schooling practices (Weinstein, 1986; Marshall and Weinstein, 1984). When we look more deeply at the nature of these clues, we see that information about expected ability lies not only in teacher-child interaction patterns but also in the structural organization of classroom and school life in which this interaction is embedded. The distinctions children make are often subtle, and children are sensitive observers. For example, they distinguish between different types of "call upon" as well as levels of "praise," drawing on nonverbal messages and the larger context for interpretation. Often, just a single incident is vividly reported by many within a classroom and is sufficient to communicate clear expectations. This suggests that our reliance on behavioral categories and their frequency may mislead us. For classroom participants, these messages have a history and a broader context that can serve to either *soften or accentuate* the clues about ability contained in a single interaction (Marshall and Weinstein, 1984).

In using children's perspectives to describe these interrelated features, we found it helpful to elaborate Rosenthal's (1973) four-factor mediation model where teacher expectations are expressed through differential allocation to students of (a) inputs (material presented), (b) outputs (opportunity to respond), (c) feedback (praise and criticism), and (d) climate (warmth). First detailed in Marshall and Weinstein (1984) and expanded in Weinstein, Soule, Collins, Cone, Mehlhorn, and Simontacchi (1991), at least eight aspects of classroom and school practice are viewed as providing information to children about expected ability:

Input Factors
- Grouping practices
- Task system (Curriculum)

- Motivational system
- Student responsibility for learning

Output and Feedback Factors
- Evaluation system

Climate Factors
- Class relationships
- Parent-class relationships
- School-class relationships

In examining these aspects of the instructional environment, it is important to *underscore three sources of effects*: instructional choices create (expand or constrain) opportunities for children, provide (accentuate or minimize) information about ability, and may also result in differential allocation of school experiences to different groups of children. These aspects of instructional choices are important in the communication of expectations.

Expectancy research has documented that the educational inputs, outputs, feedback, and climate received by children vary widely as a function of their perceived ability (Brophy, 1983). At least four aspects of instructional practice characterize the inputs that children receive: the learning groups in which children are instructed, the tasks through which the curriculum is delivered, the motivating strategies teachers use to stimulate learning, and the role of the student in learning. What Rosenthal has referred to as the output and feedback factors reflect the ways in which student work is evaluated: the beliefs about ability that underlie evaluation, the nature of the performance opportunities provided to assess capability, and the feedback given. Finally, interactions around tasks and their evaluation occur in the context of relationships (a) between teachers and students individually and as a class, (b) between parents, teachers, and students, and (c) between the class and the school as a whole. These relationships not only generate opportunities for interaction but also evoke feelings between participants, which make up the climate of the classroom and school.

Grouping Practices. Children can easily describe differences between their classroom groups and the implications that group membership has for perceived ability. A fourth grader acknowledges: "[The teacher] kinda like she separates and whoever is the best readers, they get to be in Kaleidoscope 1. And the second best readers to be in Kaleidoscope 2. And then Open Highways is the last group." And another example: "And so you know they're smart cause they're in the highest group."

Children also are aware that task difficulty varies by groups: "they (high group members) do harder work." Further, a teacher's instructional strategies depend on his or her perceptions of the ability of group members. High groups are given more independence, for example:

They put 'em (smart kids) each in the corners and give them their work and they all, like one person tells the answer, and the other person tells her and then everyone gets a turn. . . . And then the other kids that are not smart, they have to sit . . . in the groups . . . what need more help. And they have to work with the teacher.

The ways in which we group children for instruction and the qualities of our grouping practices (for example, ability-based instruction through reading groups, tracks, and pull-out programs, the extent of mobility between groups) not only provide differential opportunity to learn and to interact with peers but also heighten students' awareness of ability differences through labeling and social segregation.

Task System. Both the tasks children are assigned in the classroom and the ways in which they are paced and monitored by teachers prove informative about relative ability differences among students. Children note ability by the sequencing of materials ("he is the only one in the highest book in the class" and "'cause I gotta skip a lotta math books and was getting into some very complicated things") or by its special characteristics ("they read more books like thick books . . . like in one day, it doesn't take 'em that long"). Children know that high achievers are given more difficult work and that whether one is doing well can be inferred from the following: "When they give you harder work and stuff so you know that they're doing better than some other people who are doing easier work for them and they're having trouble."

As Doyle (1983) has argued, curriculum is delivered through the tasks that children engage in and the properties of these tasks (e.g., operations called for, products required, resources provided, and the accountability system). These characteristics of tasks create opportunities for children as well as reflect messages about children's capabilities. Research on expectancy processes has shown that teachers teach more, provide more challenging material, and allow more resources for students for whom they hold higher expectations. High achievers are more likely to be enriched and low achievers to be remediated. Further, certain task characteristics (such as sequenced readers, for example) and how they are implemented (for example, with limited mobility between readers) simply heighten ability comparisons in the classroom setting.

Motivational System. Teachers choose strategies to engage the motivation of their students. These strategies appear in the introduction to tasks, in the goals set for tasks, and in the rewards given for performance. Theorists have differentiated between competitive, cooperative, and individualistic goal and reward structures (Slavin, 1983), between learning and performance goals (Ames and Archer, 1988) or task-mastery and ego-mastery goals (Nicholls, 1989), and between intrinsic and extrinsic motivation (Lepper, 1981). Competitive, ability-driven motivational systems focus children's attention on "how I am doing" rather than "what I am doing," evoking defensive strategies to preserve self-worth (Covington, 1989) and diminishing intrinsic motivation. Children are attuned to the clues about ability inherent in these motivational strategies: "Like today, the teacher gave me an award saying that I was the second top in the class. And the first top—she had a big grin on her face." Heavy competition also changes relationships among peers: "We do our work and some people copy off of you and . . . we put the wrong answer and then we go back and put the right answer. Because the person who's copying is going to get it wrong and you are going to get it right."

Competitive ability-driven motivational strategies heighten ability comparisons, limit interaction among peers, and decrease intrinsic motivation. Further, research has demonstrated that different motivators are used for high and low achievers. Low achievers are viewed as needing more extrinsic rewards to motivate their learning. High achievers, when they finish their work early, are provided opportunities that are more intrinsically motivating.

Student Responsibility for Learning. Instruction that is largely teacher-centered and under teacher control minimizes opportunities for the participation of students. Limited student agency, that is, choice in and responsibility for instruction and its evaluation (often saved for high achievers who finish first), restricts the uncovering of talent and competence in students and diminishes intrinsic motivation. It is also true that there are differential opportunities for responsibility and choice for high and low achievers. As students note: "The teacher doesn't actually work with (the smart kids) because they know how to do their stuff." The high achievers "are let on their own more." In being let on their own, the high achievers can exercise more choice and more responsibility for their learning.

Evaluation System. Not only do educational inputs to students vary by ability level but the performance opportunities to demonstrate knowledge (outputs) and the feedback provided are differentially accorded to high and low achievers. High achievers have been found to be called on more often to perform and to receive more positive feedback from teachers. Further, choices made in evaluating student performance heighten or diminish the effects of social comparison. Certain beliefs about ability (that intelligence is stable, global, and distributed along a normal curve) also limit the provision of *varied* (reflecting multiple abilities) performance opportunities for evaluation and create scarcity of rewards. The end result is a single set of academic winners and losers in the classroom and a heightened salience of achievement differences.

Children are sensitive to these clues. They can articulate both a global view of ability ("They think that just because they are in a higher level, they're smarter than them in everything") as well as a multiple-ability view ("He's in a higher level than I am but that doesn't mean he's smarter than I am. He might know a lot of things that I don't know in math but I could be better than him in a lot of other things").

They are also sensitive to the nonverbal and more subtle nuances of teacher feedback ("It's a way that they [teachers] talk to you . . . about your grades . . . tone of voice. . . . A very soft voice lets you know you're doing well and a hard tone of voice—they shout and scream to let you know that you're not doing well") and to the public nature of performance comparison ("Like she likes to call out the grades and see how poorly some people did").

Class Relations. The quality of relationships that teachers have with each student is also reflected in the quality of relationships among classroom peers. Expectancy research both from the observer and the student perspective has documented that teachers differentially allocate warmth, trust, humor, and concern to high and to low achievers in the classroom. It also follows that in classrooms with a narrow academic agenda (as described above), the agenda frames the relationships within the class, creating a bimodal distribution of "stars" and "isolates" among peers and a devaluing of diversity and community for all. In children's eyes the relationship among peers is an uneasy one: "Not so smart girls can't play with the smart, smart girls because smart girls just act like they ignore 'em." This uneasy relationship also promotes continued strife: "When the kids they don't pay attention, when they see they have a sad face on their paper, they say I'm not smart. . . . They be mad then they start kickin' the college kids."

Parent-Class Relations. An important source of student support comes from close parent involvement in the educational process. As one fourth grader describes it, "Anyway I just practice my reading when my mother an' father is home—that's how I get my reading up to third."

In contrast, the parents of low achievers are viewed in this way: "They mother and father don't teach 'em anything at home and then they come to school, act the same way they do at home." Children express: "And you're glad that you have the kind of parents that teaches you, and the teacher that teaches you."

Clearly, there are differential parent-class relationships for high and low achievers. Further, limited and narrow communication opportunities (left to problems or parent initiation) create winner and loser families.

School-Class Relationships. "The way you know a person is smart, Miss _____ always picks on them to go different places." The expectancy research has shown that there are differential opportunities for school involvement, leadership, and reward for high and low achievers. Opportunities to get outside the classroom and for school-level recognition are most often accorded to high rather than low achievers. Further limited attention to creating opportunities for participation and recognition at a schoolwide level leaves success experiences and strong school identification just to the classroom setting and to individual teachers.

Consequences of Differential Treatment: Accentuating Student Differences

A number of studies using different methodologies provide converging evidence that classroom conditions are related to the formation of children's perceptions of ability (Rosenholtz and Simpson, 1984; Stipek, 1988). Children learn about their ability relative to their peers from clues inherent in the organizational and interactional processes of the classroom, such as those detailed above.

We have found that children's perceptions of differential treatment by teachers predict the degree to which children perceive ability differences among themselves. In classrooms where children report a great deal of differential treatment by teachers, children's expectations of themselves more closely match teachers' expectations than is the case in classrooms where teachers treat students equitably (Brattesani et al., 1984; Weinstein et al., 1987). Thus, the gap in self-expectations between students of whom teachers expect much and those of whom they expect little is accentuated and more closely follows teachers' expectations. These findings were moderated by a developmental trend (at least apparent earlier in the school year) whereby older children (fifth graders) were less likely than younger students to be influenced by the perceived classroom environment in their ability perceptions. Older students of whom teachers had low expectations held more negative-ability perceptions in both high and low differential treatment classrooms.

These studies provide evidence for a link between children's awareness of differential treatment by teachers and their perception of ability differences among their peers. Other studies, using observer-derived rather than student-derived measures of differential treatment by teachers in classrooms, confirm these relationships. Rosenholtz and her colleagues provide evidence from a sample of fifth and sixth graders that children's self-reported ability levels as well as reports of peers' ability levels are more dispersed, more consensual, and more closely matched to teachers' ratings in unidimensional classrooms (i.e., classrooms with similar tasks, low student autonomy, ability-based groups, salient performance evaluations) than in multidimensional classrooms (Rosenholtz and Rosenholtz, 1981; Rosenholtz and Wilson, 1980). In a study by Filby and Barnett (1982), class consensus about the best readers was found to be greater in whole-class reading instruction than in staggered reading instruction where performance comparisons were likely more private. Mitman and Lash (1988) contrasted third-grade classrooms across three observer-rated expectation cues (use of seating by ability level, differential allocation of sequenced instruction, and frequency of comparative evaluations) and found that the gap in perceived ability between high and low achievers was much greater in the higher-cue classrooms than in the lower-cue classrooms.

Stipek and Daniels (1988) used observation and interviews with teachers to characterize the salience of comparative evaluation in kindergarten and fourth-grade classrooms. They documented lower ratings for competence and future attainment for kindergarten children in the more comparative classrooms. By fourth grade, however, the relative emphasis on comparative evaluation in the classroom did not affect children's competence ratings (replicating the findings of Weinstein et al., 1987). This study provides evidence that the decline in children's perceptions of competence associated with age (Blumenfeld, Pintrich, Meece, and Wessels, 1982; Stipek and Tannatt, 1984) may reflect in part the environmental shift of increasing comparative evaluation across grades rather than simply a developmental phenomenon.

MacIver (1988) explored possible mediators of these relationships between classroom practices and children's perceptions of ability, highlighting the degree of talent dispersion in a classroom (that is, the range of ability as rated by teachers). He found that among fifth and sixth graders, an undifferentiated task structure (that is, the use of same tasks for all students) was related to stratification in children's ability perceptions, but only in classrooms where talent dispersion was high. Although there still remains much to learn about which classroom conditions trigger perceived ability stratification, these studies all suggest that, at least in part, children judge their ability from the organization of instruction as reflected in teacher practices.

IMPLICATIONS FOR EQUITY OF MOTIVATIONAL OPPORTUNITY

That different lives are lived within the same classroom, that children learn to read these clues for information about their own ability, and that teaching practices that heighten ability comparisons also accentuate the stratification of children's ability perceptions all suggest important implications for equity of motivational opportunity.

Jussim (1986) highlights three constructs (self-views, perceived control over outcomes, and valuing of achievement) that may mediate the impact of differential treatment (as a reflection of teachers' expectations) on children's motivation and performance. Evidence from Harter (1982) demonstrates a relationship between high self-esteem in children and positive motivational attitudes, such as intrinsic motivation, task orientation, and preference for challenge. Attributional theorists explain these relationships as reflecting different attributions for failure: low achievers to lack of ability, which erodes further motivation, and high achievers to lack of effort, which enhances persistence (Weiner, 1990). Covington (1989) further argues that low achievers avoid demonstrating effort to preserve a sense of self-esteem, a type of self-enhancement strategy. If they fail after giving minimal effort, the failure indicates the need for additional effort rather than reflecting a lack of ability. Social-psychological research on self-fulfilling prophecies in social interaction also points to the press for self-verification as well as self-enhancement strategies in support of self-esteem. Swann (1987) postulates that people low in self-esteem seek verification of self-views by attending more strongly to evidence of negative feedback despite its damaging emotional effects. This process suggests that for older children the changing of self-views (and the persistence of low effort) may prove to be a more complex process.

Theorists have also documented relationships between perceived ability and motivation in the context of different classroom conditions or student belief systems. In the work of Ames and Archer (1988), secondary students who perceive mastery or learning goals in the classroom ("What am I learning?") prefer more challenging tasks, feel more positive about school, and believe that success follows from effort. On the other hand, students who perceive performance goals ("How am I doing?") focus on their ability, evaluate themselves in negative terms, and attribute failure to lack of ability. Dweck and Leggett (1988) suggest that theories of intelligence underlie these linkages between motivational orientations and ability. Children who believe that intelligence is malleable (incremental theorists) embrace learning goals: they ignore ability information and exhibit mastery behaviors. Children who are entity theorists view intelligence as fixed: they adopt performance goals ("How am I doing?") and are driven to gain positive judgments and avoid failure. Given these latter beliefs, perceived low ability may lead to a disabling pattern of helpless avoidance.

In classrooms in which children perceive differential treatment by teachers, children learn quickly whether they are high or low achievers, and this stratification of ability differences likely widens the circle of perceived low achievers. The classroom context that accentuates ability differences promotes the conditions under which being a low achiever is associated with low motivation. Further, the costs of "ability-driven" classrooms extend to the high achievers as well. Botkin (1990) has demonstrated that in classrooms where teachers differentiate treatment, children are likely to report more defensive processes in coping with their anxiety about school. High use of psychological defenses leaves little energy for productive learning. Both high and low achievers suffer in such classroom environments, with high achievers experiencing anxiety about keeping up their good performance and low achievers giving up and turning off in the face of expected failure (Rose, 1989). Phillips (1987) points out as well the illusion of incompetence among academically competent children.

There are still other potential routes from differential treatment by teachers to the erosion of motivation. Another possible consequence of awareness of differential treatment by teachers is a change in the value placed on achievement. If children perceive that their efforts and their selves are devalued in classrooms, they will likely devalue education as a vehicle for their achievement in society (Cummins, 1986). Fordham and Ogbu (1986) also make this point about the distrust of some African-American youth of the educational establishment and their view that achievement means "acting white." Still other theorists suggest the importance of perceptions of control over academic outcomes or efficacy beliefs as the critical link between differential treatment by teachers and motivational failure. Either differential treatment (rewarding highs but not lows for effort) or differential patterns of success (linking effort with positive outcomes) can erode low achievers' beliefs that trying leads to successful performance (Bandura, 1977; Cooper, 1979; Cooper and Good, 1983).

This process of accentuating perceived ability differences within the classroom and the accompanying erosion of student motivation wastes academic talent during a formative period of growth where development might be without limits. Further, an examination of population groups most at risk for low expectations reveals an overrepresentation of ethnic minorities and the poor in the low-achieving sector (Jones and Weinstein, forthcoming; Oakes, 1987). Another group at particular risk for low expectations is girls with regard to mathematics and science, particularly in the later grades (Oakes, 1990). Still other examples include the bottom half of the achievement distribution in any school district. Children achieving at the bottom of the distribution of a high socioeconomic status, high-achieving school district, might, given another setting, appear as average or even high achievers.

Finally, much of the research described is cross-sectional, focusing on these processes at one point in time, yet children spend long days and twelve years in one classroom after another forging a school career rather than engaging in a set of disparate experiences. Classroom practices that differentiate the treatment of high and low achievers have implications that carry over from year to year. For example, a year spent in the lowest reading group with remedial material may relegate a child to a low group or low track in subsequent years. Equally important, children carry images of themselves as learners from subject to subject and from classroom to classroom. If anything, the power of these differential experiences and their meaning to children is underestimated. These effects are generalized across subject matter and compounded across school years to yield cumulative effects. Research has demonstrated a widening gap over the course of schooling in the achievement of minority and nonminority children (Alexander and Entwisle, 1988), and minorities are found to be at higher risk for school dropout (Rumberger, 1987). Research on school dropouts also suggests that the final school withdrawal is the result of a longitudinal process of successive changes in the level of school participation from early failure to marginal school attendance (Finn, 1989).

CREATING CONDITIONS FOR EQUITY IN MOTIVATIONAL OPPORTUNITY

Not surprisingly, we have control over the conditions that stratify the ability perceptions of children and thereby erode motivation. Currently, there are new initiatives, theory-driven and intervention-oriented, targeted toward creating practices that promote the engagement of all students. These initiatives emanate from alternative conceptions of the same eight classroom factors that have been implicated in expectancy research.

New Initiatives

Paris (1988) has argued that our theories and our interventions about motivation must fuse skill and will. Addressing the motivational or affective side of the equation without paying attention to the *curriculum* and its characteristics leads ultimately to failure. Levin's (1987) intervention program in inner-city schools is targeted toward curricular changes where the goal is to enrich and accelerate learning rather than to provide unending remediation, a common practice in work with low achievers.

With regard to *grouping*, researchers such as Oakes (1985) have provided strong evidence for the negative effects of high school tracking on the differential allocation of curricular opportunities to minorities. Currently, a number of school districts (e.g., San Diego, Boston) are working toward a districtwide policy of equity of educational opportunity that promotes teaching to students of mixed ability and eliminates tracking and ability-based grouping for instruction. Other districts are reexamining their retention practices and suspension policies as mechanisms of grouping students that may retard their progress rather than promote their entrance into the mainstream. The special education community has also developed a new set of initiatives based on the reintegration of children with handicaps into the regular classroom (Wang, Reynolds, and Walberg, 1986).

Other researchers such as Wang (1983) and Corno and Rohrkemper (1986) have addressed ways in which *student responsibility for learning* can be enhanced. A focus on the problem-solving processes of students (self-regulated learning) and the opportunities inherent in responsibility and choice changes the nature of the relationship between teachers, students, and curricular materials.

Motivation theorists such as Nicholls (1989) and Covington (1989) have called for an end to competitive classroom settings where the protection of self-worth is continually at issue. As alternatives, intervention programs target cooperative learning groups (e.g., Aronson, 1978; Slavin, 1983) and performance mastery strategies (e.g., Csikszentmihalyi, 1990) as the motivational context for learning.

Newer theories of *ability* such as Gardner's (1983) seven types of intelligence and Sternberg's (1986) concept of practical intelligence suggest ways of expanding the range of performance opportunities for children in the classroom with greater chances for successful and valued performance. School districts are developing curricula addressing the artistic and human knowledge aspects of intelligence identified by Gardner but largely underrepresented in our current programs. Research on incremental views versus entity views of intelligence suggests that the belief of an "increasing" intelligence alters the conditions for learning in the classroom, promoting more mastery-oriented behavior (Dweck and Leggett, 1988). In changing our views of intelligence, and ultimately promoting greater development of talent, we also need to address changes in the nature, use, and frequency of our assessments of performance (National Commission on Testing and Public Policy, 1990). Practices that address the process of learning rather than the evaluation of narrow products of learning are important steps in mitigating the negative effects of differential praise and criticism from teachers.

Sarason (1982) and Comer (1988a) focus on the psychological sense of community within schooling and the *relationships* between teachers, students, parents, and the school as a whole. Sarason argues that successfully coping with student diversity is as essential to education as instilling knowledge and that the increasing diversity of our school population (if valued and respected) represents an opportunity rather than a problem. Comer's intervention program focuses specifically on enhancing the collaborative partnership of all individuals committed to schooling and involves the parents, a largely underutilized resource, as contributors to the improvement of the social climate of schools. Other programs introduce affective curricula that focus on prosocial behavior in the classroom as a means of creating a respectful community in schooling (e.g., Solomon, Watson, Delucchi, Schaps, and Battistich, 1988).

Focusing on opportunities and relationships in the school as a whole, still other interventions expand the range of schoolwide activities such as government, school economy, and community service as vehicles for stimulating curricular and personal development beyond individual classrooms and enhancing an identification with the school (Butterworth and Marrotta, 1986). Ecological theory on setting size and the ratio of roles to number of individuals needed to fill them provides clues to how the expansion of schoolwide opportunities (such as two casts for a play) can enhance the demand characteristics for participation and the opportunities for development.

Within the arena of human relationships, other interventions focus on creating a legacy of hope in the relationships between teachers and students, parents and students, and the community and students. Individuals, businesses, and teachers have come forward with hope and often the financial backing or the critical educational and emotional support necessary to support its realization. The "I Have a Dream" program, the film *Stand and Deliver*, and Comer's (1988b) *Maggie's American Dream* are all examples (albeit without evaluative data) of how a belief in a child's potential in the context of a supportive relationship may become a self-fulfilling reality.

Initiatives for Change as Reflections of "Linked" Expectancy Processes

The above are important initiatives for change. The need is urgent to collect careful evaluative data about efficacy in the "broadest sense," reflecting newer ideas about achievement and knowledge about self and peers.

However, without considering the *interrelationships* between these aspects of educational practices, we are missing a crucial opportunity. The systemic structures addressed by these initiatives are all contexts in which expectations for success or failure are communicated to students. The goal of equitable motivational opportunity is possible only when one examines the constraints and possibilities inherent in the interrelationships between the inputs we provide children, the diverse performance opportunities and the feedback we use to assess learning, and the relationship context in which that learning takes place. Without taking into account a theoretical understanding of the relationships between these aspects of schooling and how they may work *for or against each other*, we face a possibility of a subversion of the impetus for change. As one example, consider the legislative mandate to desegregate schools by regrouping minority and nonminority children within single schools. The available evidence suggests that in many cases, children were simply regrouped into separate ability-based reading groups and tracks. The racial segregation that earlier occurred between schools now occurs within schools in separate groups and tracks (Epstein, 1985).

An Integrated and Collaborative Expectancy Intervention

There have been surprisingly few evaluated interventions directed toward changing such school expectancy processes, despite the fact that promoting "higher expectations" is the stated goal of every school effectiveness program. The best-known program is Teacher Expectations and Student Achievement (TESA) which is based on teaching teachers to equalize their interactions with high and low achievers (Kerman, 1979). It focuses largely on the feedback and opportunity aspects of differential treatment but does not address the institutionalized nature of such feedback in the set of instructional choices that teachers make.

Growing from our research on students' perspectives about expectancy processes in the classroom, we designed an intervention program to promote high expectations for all students by systematically targeting for change the eight factors addressed here (Weinstein, Soule, Collins, Cone, Mehlhorn, and Simontacchi, 1991). Collaborative rather than prescriptive in design, the program engaged a team of researchers, teachers, and administrators at a high school in the reading of research, in the observation of classroom and school practice, and in the redesign and implementation of new practices along the lines of alternative conceptions of the eight-factor expectancy communication model.

In this project, we targeted low-achieving ninth graders at risk for school failure (largely a minority population) and achieved promising but partial success. Using qualitative and quantitative methods to track the process and effects of our intervention, we found evidence for an evolving but uneven implementation of alternative practices as the school struggled with the constraints that kept existing practices in place. We were successful in bringing about policy change in the direction of detracking the high school. We achieved change among teachers in the development of staff collaboration and teacher leadership. Finally, we were able to reduce dropout rates for the targeted group at the one-year followup as compared to a comparable cohort from previous years, but this success was not accompanied by more favorable grades. What must be noted here is that the higher attrition of the control cohort makes this comparison a biased one against the wider band of "intervention" students still enrolled in the high school. Or alternatively, one year of an "evolving" program proved insufficient to fully turn around the trajectory of school failure, deeply embedded by the time students reach high school. However, our intervention, still evolving under direction from teachers, proved promising in both empowering teachers to address multiple expectancy components in their own and in students' lives and also in engaging youngsters in schooling.

Lessons Learned

The process of systematically changing communication about expectations in schooling taught us important truths about its complexity. First, we learned that the institutionalized assumptions concerning curriculum, grouping, ability and evaluation, motivators, locus of responsibility for learning, and human relationships within and between the classroom, the school, and the community constrain the lives of us all—trainers of teachers, teachers, and students alike. Second, we learned that high expectations cannot be imposed; rather they emerge from changed working (teaching and learning) conditions wherein talent is seen for the first time.

Teachers suffer from many of the same conditions of schooling that students do. As Finley (1984) notes, teachers are tracked in the eyes of their peers (the "gifted" teachers) in the same ways that students are tracked, with the high-status assignments reserved for those perceived as the best teachers or with the most seniority. Further, one of the reasons that teachers have difficulty with implementing cooperative rather than competitive learning processes in the classroom lies with their lack of experience as collaborators within their own work setting (Palincsar, Stevens, and Gavelek, 1989).

The complementarity of such processes between levels of schooling extends to the world of the university, which houses the trainers of teachers. The widening gap between the haves and the have-nots of academe (the "stars" against the others) reminds one of the differential treatment of high and low reading group members within elementary school classrooms. In the university of today, highly entrepreneurial and professionalized, increasing quantities of publications are expected and at faster rates, akin to the elementary school child's belief that smartness is getting the work done fast and first. Finally, the same tension between selecting the already motivated or talented or seeking to develop talent is reflected in the squabbles over special treatment or extended time for tenure for women during the pretenure years to ease their overtaxed position. Goodlad (1990) makes clear the need to examine all the levels of the educational system and their interrelationships in order to effect change at the classroom level.

A second truth lies in the process of changing one's expectations. Simply mandating higher expectations or imparting false information about latent ability failed in our experience to shape teachers' beliefs about themselves or their students. Rather, it was only by changing the conditions of teaching and learning that hidden talents were seen for the first time. When performance opportunities were widened in the classroom, more students appeared talented in new ways. When teachers successfully collaborated in their work, they were able to learn from colleagues they had previously written off. Change in stereotypes comes about from disconfirming experiences. As Merton (1948) argued: "The specious validity of the self-fulfilling prophecy perpetuates a reign of terror. For the prophet will cite the actual course of events as proof that he was right from the very beginning" (p. 195). Only a change in course can break this recursive cycle. A change in the circumstances of teaching and learning can call forth new behavior that may disconfirm an earlier and faulty view of human potential.

Against the Tide

In its approach to stemming the tide of school failure and engaging student motivation, the current educational climate emphasizes more requirements, rigorous school standards, and frequent testing or accountability, paying scant attention to the broader and interactive social context in which motivated learning takes place. The predominant call is for more of the same (working "harder" not "differently") without challenging the institutionalized practices that erode motivation for many students.

Even the direction of educational research leans toward subject matter specialization and farther from the social and motivational context in which the disciplines are taught. Although it is clear that curriculum has been inadequately addressed in much of educational research, it is also apparent that there are important processes that transcend disciplinary differences and serve to create a learning context that is either safe and motivating for children or threatening and destructive for the development of a self-concept as a learner. Until attention is paid to the variables that facilitate or hinder children's valuing of themselves and their learning, we will never achieve equitable motivational opportunity, especially among an increasingly diverse population of learners. This very diversity requires a learning setting that explores and appreciates these differences, that calls for high expectations but within a broadened view of the qualities of academic development. The active role of teachers, administrators, and trainers of teachers in re-examining these interrelated conditions at all levels of schooling, both for themselves and for their students, is critical to making changes in the classroom. As Sarason (1990) points out, the predictable failure of educational reform lies partly in our inability to acknowledge that schooling exists for both teachers and students—what is motivating for both will promote engagement in a continuing process of growth.

CONCLUSION

This chapter began with a call to listen to the voices of children, telling us about their experience of schooling. Children teach us that educational practices that heighten awareness of ability differences threaten their identity as learners and erode motivation to learn. With systemic and integrative change in such practices, we may highlight for children the joys of learning rather than the pain of comparative evaluations of performance. If not in schooling, then where might we increase the possibility that children *will grow*? Rose (1989), in *Lives on the Boundary*, captures the need so well:

More often than we admit, a failed education is social more than intellectual in origin. And the challenge that has always faced American education, that it has sometimes denied and sometimes doggedly pursued, is how to create both the social and cognitive means to enable a diverse citizenry to develop their ability. It is an astounding challenge. [P. 225]

Recent advances in educational theory and research suggest that we have the knowledge to meet this challenge.

REFERENCES

Alexander, Karl L., and Entwisle, Doris R. "Achievement in the First Two Years of School: Patterns and Processes," *Monographs of the Society for Research in Child Development* 53 (1988): 1–157.

Ames, Carole, and Archer, Jennifer. "Achievement Goals in the Classroom: Students' Learning Strategies and Motivational Processes," *Journal of Educational Psychology* 80 (1988): 260–267.

Aronson, Elliot. *The Jigsaw Classroom*. Beverly Hills, Calif.: Sage Publications, 1978.

Bandura, Albert. *Social Learning Theory*. Englewood Cliffs, N.J.: Prentice-Hall, 1977.

Blumenfeld, Phyllis C.; Pintrich, Paul R.; Meece, Judith J.; and Wessels, Kathleen. "The Formation and Role of Self-perceptions of Ability in Elementary Classrooms," *Elementary School Journal* 82 (1982): 401–420.

Botkin, Meryl. "Differential Teacher Treatment and Ego Functioning: The Relationship between Perceived Competence and Defense." Doctoral dissertation, University of California, Berkeley, 1990.

Brattesani, Karen A.; Weinstein, Rhona S.; and Marshall, Hermine H. "Student Perceptions of Differential Teacher Treatment as Moderators of Teacher Expectation Effects," *Journal of Educational Psychology* 76 (1984): 236–247.

Braun, Carl. "Johnny Reads the Cues: Teacher Expectations," *Reading Teacher* 26 (1973): 704–712.

Brophy, Jere E. "Research on the Self-fulfilling Prophecy and Teacher Expectations," *Journal of Educational Psychology* 75 (1983): 631–661.

Butterworth, Barbara, and Marrotta, June. "Our Economic World in Microcosm: The Keys School Community." Unpublished paper, 1986.

Comer, James. "Educating Poor Minority Children," *Scientific American* 259 (1988a): 42–48.

Comer, James. *Maggie's American Dream: The Lives and Times of a Black Family*. New York: NAL Books, 1988b.

Cooper, Harris M. "Pygmalion Grows Up: A Model for Teacher Expectation Communication and Performance Influence," *Review of Educational Research* 49 (1979): 389–410.

Cooper, Harris M., and Good, Thomas L. *Pygmalion Grows Up: Studies in the Expectation Communication Process*. New York: Longman, 1983.

Corno, Lyn, and Rohrkemper, Mary M. "The Intrinsic Motivation to Learn in Classrooms." In *Research on Motivation in Education: The Classroom Milieu*, edited by Carol Ames and Russell E. Ames. New York: Academic Press, 1986.

Covington, Martin V. "Self-esteem and Failure in School: Analysis and Policy Implications." In *The Social Importance of Self-esteem*, edited by Andrew M. Mecca, Neil J. Smelser, and John Vasconcellos, pp. 72–111. Berkeley: University of California Press, 1989.

Csikszentmihalyi, Mihaly. *Flow: The Psychology of Optimal Experience*. New York: Harper and Row, 1990.

Cummins, Jim. "Empowering Minority Students: A Framework for Intervention," *Harvard Educational Review* 56 (1986): 18–36.

Darley, John M., and Fazio, Russell H. "Expectancy Confirmation Processes Arising in the Social Interaction Sequence," *American Psychologist* 35 (1980): 867–881.

Doyle, Walter. "Academic Work," *Review of Educational Research* 53 (1983): 159–199.

Dusek, Jerome B., ed. *Teacher Expectancies*. Hillsdale, N.J.: Erlbaum, 1985.

Dweck, Carol, and Leggett, Ellen. "A Social-Cognitive Approach to Motivation and Personality," *Psychological Review* 59 (1988): 256–273.

Eckert, Penelope. *Jocks and Burnouts: Social Categories and Identity in the High School*. New York: Teachers College Press, 1989.

Epstein, Joyce L. "After the Bus Arrives: Resegregation in Desegregated Schools," *Journal of Social Issues* 42 (1985): 23–43.

Filby, Nikola N., and Barnett, Bruce G. "Student Perceptions of 'Better Readers' in Elementary Classrooms," *Elementary School Journal* 82 (1982): 435–449.

Finley, Merrilee K. "Teachers and Tracking in a Comprehensive High School," *Sociology of Education* 57 (1984): 233–243.

Finn, Jeremy. "Withdrawing from School," *Review of Educational Research* 59 (1989): 117–142.

Fordham, Signithia, and Ogbu, John U. "Black Students' School Success: Coping with the Burden of 'Acting White'," *Urban Review* 18 (1986): 178–206.

Gardner, Howard. *Frames of Mind: The Theory of Multiple Intelligences*. New York: Basic Books, 1983.

Goodlad, John I. *Teachers for Our Nation's Schools*. San Francisco: Jossey-Bass, 1990.

Harter, Susan. "A Developmental Perspective on Some Parameters of Self-regulation in Children." In *Self-management and Behavior Change: From Theory to Practice*, edited by Paul Karoly and Frederick H. Kanfer. Elmsford, N.Y.: Pergamon Press, 1982.

Jones, Lauren, and Weinstein, Rhona. *Teacher Expectations for Black and White Students in Contrasting Classroom Environments*. Berkeley: University of California, forthcoming.

Jussim, Lee. "Self-fulfilling Prophecies: A Theoretical and Integrative Review," *Psychological Review* 93 (1986): 429–445.

Kerman, Sam. "Teacher Expectations and Student Achievement," *Phi Delta Kappan* 60 (1979): 716–718.

Lepper, Mark. "Intrinsic and Extrinsic Motivation in Children: Detrimental Effects of Superfluous Social Controls." In *Aspects of the Development of Competence: The Minnesota Symposia on Child Psychology*, Vol. 14, pp. 155–214, Hillsdale, N.J.: Erlbaum, 1981.

Levin, Henry. "Accelerated Schools for Disadvantaged Students," *Educational Leadership* 44 (1987): 19–21.

MacIver, Douglas. "Classroom Environments and the Stratification of Pupils' Ability Perceptions," *Journal of Educational Psychology* 80 (1988): 495–505.

Marshall, Hermine, and Weinstein, Rhona S. "Classroom Factors Affecting Students' Self-evaluations: An Interactional Model," *Review of Educational Research* 54 (1984): 301–325.

Merton, Robert K. "The Self-fulfilling Prophecy," *Antioch Review* 8 (1948): 193–210.

Miller, Dalte T., and Turnbull, William. "Expectancies and Interpersonal Processes," *Annual Review of Psychology* 37 (1986): 233–256.

Mitman, Alexis L., and Lash, Andrea A. "Students' Perceptions of Their Academic Standing and Classroom Behavior," *Elementary School Journal* 89 (1988): 55–68.

National Commission on Testing and Public Policy. *From Gatekeeper to Gateway: Transforming Testing in America.* Chestnut Hill, Mass.: Boston College, 1990.

Nicholls, John. *The Competitive Ethos and Democratic Education.* Cambridge, Mass.: Harvard University Press, 1989.

Oakes, Jeannie. *Keeping Track: How Schools Structure Inequality.* New Haven, Conn.: Yale University Press, 1985.

Oakes, Jeannie. "Tracking in the Secondary Schools: A Contextual Perspective," *Educational Psychologist* 22 (1987): 129–153.

Oakes, Jeannie. *Multiplying Inequalities: The Effects of Race, Social Class, and Tracking on Opportunities to Learn Mathematics and Science.* Santa Monica, Calif.: Rand Publication Series, 1990.

Palincsar, Annemarie S.; Stevens, Dannelle D.; and Gavelek, James R. "Collaborating with Teachers in the Interest of Student Collaboration," *International Journal of Educational Research* 13 (1989): 41–53.

Paris, Scott G. "Fusing Skill and Will in Children's Learning and Schooling." Paper presented at the Annual Meeting of the American Educational Research Association, New Orleans, 1988.

Phillips, Deborah A. "Socialization of Perceived Academic Competence among Highly Competent Children," *Child Development* 58 (1987): 1308–1320.

Rose, Mike. *Lives on the Boundary: The Struggles and Achievements of America's Underprepared.* New York: Free Press, 1989.

Rosenholtz, Susan, and Rosenholtz, Steven. "Classroom Organization and the Perception of Ability," *Sociology of Education* 54 (1981): 132–140.

Rosenholtz, Susan J., and Simpson, Carol. "The Formation of Ability Conceptions: Developmental Trend or Social Construction?" *Review of Educational Research* 54 (1984): 31–63.

Rosenholtz, Susan J., and Wilson, Bruce. "The Effect of Classroom Structure on

Shared Perceptions of Ability," *American Educational Research Journal* 17 (1980): 75–82.

Rosenthal, Robert. *On the Social Psychology of the Self-fulfilling Prophecy: Further Evidence from Pygmalion Effects and Their Mediating Mechanisms*. New York: MSS Modular Publications, 1973.

Rumberger, Russell W. "High School Dropouts: A Review of Issues and Evidence," *Review of Educational Research* 57 (1987): 101–121.

Sarason, Seymour B. *The Culture of the School and the Problem of Change*, 2nd edition. Boston: Allyn and Bacon, 1982.

Sarason, Seymour B. *The Predictable Failure of Educational Reform*. San Francisco: Jossey-Bass, 1990.

Slavin, Robert E. *Cooperative Learning*. New York: Longman, 1983.

Solomon, Daniel; Watson, Marilyn S.; Delucchi, Kevin L.; Schaps, Eric; and Battistich, Victor. "Enhancing Children's Prosocial Behavior in the Classroom," *American Educational Research Journal* 25 (1988): 527–554.

Sternberg, Robert. "Intelligence, Wisdom, and Creativity: Three Is Better Than One," *Educational Psychologist* 2 (1986): 175–190.

Stipek, Deborah J. *Motivation to Learn: From Theory to Practice*. Englewood Cliffs, N.J.: Prentice-Hall, 1988.

Stipek, Deborah J., and Daniels, Denise. "Declining Perceptions of Competence: A Consequence of Changes in the Child or the Educational Environment?" *Journal of Educational Psychology* 80 (1988): 352–356.

Stipek, Deborah J., and Tannatt, Lupita M. "Children's Judgments of Their Own and Their Peers' Academic Competence," *Journal of Educational Psychology* 76 (1984): 75–84.

Swann, William B. "Identity Negotiation: Where Two Roads Meet," *Journal of Personality and Social Psychology* 53 (1987): 1038–1051.

Wang, Margaret C. "Development and Consequences of Students' Sense of Personal Control." In *Teacher and Student Perceptions: Implications for Learning*, edited by John M. Levine and Margaret C. Wang. Hillsdale, N.J.: Erlbaum, 1983.

Wang, Margaret C.; Reynolds, Maynard C.; and Walberg, Herbert J. "Rethinking Special Education," *Educational Leadership* 44 (September 1986): 26–31.

Weiner, Bernard. "History of Motivational Research in Education," *Journal of Educational Psychology* 82 (1990): 616–622.

Weinstein, Rhona S. "The Teaching of Reading and Children's Awareness of Teacher Expectations." In *The Contexts of School-based Literacy*, edited by Taffy E. Raphael. New York: Random House, 1986.

Weinstein, Rhona S. "Perceptions of Classroom Processes and Student Motivation: Children's Views of Self-fulfilling Prophecies." In *Research on Motivation in Education*, edited by Russell Ames and Carol Ames, Vol. 3. New York: Academic Press, 1989.

Weinstein, Rhona S.; Marshall, Hermine H.; Brattesani, Karen; and Middlestadt, Susan E. "Student Perceptions of Differential Teacher Treatment in Open and Traditional Classrooms," *Journal of Educational Psychology* 74 (1982): 678–692.

Weinstein, Rhona S.; Marshall, Hermine H.; Sharp, Lee; and Botkin, Meryl.

"Pygmalion and the Student: Age and Classroom Differences in Children's Awareness of Teacher Expectations," *Child Development* 58 (1987): 1079–1093.

Weinstein, Rhona S., and Middlestadt, Susan E. "Student Perceptions of Teacher Interactions with High and Low Achievers," *Journal of Educational Psychology* 71 (1979): 421–431.

Weinstein, Rhona S.; Soule, Charles C.; Collins, Florence; Cone, Joan; Mehlhorn, Michelle; and Simontacchi, Karen. "Expectations and High School Change: Teacher-Researcher Collaboration to Prevent School Failure," *American Journal of Community Psychology* 19 (1991): 333–363.

Wineburg, Samuel S. "The Self-fulfillment of the Self-fulfilling Prophecy," *Educational Researcher* 16, no. 9 (1987): 28–44.

Chapter 10

PERCEIVING AND DISPLAYING EFFORT IN ACHIEVEMENT SETTINGS

Sharon Nelson-Le Gall

The quality and quantity of effort that students devote to academic tasks has become a topic that generates a great deal of interest and concern among educators, families, economists, businesspeople, and the public in general. The concern is over why students do not appear to be investing in academic tasks the time and energy necessary to attain higher levels of academic achievement. However, we cannot define in absolute terms what exactly *trying* is, although we act as if we know very well how to tell when a person is trying hard or not trying very much at all. Educators do not have a straightforward way to assess effort devoted to school tasks. Questions such as these remain unanswered: How do students decide that they should or must try hard at school tasks? When and under what conditions do students undertake self-assessment of their effort? How do students know how much effort they exerted in accomplishing a particular task? What is the standard they use for determining that the level of effort they are expending represents their "best effort" or "really trying very hard?"

The purpose of this chapter is to examine some of the developmental and social contextual influences (e.g., self-knowledge or perceptions, teacher beliefs, classroom structures, group norms and values, and societal rewards) on the student's displays of personal effort and his or her motivation to learn in academic settings. First, traditional work on the development of children's reasoning about effort and motivation will be briefly examined, followed by a discussion of why and how (from the student's point of view) motivation

225

might be displayed in school settings. I then will describe alternative achievement behaviors that are adaptive in learning and how these alternative modes of displaying personal effort and motivation are conditioned by cultural and classroom features.

DEVELOPMENT OF THE CONCEPT OF EFFORT

When we talk about student effort we tend to treat it like a variable, personal causal factor that is under volitional control (Heider, 1958). It is important, therefore, that students' beliefs and perceptions about their effort be a central focus of inquiry. Indeed, a key component of students' beliefs about their academic performance is their understanding of personal effort (Paris and Byrnes, 1989). A specific feature of this understanding is that there should be thoughtful and flexible (i.e., effective) application of effort in pursuit of goals and that this aspect of academic performance is particularly important in the face of task difficulty or failure.

An individual's formation of the concept of effort depends on his or her experience that success and failure covary with the perceived degree of effort he or she has expended. This experience can occur only with tasks that require exertion or persistence. Research suggests that three-year-olds have a rudimentary concept of effort as a causal factor in achievement outcomes (see Heckhausen [1982] for a review). Moreover, it appears that most children over age five can perceive a causal relationship between performance outcomes and intended and actual effort by self or by others.

From the time of school entry and on into the primary grades children view effort as an important, and perhaps the most important, determinant of achievement outcomes (Surber, 1984). Greater achievement is judged to be due to greater effort, and greater effort is taken as a sign of greater ability. With increasing age and schooling, however, judgments of ability become related to judgments of effort in a compensatory causal schema such that for some students and in some academic achievement settings trying harder comes to imply lesser ability, and greater achievement is more likely to be explained by greater ability than by greater effort (Nicholls and Miller, 1984).

Blumenfeld, Pintrich, Meece, and Wessels (1982) have suggested that the concept of effort may be more globally defined for younger than for older children. According to these researchers, children do not explicitly consider the nature or quality of effort displayed (e.g., persisting, applying alternative strategies on their own, or seeking the help of others). Rather, for young students good conduct (i.e., not fooling around, working quietly) is synonymous with effort or trying hard.

WHY TRY HARD OR WORK AT ALL?: GOALS AND EFFORT

When educators or parents worry about children's motivation they are not raising the issue of whether the child has the requisite energy. Instead, they are concerned about how (i.e., to what end or purpose) the energy is invested. Hence, it is important that when we talk about student effort we distinguish between the availability and the allocation of motivational resources.

In most everyday tasks (e.g., reading a magazine, calculating change due from a purchase) what is done and the manner in which it is done are subordinated to some larger purpose or goal. The motivation for task engagement and a meaningful basis for evaluation of task performance are defined by situating the "action" in a web of personally and societally meaningful social practice. That is, in everyday learning, the task confronting the "student" clearly has a meaningful place in a broader system of activity (with related goals and purposes) that both the students and the teacher clearly understand. Yet, the relationship between action and activity in school seems to be rather peculiar. It could be argued that the evaluation of competent performance is probably a nearly universal characteristic of human activity, and that the evaluation of competent performance by others (whether by "superiors" in power or knowledge, by peers, and/or by consumers or customers of one's products) is hardly unusual. Nevertheless, production for the purpose of evaluation and certification is peculiar (if not unique) to the institution of formal schooling (see Wertsch, Minick, and Arns [1984] for a discussion of some of the implications of the peculiar relationship created between action and activity when the "motives" of evaluation and learning are isolated from productive activity through the emergence and development of institutions of formal schooling).

Minick (1990) has argued that there is an important sense in which the institutional arrangement of the school makes it extraordinarily difficult to create or maintain the kind of "engagement" in activity (task motivation) that most educators would like to see. It is extremely difficult to engage people for very long in carrying out tasks for the purpose of evaluating how well they carry them out. There are, of course, instances in which this may happen. Some students, especially young ones, find the social relationship with the teacher sufficient; others become embroiled in competition for grades. In general, however, even when the subject matter dealt with in school engages students, the engagement seems short-lived because the institutional organization tends to frustrate rather than foster this type of engagement. For example, the act of reading a text about the life cycles of tuna and the supporting marine ecology is isolated from a practice that would link the child's initial fascination with a science-like practice of pursuing deeper understanding over time (possible in school) or from a business-like practice of linking this information to, say, the profitable fishing of tuna (probably not possible in school). By dislocating the performances being acquired from any meaningful frame within which the student or teacher can evaluate it, the school introduces a heavy dose of arbitrariness, and engagement takes on the nature of mere "compliance."

In brief, Minick suggests that the shift from broader purposes (social, intellectual, economic) to the way an action is carried out, or a classification made, or a concept formulated, permits some reasonable evaluation. By isolating the action from such purposes—and locating it in "performance for evaluation"—evaluation (value for what?) becomes arbitrary and dependent on the authority of the teacher or the text. I suggest here that motivation not be seen as something existing solely in the student that he or she brings to the classroom and academic tasks, but rather as an outcome of meaningful participation in the classroom and the social practices that accomplish its everyday practical activities.

The issue of examining goals in order to understand achievement can be considered from several vantage points: that of the person, that of the learning group, and that of the society and its norms and values. Individual differences in achievement orientation are important influences on children's responses to academic difficulties. Several researchers (e.g., Ames, 1983; Dweck and Leggett, 1988; Elliott and Dweck, 1988; Nicholls, 1984) have posited that individual differences in the goals pursued in achievement situations can influence expectancies of success, actual task behaviors, and evaluation of task outcomes as well. For example, Dweck and Leggett (1988) have distinguished two groups of children who appear to differ in their tendencies to pursue learning versus performance goals in achievement situations. Some children are characterized by a strong orientation to mastery and are thought to pursue learning goals. When faced with obstacles to achievement these children are likely to focus on the task, attempt to generate alternative strategies, and garner resources for problem solving both internal and external to themselves. In general, these children display continued high, and even increasing, levels of task-related effort in response to difficulty. In contrast, other children are characterized by a weaker orientation to mastery and are thought to pursue performance goals in achievement situations. When faced with task difficulties these children are likely to display helplessness, focus on their perceived lack of ability, and resort to ineffectual strategies. Children with this orientation show decreasing effort, or even a complete lack of task-related effort such as abandoning the task, if possible (Miller, 1986).

HOW TO WORK: DISPLAYS OF EFFORT

Effort-Engagement Behavior

What do we see that leads us to say that a person is or is not motivated, is or is not putting forth effort? In a survey study of secondary students and their teachers, Natriello and Dornbush (1984) measured student effort and achievement. Two academic subject-specific measures of effort were used. The first measured what Natriello and Dornbush referred to as effort-engagement behaviors (e.g., cutting class, doing homework, daydreaming in class, and paying attention to the teacher). The second measure was a self-assessment of effort. For this measure students were required to rate their own level of effort in each of four academic subjects. These researchers found that students' report of high levels of effort-engagement behaviors was positively related to student learning and achievement outcomes as measured by course grades and achievement tests. Self-assessments of effort were less closely related to learning outcomes, but tapped instead subjective interpretations of student effort.

For some students or under some assessment circumstances

self-assessments may entail mostly intrapersonal (e.g., temporal and situational) comparisons of effort, for example, believing that one is working harder on one task than on another, or working harder than ever before on a task. For other students, or under other assessment circumstances, the level of effort experienced may be determined by comparison to other students. For example, some students feel they are working hard when they perceive that they have spent more time studying, doing homework, or preparing an academic product than other students. This comparative standard can, at times, have a negative influence on student motivation in that students have been noted to express concerns about student effort in academic settings. Unfortunately, at advanced grades (i.e., junior high, high school, and college) the most salient student concern is often that other students work too hard or study too much.

How is effort perceived in goal-directed action? A commonsense analysis suggests that signs of interest, attention, enthusiasm, and participation on the part of the student in academic activities would indicate to an observer that the student is motivated. The multiplicity of cues about the display of effort is found, for example, in the Intellectual Achievement Responsibility (IAR) Questionnaire (Crandall, Katkovsky, and Crandall, 1965), a widely used measure of children's and adolescents' academic achievement motivation. Several questions in the IAR present response options that are often taken to represent the causal attributional category of effort. The actual items refer to a variety of behaviors on the part of the individual that range from specific acts such as "listening carefully" and "not answering too quickly" to global behaviors or states such as "working very hard" and "being interested in the assignment." In experimental research on motivation (e.g., Touhey and Villemez, 1980), instructions to subjects that are intended to evoke high effort request that subjects put everything else out of their minds.

Perception of the level in effort exerted may be linked to perceptions of changes in the quantity, quality, or both quantity and quality of the performance and performance outcomes (Heckhausen, Schmalt, and Schneider, 1985). In this case what constitutes sufficient and effective effort may vary depending on whether the desired or sufficient level of performance is measured in terms of quantity or quality of performance. According to the analysis of Heckhausen and colleagues (1985) the substitution of quantity of performance for quality of performance occurs primarily when the task has a prescribed sequence of steps. In perceiving student effort in the classroom, one must ask not only whether the task is easy or difficult, but also whether measurement of performance on the task is in terms of quantity or quality. Among adult workers there is some evidence that the experience of effort is determined primarily by the quantity of work experienced.

A definition of effort cannot easily be made outside of the task conditions and demands. A key question in this area, then, is to develop and test out concepts for how task-related effort is translated into various strategies of task processing and thus into different measures of achievement for different tasks and task settings. Consider, for example, that task persistence is a commonly used index of effort. Yet, little is known about what constitutes sufficient persistence (i.e., active goal pursuit) in the view of students and their teachers. For example, children's judgments of what constitutes adequate persistence in the face of task difficulty may depend on their perception of the appropriateness of producing different manifestations of effort. We know little about the specific signs of effort in the classroom that are valued jointly by students and teachers.

Moreover, persistence has both positive and negative meanings (Dewey, 1966; Feather, 1962). In its positive sense persistence means that an individual is protecting his or her pursuit of a chosen goal from interference that might come either from the individual him- or herself or from external sources. In its negative sense persistence may reflect an individual's inflexibility and lack of reflection on the application of means to the end goal. In this sense, however, persistence may reveal more about the individual's value for independence than about his or her value for task mastery. When independence becomes more important or salient than task mastery as a goal, the development of skills necessary for competence in the task domain may be compromised. Whereas task mastery provides its own feedback and rewards that promote learning, independence does not necessarily promote learning because it may or may not involve mastery.

For example, children may continue to work at a task without help, in spite of prolonged lack of success and the availability of more productive alternative strategies, in order to forestall judgments of failure (Diener and Dweck, 1978). In these cases children may inappropriately be regarded as highly motivated because they have spent a long time working on the task. It appears, then, that the length of time spent working independently on a task may not be as sensitive an indicator of achievement as would some measure of whether the time was spent in active pursuit of a solution. Thus, independent striving may not always lead to task mastery and when used unproductively despite prolonged lack of success and the availability of more productive alternatives, may be maladaptive.

This distinction between blind personal exertion or arbitrary effort and productive, goal-directed effort has been drawn clearly by John Dewey (1966), who wrote,

The really important matter in the experience of effort concerns its connection with thought. The question is not the amount of sheer strain involved, but the way in which the *thought of an end* persists in spite of difficulties and induces a person to reflect upon the nature of the obstacles and the available resources by which they may be dealt with. [P. 171]

All too often the message students pick up is that persistence, even arbitrary solitary persistence, is the preferred option for academic tasks. Hanging in there to the end, putting in time, and the quantity of product produced have become indices of effort without much concern given to the quality of the outcome or the level of understanding acquired by the student. However, Dewey's emphasis on evaluating and garnering available resources suggests an alternative and potentially adaptive strategy that could be used to master a task that is beyond a student's current level of competence, namely, to seek help from others. It is this strategy that I would like to consider in some detail because it represents an adaptive alternative that can strengthen a student's motivation to learn and perform in the social context of the classroom.

HELP SEEKING AND MOTIVATION FOR LEARNING

Set against the mythical ideal of individualism and autonomy that is emphasized in American culture as a sign of competence and mature psychosocial functioning, help seeking may appear to be a sign of immaturity or of inadequate personal coping skills. However, help seeking can be conceptualized as a mature, even sophisticated strategy for coping with difficult tasks. As a self-initiated behavior, help seeking is regarded by some theorists (e.g., Ames, 1983; Nelson-

Le Gall, 1981) as an act of effort in that the child seeking help is actively using available resources to increase the probability of future success. The classification of help seeking as a learning strategy is particularly appropriate in those instances in which the help requested is focused on acquiring the processes of problem solving and is limited to the amount and type needed to allow children to acquire new skills, master current skills, or solve problems in the future for themselves. Teachers tend to believe that seeking help from others is an appropriate and adaptive achievement strategy for children to use, but only after a child's independent sustained effort fails (Nelson-Le Gall and Scott-Jones, 1985).

This point of view, which treats such acts of help seeking as adaptive and instrumental to achievement, is in sharp contrast to that underlying studies of achievement motivation in which help seeking is considered to be the antithesis of achievement behavior (e.g., Winterbottom, 1958). When the conceptual links between independence, task mastery, and achievement are fully considered, it becomes evident that the link between help seeking and achievement conceived of as task mastery, rather than simply as task independence, has not been explored adequately. Consideration of the adaptive functions of help seeking is particularly important for a more complete understanding of knowledge acquisition and mastery.

The Efforts of Active Learners in Social Context

Recent reconceptualizations of help-seeking behavior by Ames (1983) and Nelson-Le Gall (1981; 1985) emphasize the individual's value priorities and goals related to achievement. The major contribution of this achievement-related view of help seeking is its focus on the costs of not seeking help, and importantly in its treatment of help seeking as a part of an ongoing process rather than as a dichotomous (i.e., help seeking—no help seeking) decision. Within this perspective the role of help seeker is not a static one; nor is it continually occupied by the same learners in a group. Individuals in a learning group may move in and out of this role during the course of work on a task such that donors of help become recipients and vice versa. This achievement-related view of help seeking identifies it as a critical process variable in didactic (teacher-learner) interactions and in collaborative (doer-doer) interactions in learning groups.

The conceptualization of help seeking as an adaptive general learning skill is compatible with currently influential theories of mental development and learning (e.g., Brown, Bransford, Ferrara, and Campione, 1983; Brown and Reeve, 1987; Vygotsky, 1978). In Vygotsky's view knowledge and understanding have their roots in social interactions with more mature learners who plan, direct, monitor, and evaluate the child's task activity. Mental functions are thought to develop first on a social level as children interact with adults or more highly skilled peers, who serve as supportive, knowledgeable others. After interacting with others in learning situations, children gradually internalize the supportive-other role and begin to perform these regulatory behaviors for themselves. When children are able and willing to take the initiative to gain the assistance of more mature and expert others, the child can participate, in a supportive social context, in the interrogatory process that mature learners employ to construct the relevant contextual knowledge for task solution. Instrumental help seeking, thus, may serve as a mechanism of transition from a state of other-regulation in problem solving to one of self-regulation.

Learning and understanding are not merely individual processes supported by the social context; rather they are the result of a continuous, dynamic negotiation between the individual and the social setting in which the individual's activity takes place. Both the individual and the social context are active and constructive in producing learning and understanding. In a group learning situation, such as a classroom, the social environment is provided by the teacher and students. Effective learning in this setting should occur when this environment constrains the information and tasks available to a child so as to fit the child's current understanding and cognitive abilities. Furthermore, the nature of the constraints changes as children gain understanding and skill (e.g., Levin and Kareev, 1980; Rogoff and Gardner, 1984; Wood, Bruner, and Ross, 1976; Wood and Middleton, 1975). Indeed, children depend on such socially imposed constraints when seeking help in the form of input and feedback from others in situations where they are aware of their lack of understanding. However, children also take responsibility for structuring and using that support as necessary.

The conceptualization of an active mutual influence between the individual learner and the social environment is characteristic of achievement-related perspectives on help seeking. In achievement-related frameworks personal characteristics of the individual help seeker, such as perceived competence and mastery orientations (e.g., Ames, 1983; Harter, 1981), and situational characteristics of the achievement setting are used to predict and explain help seeking. For example, a distinction between dependency-oriented help seeking and mastery-oriented help seeking has been drawn by Nelson-Le Gall (1985).

Dependency-oriented help seeking refers to those instances in which individuals allow someone else to solve a problem or attain a goal on their behalf without their active participation in the solution of the problem. Learners seeking help with problems within and beyond their current level of competence, who are willing to relinquish involvement in and responsibility for problem solving, and who appear to be more interested in the product or successful outcome than in the processes or means of achieving the outcome would be viewed as dependency oriented. Thus, it is help seekers' continued reliance on others to provide more help than is needed, and a lack of participation in the task in a way that allows them to acquire some of the more masterful helper's understanding of the problem and its solution, that would characterize help seeking as dependency oriented (Nelson-Le Gall, 1981; Rogoff and Gardner, 1984). It is just this sort of help seeking that is properly considered antithetical to achievement (cf. Winterbottom, 1958).

Mastery-oriented help seeking, in contrast, is likely to be instrumental to skill acquisition. It refers to those instances in which the help requested appears to be focused on acquiring successful processes of problem solution and is limited to the amount and type needed to allow learners to solve similar problems in the future for themselves. Learners with effective instrumental help-seeking skills are able to refuse help when they can perform a task by themselves, yet can obtain help when it is needed. From this perspective, help seeking represents competent, coping behavior. Whether as the less skilled novice in the interaction or as an equally competent collaborator, learners seeking mastery-oriented help mediate their learning and problem solving by taking the initiative to question, suggest, observe, and imitate. In sum, they are self-regulating learners.

Self-Regulated Learning and Effective Help Seeking

Awareness of the Need for Help. Seeking help is an intentional act and therefore is contingent on the individual becoming aware of the need for help (i.e., knowing that his or her own available resources are not sufficient to reach a goal). Determination of the need for help may be made by the individual or by others. An incorrect answer or lack of progress after diligent attempts to solve a problem might indicate to children, or to someone else concerned with their performance, that seeking help is necessary (Nelson-Le Gall and Scott-Jones, 1985). Individuals' knowledge about the compatibility between themselves as learners and the learning situation plays an important role in effective problem solving (Brown, 1978). If individuals have some awareness of the complexity of the task and can monitor their progress on the task well enough to detect a problem, they are in a relatively good position to utilize help seeking as an alternative strategy to respond to anticipated difficulties or to recover easily from difficulties encountered.

Decision to Seek Help. It might be assumed that awareness of the inadequacy of one's knowledge and skill would be sufficiently motivating to cause a person to seek help. Once aware of the need for help, however, an individual must also take responsibility for alleviation of the problem and for task completion. Very young children, for example, often perceive a need for help but fail to seek help actively because they may feel it is the adult's responsibility to determine that help is needed and to offer assistance (Gumerman, 1982).

In addition, research on help seeking in adults indicates that there are costs perceived to be associated with asking for and accepting help, such as loss of perceived competence or diminished credit or reward for a successful outcome, which may deter the individual from attempting to obtain assistance (e.g., DePaulo and Fisher, 1980). These costs must be outweighed by perceived benefits (e.g., avoiding task failure, increasing or mastering task skills) if help seeking is to occur. Certain individual differences such as achievement goal orientation (Dweck, 1988), intellectual self-esteem, and preferences for challenge and independent mastery (Harter, 1981) may influence the perception and weighing of these costs and benefits. Thus, the decision to seek help may be affected not only by the need for help, but also by the achievement orientation and goals that characterize the help seeker in a given problem context (Ames, 1983; Nelson-Le Gall, 1990; Nelson-Le Gall, DeCooke, and Jones, 1989; Nelson-Le Gall and Jones, 1990).

For example, it has been suggested (Murphy, 1962; Nelson-Le Gall, 1981) that help seeking may serve multiple purposes. The child's primary goal in seeking help may be merely task completion, without comprehension or mastery as an objective, or the child's primary goal could be to avoid criticism from an agent of evaluation. Alternatively, help may be sought to increase the child's mastery in current and future learning tasks. These distinctions map onto distinctions made by achievement motivation theorists, who describe individual differences in children's achievement goals and orientations as indicators of how children will cope with difficulty in learning and problem solving (Dweck and Elliott, 1983; Harter, 1981; Nicholls, 1984). Children with a mastery achievement orientation will usually adopt learning goals (Dweck and Elliott, 1983), show a preference for challenge, show curiosity and interest in problem-solving and learning contexts, and strive toward independent mastery in their undertakings (Harter, 1981). These children focus their attention on mastery of tasks and do not tend to be concerned with explaining their errors or failures, which they see as a natural and useful source of feedback in the learning process (e.g., Ames and Archer, 1988; Elliott and Dweck, 1988). When they do make causal attributions about their task failures, mastery-oriented children attribute poor performance to insufficient effort (Diener and Dweck, 1978), a personal characteristic over which they have control. Mastery-oriented children will tend to have high perceived cognitive competence and, thus, will be more likely to view help seeking as a relevant and viable achievement strategy than will children who are not mastery oriented (e.g., Nelson-Le Gall, 1990).

SOCIOCULTURAL ORIGINS OF MOTIVATION

Socialization in the Family

The analysis of help-seeking behavior outlined here is of particular interest in the case of racial- and ethnic-minority children whose achievement behavior has often been characterized as deviant or deficient. For example, an examination of the cultural patterns of socialization that many black children experience in their families, and of the changes in the nature of the typical classroom environment encountered by these children across the elementary school years, suggests the potential for conflict between learner and task environment.

Bloom (1976) has noted that the individual characteristics that learners bring to a task may set the stage for learning and performance in the task environment. Every learner brings to the task a prior history of learning. For black Americans, these entry characteristics are thought to include a preference for people-oriented situations and a highly affective orientation toward ideas, people, and things (Shade, 1982).

For example, many black Americans participate in a multigenerational kinship network of relatives (e.g., Harrison, Wilson, Pine, Chan, and Buriel, 1990). As members of this network, children are socialized to orient toward interpersonal relatedness, to respond to the authority of a dominant family member, and to recognize collective responsibility. Combined with the emphasis on giving and receiving support within the network, the caregiver-child relationship within black families encourages the child to seek help while moving toward independence (Aschenbrenner, 1973; Tolson and Wilson, 1990).

An interdependent and cooperative-functioning orientation entails individuals assuming particular responsibilities but functioning as a collective unit in efforts to meet task demands. It has been reported that group-oriented cultures, such as Afro-Americans (Rotheram and Phinney, 1987), tend to value collective efforts more than competition as viable strategies in goal-oriented situations (Boykin, 1986; Ogbu, 1982; Tolson and Wilson, 1990). Therefore, it seems reasonable on conceptual grounds to expect that seeking and accepting help when necessary would be utilized by black children as an adaptive strategy in achievement-oriented situations.

A substantial body of literature associates positive achievement outcomes with black socialization patterns (Shade, 1978). Researchers have found that black children who do well in school have parents who are responsive to their help seeking and encourage an active coping style (Garmezy, 1983; Holliday, 1985; Shade, 1978). An active coping style is characterized by initiating change and manipulating the environment to produce and employ resources that can help overcome obstacles to the achievement of personal goals and desired outcomes. Children who evidence an active coping style in problem-solving situations tend to initiate solutions to problems and demonstrate competence in terms of handling various situations themselves.

Grade-related changes in the classroom environment may determine the effectiveness of help seeking as an achievement strategy. The socially interactive style many black children bring to school is compatible to a degree with the task environment typically encountered in the first few years of formal schooling (i.e., kindergarten through second grade) because of the teacher's concern with the child's socialization into the student role (Brophy and Evertson, 1978; Nelson-Le Gall and Scott-Jones, 1985). However, around approximately grade three the dynamics of teacher-child interactions change and the teachers in typical elementary classrooms function less like parent substitutes. Student-teacher relationships are less personalized and standards for classroom performance are redefined with more emphasis being placed on individual achievement and competition among students (Eccles, Midgley, and Adler, 1984). It is important to note that this change in classroom environment coincides with what has been frequently observed as the beginning of divergence of black students' achievement levels from those of their white counterparts. Indeed, studies of teachers' effects on achievement have indicated that continuing academic excellence among black students is associated with interpersonal contact with a nurturant, supportive, child-oriented teacher (see Shade, 1982). It may also be the case that successful children tend to change their support-seeking behavior to reflect changes in the classroom environment. This possibility has not been adequately explored.

Racial Stratification and Academic Motivation

For black Americans, and other low-status ethnic minorities, forces operating beyond the family and immediate social context of the school can influence motivation to pursue specific goals and the motivation to work hard to achieve them. John Ogbu (1978) argued that explanations of black children's school performance "stress the personal and social inadequacies of blacks and the inadequacies of the schools they attend, or both, as the causes of their academic retardation. Such explanations ignore the system of racial castes under which blacks must live and study—the source of their personal, social, and institutional adaptation" (p. 369).

Ogbu suggests that educators have not studied how racial

stratification affects minorities' school performance. In part because of their ease of identification, black Americans cannot be absorbed readily into the mainstream of a race-caste society. Minority achievement cannot be understood when taken out of the context of the status of minorities in America. For Ogbu, "The caste system which relegates blacks to the pariah status and excludes them from full social and technoeconomic participation in adult life determines black economic status; childrearing practices; and linguistic, cognitive, and motivational skills. The latter, in turn, influence black school performance more directly" (p. 369). In almost every aspect of the political, economic, and social orders, opportunity and rewards for equal effort are lower for the lower-caste members. In the presence of this differential in the opportunity and reward structure, blacks and other low-status ethnic minorities may respond with reduced or less than optimal effort. According to Ogbu, this is particularly obvious in school learning situations and may account for the depressed achievement so often seen in those groups. Since the post-school world does not reward equally for equal effort in school, effort invested in school is reduced.

CONCLUSIONS

In conclusion, I am suggesting that students may not display optimal effort and motivation to achieve in school settings for many reasons, not the least of which being that they receive ambiguous and even conflicting messages about the "Why" and "How" of displaying effort in school. In this chapter I have discussed at length a particular manifestation of student effort, namely instrumental help-seeking behavior. Instrumental help seeking can and should be promoted as a general learning skill in classroom groups because it allows students to participate more effectively in socially mediated learning experiences. It is important to underscore that help be actively sought out by the student in response to perceived need. By attempting to study and account for this type of active, help-seeking behavior that is concerned with extending knowledge and understanding, attention is drawn to the reality that learners actively construct and practice academic as well as social knowledge in the contexts of classroom learning.

A task for educational practitioners, administrators, researchers, and policymakers concerned with understanding and enhancing students' motivation to learn and achieve, then, is to find ways to build and support a community of learners in the educational setting. This must be a community in which students take personal responsibility to exert personal effort and cultivate social supports to achieve academically. Classrooms can then be communities of learners wherein more experienced members of the community are sought out to guide the less experienced in accomplishing culturally meaningful tasks. Accordingly, the rewards for such accomplishment must be equally accessible to all who participate actively in the community's work.

REFERENCES

Ames, Carol, and Archer, Jennifer. "Achievement Goals in the Classroom: Students' Learning Strategies and Motivation Processes," *Journal of Educational Psychology* 80 (1988): 260–267.

Ames, Russell. "Help-seeking and Achievement Orientation: Perspectives from Attribution Theory." In *New Directions in Helping*, Vol. 2, *Help-seeking*, edited by Bella DePaulo, Arie Nadler, and Jeffrey Fisher, pp. 165–186. New York: Academic Press, 1983.

Aschenbrenner, Joyce. "Extended Families among Black Americans," *Journal of Comparative Family Studies* 3 (1973): 257–268.

Bloom, Benjamin. *Human Characteristics and School Learning*. New York: McGraw-Hill, 1976.

Blumenfeld, Phyllis; Pintrich, Paul; Meece, Judith; and Wessels, Kathleen. "The Formation and Role of Self-perceptions of Ability in Elementary Classrooms," *Elementary School Journal* 82 (1982): 401–420.

Boykin, A. Wade. "The Triple Quandary and the Schooling of Afro-American Children." In *The School Achievement of Minority Children*, edited by Ulric Neisser. Hillsdale, N.J.: Erlbaum, 1986.

Brophy, Jere, and Evertson, Carolyn. "Context Variables in Teaching," *Educational Psychologist* 12 (1978): 310–316.

Brown, Ann. "Knowing When, Where, and How to Remember: A Problem of Metacognition." In *Advances in Instructional Psychology*, edited by Robert Glaser, pp. 77–165. Hillsdale, N.J.: Lawrence Erlbaum Associates, 1978.

Brown, Ann; Bransford, John; Ferrara, Roberta; and Campione, Joseph. "Learning, Remembering, and Understanding." In *Handbook of Child Psychology*, Vol. 3, *Cognitive Development*, edited by Paul Mussen, pp. 77–166. New York: Wiley, 1983.

Brown, Ann, and Reeve, Robert. "Bandwidths of Competence: The Role of Supportive Contexts in Learning and Development." In *Development and Learning: Conflict or Congruence?*, edited by Lynn Liben and David Feldman, pp. 173–222. Hillsdale, N.J.: Erlbaum, 1987.

Crandall, Vaughn C.; Katkovsky, Walter; and Crandall, Virginia J. "Children's Beliefs in Their Own Control of Reinforcements in Intellectual-Academic Achievement Situations," *Child Development* 36 (1965): 91–109.

DePaulo, Bella, and Fisher, Jeffrey. "The Costs of Asking for Help," *Basic and Applied Social Psychology* 7 (1980): 23–35.

Dewey, John. "Effort, Thinking, and Motivation." In *John Dewey: Selected Educational Writings*, edited by Francis William Garforth, pp. 168–180. London: Heinemann Educational Books Ltd., 1966.

Diener, Carol, and Dweck, Carol. "An Analysis of Learned Helplessness: Continuous Changes in Performance, Strategy, and Achievement Cognitions Following Failure," *Journal of Personality and Social Psychology* 39 (1978): 940–952.

Dweck, Carol. "Motivation." In *Handbook of Psychology and Education*, edited by Robert Glaser and Alan Lesgold, pp. 187–239. Hillsdale, N.J.: Erlbaum, 1988.

Dweck, Carol, and Elliott, Elaine. "Achievement Motivation." In *Handbook of Child Psychology*, Vol. 4, *Socialization, Personality, and Social Development*, edited by Paul Mussen, pp. 643–692. New York: Wiley, 1983.

Dweck, Carol, and Leggett, Ellen. "A Social-Cognitive Approach to Motivation and Personality," *Psychological Review* 95 (1988): 256–273.

Eccles, Jacquelynne; Midgley, Carol; and Adler, Theresa. "Grade-related Changes in the School Environment: Effects on Achievement Motivation." In *Advances in Motivation and Achievement*, Vol. 3, edited by John Nicholls, pp. 283–331. New York: JAI Press, 1984.

Elliott, Elaine, and Dweck, Carol. "Goals: An Approach to Motivation and Achievement," *Journal of Personality and Social Psychology* 54 (1988): 5–12.

Feather, N. T. "The Study of Persistence," *Psychological Bulletin* 59 (1962): 94–114.

Garmezy, Norman. "Stressors in Childhood." In *Stress, Coping, and Development in Children*, edited by Norman Garmezy and Michael Rutter, pp. 43–84. New York: McGraw-Hill, 1983.

Gumerman, Ruth. "Young Children's Help Seeking and Its Implications for the Training of Professionals in Early Education." Doctoral dissertation, University of Pittsburgh, 1982.

Harrison, Algea; Wilson, Melvin; Pine, Charles; Chan, Samuel; and Buriel, Raymond. "Family Ecologies and Ethnic Minority Children," *Child Development* 61 (1990): 347–362.

Harter, Susan. "A Model of Intrinsic Mastery Motivation in Children: Individual Differences and Developmental Change." In *Minnesota Symposia on Child Psychology*, Vol. 14, pp. 215–255. Hillsdale, N.J.: Erlbaum, 1981.

Heckhausen, Heinz. "The Development of Achievement Motivation." In *Review of Research in Child Development*, Vol. 6, edited by Willard Hartup. Chicago: University of Chicago Press, 1982.

Heckhausen, Heinz; Schmalt, Heinz-Dieter, and Schneider, Klaus. *Achievement Motivation in Perspective*. Orlando, Fla.: Academic Press, 1985.

Heider, Fritz. *The Psychology of Interpersonal Relations*. Hillsdale, N.J.: Erlbaum, 1958.

Holliday, Bertha. "Toward a Model of Teacher-Child Transactional Processes Affecting Black Children's Achievement." In *Beginnings: The Social and Affective*

Development of Black Children, edited by Margaret Spencer, Geraldine Brookins, and Walter Allen. Hillsdale, N.J.: Erlbaum, 1985.

Levin, James, and Kareev, Yacov, "Problem Solving in Everyday Situations," *Quarterly Newsletter of the Laboratory of Comparative Human Cognition* 2 (1980): 47–52.

Miller, Arden. "Performance Impairment after Failure: Mechanism and Sex Differences," *Journal of Educational Psychology* 78 (1986): 486–491.

Minick, Norris. "Authenticity Again," *XCLASS: Electronic Mail Forum on Educational Practice*, August 28, 1990. Available from Norris Minick, Communication Sciences and Disorders, Northwestern University, Evanston, Ill. 60208.

Murphy, Lois. *The Widening World of Childhood.* New York: Basic Books, 1962.

Natriello, Gary, and Dornbush, Sanford. *Teacher Evaluative Standards and Student Effort.* New York: Longman, 1984.

Nelson-Le Gall, Sharon. "Help-Seeking: An Understudied Problem-solving Skill in Children," *Developmental Review* 1 (1981): 224–246.

Nelson-Le Gall, Sharon. "Help-Seeking Behavior in Learning." In *Review of Research in Education* 12 (1985): 55–90.

Nelson-Le Gall, Sharon. "Academic Achievement Orientation and Help-Seeking Behavior in Early Adolescent Girls," *Journal of Early Adolescence* 10 (1990): 176–190.

Nelson-Le Gall, Sharon; DeCooke, Peggy; and Jones, Elaine. "Children's Self-perceptions of Competence and Help Seeking," *Journal of Genetic Psychology* 150 (1989): 457–459.

Nelson-Le Gall, Sharon, and Jones, Elaine. "Cognitive-Motivational Influences on Children's Help Seeking," *Child Development* 61 (1990): 581–589.

Nelson-Le Gall, Sharon, and Scott-Jones, Diane. "Teacher's and Young Children's Perceptions of Appropriate Work Strategies," *Child Study Journal* 15 (1985): 29–42.

Nicholls, John. "Achievement Motivation: Conceptions of Ability, Subjective Experience, Task Choice, and Performance," *Psychological Review* 91 (1984): 328–346.

Nicholls, John, and Miller, Arden. "Development and Its Discontents: The Differentiation of the Concept of Ability." In *Advances in Motivation and Achievement*, Vol. 3. *The Development of Achievement Motivation.* Greenwich, Conn.: JAI Press, 1984.

Ogbu, John. *Minority Education and Caste: The American System in Cross-cultural Perspective.* New York: Academic Press, 1978.

Ogbu, John. "Socialization: A Cultural Ecological Perspective." In *The Socialization of Children in a Changing Society*, edited by Kathryn Borman. Hillsdale, N.J.: Erlbaum, 1982.

Paris, Scott, and Byrnes, James. "The Constructionist Approach to Self-regulation and Learning in the Classroom." In *Self-regulated Learning and Academic Achievement*, edited by Barry Zimmerman and Dale Schunk, pp. 169–200. New York: Springer-Verlag, 1989.

Rogoff, Barbara, and Gardner, William. "Adult Guidance of Cognitive Development." In *Everyday Cognition: Its Development in Social Context*, edited by Barbara Rogoff and Jean Lave. Cambridge, Mass.: Harvard University Press, 1984.

Rotheram, Mary, and Phinney, Jean. "Ethnic Behavior Patterns as an Aspect of Identity." In *Children's Ethnic Socialization*, edited by Jean Phinney and Mary Rotheram. Beverly Hills, Calif.: Sage, 1987.

Shade, Barbara. "Social Psychological Characteristics of Achieving Black Children," *Negro Educational Review* 29 (1978): 80–86.

Shade, Barbara. "Afro-American Cognitive Style: A Variable in School Success?" *Review of Educational Research* 52 (1982): 219–244.

Surber, Colleen. "The Development of Achievement-related Judgment Processes." In *Advances in Motivation and Achievement*, Vol. 3, *The Development of Achievement Motivation*, edited by John Nicholls. Greenwich, Conn.: JAI Press, 1984.

Tolson, Timothy, and Wilson, Melvin. "The Impact of Two- and Three-generational Black Family Structure on Perceived Family Climate," *Child Development* 61 (1990): 416–428.

Touhey, John, and Villemez, Wayne. "Ability Attribution as a Result of Variable Effort and Achievement Motivation," *Journal of Personality and Social Psychology* 38 (1980): 211–216.

Vygotsky, Lev. *Mind in Society: The Development of Higher Psychological Processes*. Cambridge, Mass.: Harvard University Press, 1978.

Wertsch, James; Minick, Norris; and Arns, Flavio. "The Creation of Context in Joint Problem Solving." In *Everyday Cognition: Its Development in Social Context*, edited by Barbara Rogoff and Jean Lave, pp. 151–171. Cambridge, Mass.: Harvard University Press, 1984.

Winterbottom, Marian. "The Relationship of Need for Achievement to Learning Experiences in Independence and Mastery." In *Motives in Fantasy, Action, and Society*, edited by John Atkinson, pp. 453–478. Princeton, N.J.: Van Nostrand, 1958.

Wood, David; Bruner, Jerome; and Ross, Gail. "The Role of Tutoring in Problem Solving," *Journal of Child Psychology and Psychiatry* 17 (1976): 89–100.

Wood, David, and Middleton, David. "A Study of Assisted Problem Solving," *British Journal of Psychology* 66 (1975): 181–191.

Chapter 11

CLASSROOM MANAGEMENT AND MOTIVATED STUDENT LEARNING

Mary McCaslin and Thomas L. Good

Classroom management touches on very basic cultural notions of children and the authority of adults and social institutions. Classroom management is an expression of these cultural beliefs. In this chapter we briefly examine cultural ambivalence about "children." We illustrate that ambivalence about children is manifested also in conceptions of "student." We will argue that discordant messages about students are mirrored in current patterns of classroom management that are antithetical to present curriculum reform and professed educational goals. We argue that classroom management can and should do more than elicit predictable obedience; indeed, it can and should be one vehicle for the enhancement of student self-understanding and the internalization of self-control.

CONSTRUCTIONS OF CHILDREN

Historically there has been a lack of consensus on what is a child. This is partly because children are cultural inventions. Societies construct an image of children that embodies beliefs about their nature,

We wish to thank Bruce Biddle, Gail Hinkel, and Mary Beth Llorens for their helpful comments. We wish also to acknowledge the support of the Center for Research in Social Behavior at the University of Missouri—Columbia. We thank Lisa Tharp for typing the manuscript.

245

development, and socialization and the role of society in those processes (Borstelmann, 1983).

Recurring tensions between issues of vulnerability and the potential of children are ever present. Thus, even within a culture children may be perceived as deficits (as crosses to bear), as responsibilities (guiltless if not innocent beings needing guidance), and as assets (economic resources and society's future).

Ambivalence toward children is not new and it continues. Our popular culture is replete with discordant messages about children. Children kill children. Children fear children. Each day 135,000 children take a gun to school (Haycock, 1990). Children are having children. Every day 2,740 adolescents get pregnant (Haycock, 1990). Minority children especially face huge problems. Reston (1991) notes, "Though there is a developing black middle class, almost half of the black teenagers in Chicago fail to graduate from high school; in Washington, D. C., four times as many blacks are jailed as graduated from the public schools" (p. 460). "Hurried children" are the measure of their parents' success, engaged in adult pressures in preschool (Elkind, 1982). "Latchkey" children assume responsibility for home, sibling, and self-care. Working children are exploited by employers and required to work long and late hours.

Given such variation in societal conceptions of children, it is not surprising that continuous fluctuations in beliefs about the restriction and/or enhancement of children are evident. Child-rearing and educational advice have varied, both across time and within the same periods. Thus, good management practices have been measured, for example, by the frequency and severity of punishment, by the absence of punishment, by submission to authority, and by internalized self-control. The barrage of sometimes competing messages about children and their care confuses questions of responsibility as well. We have difficulty deciding what children are responsible for and at what age; we also search for who is responsible for the children. Changes in families and child-care alternatives blur the identification of responsibility for children's upbringing. Clearly the time is right for assigning blame. Indeed, there are historical precedents for blaming insensitive government, inadequate schools, the failure of religion, provocative media, inept parents, and shiftless children. We take the position that the multiple facets of this society *share* a broad responsibility for proactively building an infrastructure that supports children. (See

McCaslin and Good, in press, for expanded arguments about building appropriate support systems.)

By infrastructure we mean the basic support of nutrition, health, safety, and comfort that enables children to see beyond their immediate survival needs, to image a future in which they *can* and *want* to participate. Unfortunately, in a report from the Children's Defense Fund, Haycock (1990) notes that one in five children, 12 million, live in poverty and have no health insurance. Children are the poorest Americans; and the fastest growing segment of the homeless population consists of families with children.

Experience with Head Start programs has illustrated that providing structural support can have a positive impact on helping children to develop skills and dispositions that enable them subsequently to live richer and fuller lives. However, research on Head Start and on other educational change programs such as those discussed in Chapter 9 of this volume also suggests that only long-term support is likely to make a difference—indeed, many of the immediate proximal measures of the Head Start programs were not encouraging—change takes years. There are no quick fixes, no easy right answers. The responsibility for building this infrastructure is one we all share—citizens, parents, teachers, administrators, policymakers, and children.

CONSTRUCTIONS OF STUDENT

Historical Conceptions

One starting point in building an infrastructure is an understanding of "student." Getzels (1978) argued that the view of student has evolved over time and that the physical design of classrooms reflects conceptions of how students learn. He noted that at the turn of the century classrooms were rectangular and students' chairs were bolted to the floor so that they faced the teacher at all times—a format that corresponds to the conception of student as "empty vessel" who learns to associate stimuli and response through rewards and punishments that teachers control. By the 1930s classrooms were square-shaped, pupils had moveable chairs, and the teacher's desk was no longer in front of the room—the view of student had evolved from empty vessel to "active learner" at the center of the process.

Around 1950 classrooms began to use individual pupil desks that could easily form circles—in recognition that the student is a "social being" and that at times learning involves the group. By 1970 classrooms had become "wall-less," without clearly defined space for the teacher or student—students had become "stimulus seeking," they needed to move, to explore, and to find challenges. In the 1990s we expect to hear a call for classrooms that have moveable chairs and multiple worktables for students who are "social constructivists" (see chapter 10 in this volume) and whose learning begins in the social world.

Thus, in this century images of the role of student have changed— once reproducers of teacher knowledge, they are now creators of socially situated knowledge. Note the equation of "student" with the processes of learning. Little is said about the curriculum (what should be learned) or about management (who evaluates the learning). And nothing is said about student motivation. While a case can be made that theoretical conceptions of learning have evolved into more sophisticated constructs, the parallel case can not be made for notions of student. Student is not isomorphic with processes of learning.

Present Conceptions

Indeed, present conceptions of student, like conceptions of children, reflect the ambivalence, the diffusion of responsibility, and the desire to assign blame. *Newsweek* magazine, in its back-to-school special issue (Fall/Winter 1990), could not have put it more graphically. The table of contents includes articles on curriculum innovation and the interfaces between home and school and between school and policymakers. Articles are interspersed with photographs of earnest students and dedicated teachers. The message between the covers, on the importance and viability of education, is congruent; unfortunately, it is at odds with the cover design. Under the banners, "Education: A Consumer's Handbook," and "How to Teach Our Kids," the cover portrays student-as-ruffian—disobedient, inattentive, consumed by impulse, aggressive—a sort of ready excuse, a handy scapegoat should our new curricula and greater knowledge about teaching cognitive skills fail to influence student learning and dispositions. Such a portrayal has much in common with historical conceptions of children who would not be saved, either by God or by society.

Recently, many have argued that the problem of schooling is that students do not work hard enough. Student-as-scapegoat is not a new conception, yet within the educational community and in the popular culture, there is a persistent, indeed relentless, insistence that there was a better time when students wanted to learn, took initiative and responsibility for their learning, were prepared, and *worked hard*. We did not need to consider student motivation. However, various educational reports attest to the enduring forms, practices, and problems of education (e.g., Cuban, 1984). For example, Rose (1989) notes that in 1898 the University of California began to assess student proficiency in English and soon established that 30 to 40 percent of the students who took the exam were deficient—a percentage that has remained fairly stable over time. Unfortunately, much of educational reform is driven by a false attempt to recapture a mythical past.

Perhaps no myth is stronger than the belief that a "motivated" person will succeed and, conversely, that failure is due to lack of motivation. Effort guarantees success. Rose (1989), in examining his own escape from poverty through education, expresses the myth this way: "We live, in America, with so many platitudes about motivation and self-reliance and individualism—and myths spun from them like Horatio Alger—that we find it hard to accept the fact that they are serious nonsense" (p. 47).

However, as Rose argues in compelling fashion, structural support can make all the difference in enabling students with potential but with poor backgrounds to make educational progress. He insists that students need many models to help them understand what they do not know and how to make progress. Rose maintains that students need help in understanding their emerging ideas and they need people who simply look out for them. It is time to recognize that individual effort, although typically necessary for meaningful achievement, is insufficient.

CONFLICTING CONCEPTIONS OF APPROPRIATE EDUCATIONAL GOALS

Effort is not merely an individual variable. Effort is also a function of the setting (e.g., Ames, 1984), the task (e.g., Blumenfeld, forthcoming; Doyle, 1986), and interpersonal dynamics (e.g., Good, 1981) in interaction with personal factors (e.g., McCaslin and Murdock, 1991). And, as if that is not complicated enough, we can consider the potential variation within each factor. For example, consider two of the more pervasive expectations for student success in school: "Achievement" refers to mastery of a "curriculum" that varies widely from school to school or to performance on standardized tests, themselves in the midst of criticism and revision, that may or may not match the enacted curriculum (Porter, 1988). Similarly, self-esteem is defined by some educators as an emergent concept of the self-as-competent, but increasingly too many educators define self-esteem as a "feel-good" trait. Such discontinuities in expectations for student goals further complicate our, and students', understanding of the role of effort and its relationship to achievement and pride. For example, Stevenson and Flanagan (1990) report that our students know less about mathematics, know less about their world, yet feel better about themselves than do students in Japan and China. Our students are like Buick, which advertises that its car is fifth-rated but is still the best in America. They feel good and they are doing "well enough."

Expectations for students are muddled; classroom enactments of our beliefs are at times chaotic, and our frustration with the results is obvious. Thus, even as we seek student self-initiative, we *shape* hedonism in our students through management systems that rely on blatant external provision of rewards and punishments and we expose students to unchallenging curricula that define success by speed and accuracy. And educators are saddened, if not disgusted, that students feel good. They haven't earned it. Yet, we subject students to curricula and systems of management that *obviate* the development of internalized self-control, a commitment to striving, and an emergent, competence-oriented self-concept. It is no wonder, then, that students' pride rests on abundant external rewards for quick mastery of facts and skills and not on self-evaluation of the level of their learning of fundamental concepts and problem-solving processes.

There is growing consensus that something is amiss in an education that does not include problem solving, integration, and elaboration of meaning by self-regulated learners (Good, McCaslin, and Reys, forthcoming). Current beliefs are that a problem-solving orientation should undergird the education of all students, regardless of age, ability, gender, economic status, or location (e.g., National Council of Teachers of Mathematics, 1990). We maintain that present enactments of management and instruction are incompatible within this context of professed educational goals. This is because management of students typically involves application of behavior modification and behavioral control programs. Behavior modification systems of student management are compatible with a curriculum of basic skills acquisition. In both systems concern is with the identification (by teacher), sequencing (by teacher), and reinforcement (by teacher) of student performance of discrete skills. Indeed, this definition of management and learning dominated our definitions of schooling for much of the past two decades and, unfortunately, continues to dominate practice. It is of particular consequence that even when curriculum changes are evoked to embrace problem-solving processes by active and constructive learners, *conceptions of management remain static.* Indeed, behavior-control programs stressing perfunctory punishment in addition to routinized rewards to manage student behavior are becoming increasingly popular. There is a fundamental mismatch in the promotion of a problem-solving curriculum within the context of behavior control management. We cannot expect that students will profit from the incongruous messages we send when we *manage* for obedience and *teach* for exploration and risk-taking.

To the extent that progressive school districts have responded to articulate calls for curriculum reform (e.g., documents like *Everybody Counts* [National Research Council, 1989] and *Becoming a Nation of Readers* [Anderson, Hiebert, Scott, and Wilkinson, 1985]), educators have created a difficult dilemma: a curriculum that urges problem solving and critical thinking within a management system that requires compliance and narrow obedience. The management system at least dilutes the potential power of the curriculum for many of our students. Students are asked to think and understand, but in too many classrooms they are asked to think noiselessly, without peer communication or social exchange. And the problems they are asked to think about must be solved, neatly, within (at most) 45-minute intervals. Students generally gain recognition and approval by paying close attention to recommended procedures and by taking few academic risks.

We maintain that problem solving is just as critical in the social world as it is in the physical world. The problem with obedience is that the conditions that foster quick and predictable obedience do not foster the internalization of self-control (Lepper, 1983). And it is our position that students need internalized self-control, or "self-regulation" in the current vernacular, if they are to function adaptively in the classroom and in this society. And these are linked. Students live in a world that daily challenges their ability to cope. They are in classrooms where, for many students, there is no reason to expect that successful performance will enhance the quality of life. For many students their present and predicted worlds are *not* ever-changing. Their *Future Shock* (Toffler, 1970) is the reality of *stagnation.*

CONFLICTING CONCEPTIONS OF THE VALUE OF WORK

Expectations for and attitudes about the adult world of work can hardly be enhanced when students work for employers who hold them accountable to arbitrary and unexpected changes in work schedules that interfere with homework and sleep. Youth are apt to become cynical when parents and other adults encourage them to take jobs to learn initiative and the value of money. What youth learn instead is that initiative is not valued in the workplace; indeed, initiative is often mistaken for disregard for authority (especially when youth question inconsistent policies). And too many youth learn to overvalue money and the pleasures it can provide. Students may be disgruntled employees but they are avid consumers. They are the targets of high-tech, high-pressure advertising campaigns that goad them to have fun and to take it now: You "gotta have it." Advertisements blur the distinctions between impulsivity and spontaneity, between indecision and reflection. The message, however, is clear: Money buys what you need—immediate gratification. Our youth are primed for "pleasure now" messages, whether they come from Madison Avenue or the streets. The choice between working extra hours on the job or on homework is not much of a dilemma because students have not been taught how to say no to immediate gratification. And if they do not say no to at least some of these pleasures (e.g., drugs) then anything else we do does not matter. The best way to lose our next generation is not to teach them problem-solving and coping skills—self-regulated learning—in the social domain.

CLASSROOM MANAGEMENT AND SELF-REGULATED LEARNING

If our students are to be able to engage in problem solving in social contexts as well as in subject-matter domains, then they must be encouraged to reflect on their decision making, behavior, and the social and personal consequences of their actions. Instead, unfortunately, our students are taught to trade apparent attention for predictable routines. There are data to support that student obedience can be elicited under certain conditions. Indeed, historically, management research has focused on the administration of rewards and punishments to shape or control student behavior. More recently, research has focused on student compliance through teacher control of classroom momentum (e.g., pace, transitions, alerting, etc.) that prevents or reduces the opportunity for student noncompliance to occur (e.g., Kounin, 1970). Substantial research also indicates that teachers can negotiate "academic bargains" with their students through the nature of the work they assign. Doyle (1986) has provided clear evidence to suggest that this is readily accomplished by manipulating task features (e.g., reducing risk and ambiguity of a task can increase students' work-completion rates). There have been some important advances in conceptions of classroom management (see, for example, Doyle, 1986; Good and Brophy, 1991). Despite these research advances, however, classroom management in practice typically remains rooted in a behavioral conception of teaching that places the responsibility for student motivation and effort largely on the shoulders of teachers. Teachers demand; students obey. We maintain that our present focus in classroom management on student obedience (or "cooperation")—even when it can be obtained—is not only not enough, it may be dangerous. Some time ago, Milgram (1974) taught us about the crimes of obedience; more recently, Kelman and Hamilton (1989) inform us of the enormous complexity of obedience and its potential for destructiveness.

Our management systems must do more than elicit submission. Research on families and the socialization of children and work in social psychology can inform the design of management systems more appropriate for students' internalization of goals; the motivation to commit, challenge, or reform them; and the strategic competence to enact and evaluate those commitments. We term this the fostering of student adaptive learning.

RESEARCH ON PARENT MANAGEMENT STYLES

Baumrind's research on parenting focuses primarily on issues of management and control (Baumrind, 1971, 1987). Parental control is viewed as a dimension anchored by "laissez-faire" or "permissive" parenting at one extreme. These are parents who exercise little control and provide little instruction to their child. Laissez-faire parents are benign resources that the child may or may not wish to use. "Authoritarian" parenting anchors the dimension at the other extreme. These parents maintain control over their child's decision making and behavior independent of the child's emerging capacities. Authoritarian parents are less likely to discuss the reasons behind the rules. They order. The goal is child obedience, not understanding. A third profile on the parental control dimension, "authoritative," lies between these anchors. Authoritative parents provide explanations for their "firm but flexible" limits on child behavior. They discuss their standards, teach their child how to meet them, and value behavior that is monitored by self-discipline and self-control (see also McCaslin and Murdock, 1991). Thus, these parents provide their children with opportunities to reflect on their behavior and its consequences in various contexts. By providing parental guidelines and affording experiences, these parents help their children learn to value and understand responsible action and the problem solving it requires. Baumrind (1971) found that such a pattern of directive guidance encourages the development of responsible instrumental competence. Children of authoritative parents show the most advanced levels of autonomy and independence for their ages and have greater confidence and healthier self-concepts. Baumrind (1987) has also shown that adolescents in authoritative homes are more likely to engage in appropriate risk taking.

Baumrind's work provides a convincing and data-based argument to support authoritative over authoritarian and laissez-faire methods of management. Authoritative methods are not merely better perceived; they apparently are more effective in building the cognitive structures and behavioral control mechanisms within children that enable them to become both independent and responsible in managing their affairs—self-regulated learners who can adapt to changing expectations. Authoritative teacher behavior should help students to understand and internalize the rationales that underlie classroom rules and to operate within the rules on their own initiative.

Further, the nature of authoritative management recognizes the need for flexible rules so that students can progressively assume more responsibility for self-management: a sort of instructional scaffolding in the interpersonal domain. Authoritarian approaches do not encourage the development of such internal control mechanisms, partly because they lack instructional components and do not recognize the increasing competence of the learner. Instead, they generate conflict and tension, even when they succeed in controlling behavior. This becomes increasingly the case as students move through the grades.

COMPLIANCE AND SOCIALIZATION RESEARCH

Social psychologists have examined similar phenomena in research on conditions that promote or hinder compliance. An attributional analysis of this considerable body of research informs our discussion (Lepper, 1983). We briefly highlight just three points that are pertinent to classroom management (for more extended discussion, see Lepper, 1983; Lepper and Greene, 1978).

First, what is the goal of the management attempt? Kelman (1958, 1961) distinguishes among (1) compliance, which occurs when an attitude and behavior are expressed only when the individual expects to get a reward or avoid punishment (i.e., behavior is instrumental), (2) identification, in which the attitude and congruent behavior occur as long as the person whom the individual wishes to emulate is salient, and (3) internalization, in which the attitude and behavior endure across a variety of settings in the absence of external constraints. Internalization goals involve a shift from initially external forms of control to subsequent internalized social control. It is reasonable to assume that for some student behavior (e.g., raising your hand rather than calling out), compliance is a sufficient management goal. For others (e.g., staying with an ambiguous task) internalization seems the more appropriate goal.

A second informative construct from this research concerns the current motivational status we wish to influence. Lepper (1983) distinguishes among instilling, maintaining, and inhibiting attitudes and behavior. In the classroom instilling student motivation involves the judicious use of external rewards that are then faded. Maintaining the motivation of students who already are motivated calls for quite different management. Indeed, in these conditions external rewards consistently have been found to undermine motivation. Finally, Lepper's work reminds us that inhibiting behavior is not to be confused with instilling attitudes—student obedience does not equal student motivation.

The third point we draw from this research tradition is the need to keep an individual internally focused if we seek internalization as a management goal. Thus, when required, rewards and punishments should be subtle and informative. Lepper (1983) describes this as the "minimal sufficiency principle of social control." (For more extensive discussion of the function of incentives and disincentives in classroom performance, see also Chapter 5 in this volume.) Within this framework authoritative management successfully inculcates self-regulation because it keeps students focused on internal as opposed to external reasons for their behavior. Authoritarian management, in contrast, at best promotes compliance because the external reasons for obedience are salient.

CLASSROOM MANAGEMENT AND MOTIVATED STUDENT LEARNING

Our theoretical position—that authoritative classroom management by the teacher is similar to authoritative family management by parents—necessitates the view that the teacher will adjust a management system to changes in context and in students' needs and abilities. One of the key characteristics of authoritative parenting involves extending more responsibility and control to children as they develop more self-control and adaptive capacity and become capable of handling more responsibility. Thus, the concept of authoritative management requires that rules and structures be *adjusted* so that students progressively assume more responsibility for self-control, self-regulation.

In short, teachers' behavior, rules, tasks, and expectations should *change* over time—within a school year and across grades. Criteria for a successful management system in first- and sixth-grade classrooms should differ in important ways, for example, in the opportunity provided to students for self-regulation. Unfortunately, some conceptions of management are relatively static. This is an untenable choice if the goal is to increase students' capacity for self-regulation and adaptive learning in a problem-solving world.

Good (1986) has argued that there are notable differences in what constitutes successful learning in the home, the nursery school, kindergarten, and primary school. Differences among adults' management systems and expectations for performance in these settings are not necessarily inappropriate. Indeed, varied and increasingly more complex systems should stimulate students' academic and social development. However, Good reports that variation across settings sometimes appears to be so striking, and at times contradictory, that some students are likely to be confused by radical shifts in routines and expectations. Our own observations indicate that many nursery school students have more opportunity for self-direction, self-evaluation, and choice than do typical sixth-grade students.

It is time to examine the "connectedness" of management systems. How can we build better bridges between home and school? How can we build better bridges from grade to grade? Part of building an appropriate infrastructure that allows students to assume more responsibility for their own behavior will require schools to begin to provide structural mechanisms that allow teachers to think about students' adaptive development over time.

To achieve more congruence both across classrooms and over time, teachers will need both more information about how to play this role and more time to enact these conceptions. Although it is beyond our purpose here to discuss issues associated with the professionalism of teaching, we do want to make it clear that we are not blaming individual teachers for the ineffectual approaches to management in many classrooms. First, in many cases, reform (including management programs) is urged by external sources and/or imposed by administrative fiat (Sarason, 1990). Second, to the extent that teachers have the opportunity to alter school management policies in their classrooms, it is important to recognize that most teachers work hard but have little time or opportunity for professional growth or stimulation (Maeroff, 1988). If significant changes are to occur in how students are "managed" and if a problem-solving curriculum is to be implemented in many schools, it will be necessary to find some ways to restructure schooling so that teachers have time for continual professional development during the normal work week (e.g., time to consider new conceptualizations, time to talk and plan with peers).

Some schools may need more help than others. For example, McQuaite (1992) contends, "In many urban schools, teachers lack facilities, proper instructional materials, or support from the school administration" (p. 14). In our opinion, inner-city schools and rural areas marked by poverty and isolation would appear to need more resources than more advantaged areas. These schools need more resources in order to provide equitable learning opportunities for the youth they serve (e.g., if students do not have computers at home, there is even greater need to be sure that students have access to technology at school). Further, it would seem that children of poverty would especially need effective, indeed inspired, teachers (if such children have had less opportunity to learn to value learning and the appropriate dispositions for handling academic challenges). Unfortunately, it is common in the United States (unlike some countries) for those schools that need the most resources to receive the least. We are well aware of the fact that resources can and have been misused, and that money per se is not a solution. However, it is time to recognize the basic fact that more money must be strategically spent on education to develop creative structural supports that enable youth to acquire and develop academic interests and talents equitably. If students do not possess basic writing skills, they must have meaningful opportunities to write and to receive helpful, detailed feedback from teachers and peers. However, to allow this we must have smaller class sizes and other supports (data-processing equipment for students, aides for teachers, and instructional strategies) that allow for resources to be used effectively.

INTEGRATIVE SOLUTIONS

Classroom management must move from a concern with proximal goals of reduction of disobedience to more distal goals of self-regulation. It is now time to broaden conceptions of classroom management to include goals that we wish students to seek and realize as members of the classroom and as members of the community. "Prevention" in classroom management should adopt the connotation of the proactive goals and strategies that characterize preventive approaches in nutrition, health, and well-being programs. This broadened conception of management attends as well to the fact that students are children and adolescents; they live in and beyond the classroom. Students'—children's—lives are complicated. We argue that if they are to profit from experience and meaningfully participate in their community, they need to learn how to cope with stress, engage in self-regulation, and become adaptive learners. (For more extended discussion of the enhancement of adaptive learning, see McCaslin, 1990; McCaslin and Murdock, 1991; Rohrkemper, 1989; Rohrkemper and Corno, 1988.)

Historically, as we have argued, conceptions of the "problem" have been narrow and overly fragmented. Conceptions of the "solution" have also been narrowly drawn—at times, parent reform is argued and yet at other times, the solution lies in better schools, better curricula, better instruction, and better students; if not "better," then more effortful. It seems irresponsible to target any one group for the responsibility of failure (i.e., if only *students* would work harder) when we deal with systemic issues. Unfortunately, one ugly consequence of assigning blame and concomitant directions for reform is that it enables society to ignore the core problem: If universal education is to be successful, it requires the commitment of various resources, both financial and moral. If all children are to have the opportunity to become adaptive learners, then schools that need the most resources cannot continue to receive the least. There are no quick fixes and certainly no inexpensive solutions. And asking one group to work harder is *not* a solution.

REFERENCES

Ames, Carole. "Competitive, Cooperative, and Individualistic Goal Structures: A Cognitive-Motivational Analysis." In *Research on Motivation in Education, Vol. 1: Student Motivation*, edited by Russell Ames and Carole Ames, pp. 177–207. New York: Academic Press, 1984.

Anderson, Richard; Hiebert, Elfrieda; Scott, Judith; and Wilkinson, Ian A. G. *Becoming a Nation of Readers: The Report of the Commission on Reading*. Washington, D. C.: National Institute of Education, 1985.

Baumrind, Diana. "Current Patterns of Parental Authority," *Developmental Psychology Monograph* 4, no. 1, Part 2 (January 1971): 1–103.

Baumrind, Diana. "A Developmental Perspective on Adolescent Risk Taking in Contemporary America." In *Adolescent Social Behavior and Health*, edited by Charles E. Irwin, Jr. San Francisco: Jossey-Bass, 1987.

Blumenfeld, Phyllis. "The Task and the Teacher: Enhancing Student Thoughtfulness in Science." In *Advances in Research on Teaching*, Vol. 3, edited by Jere Brophy. Greenwich, Conn.: JAI Press, forthcoming.

Borstelmann, Lloyd J. "Children before Psychology: Ideas about Children from Antiquity to the Late 1800s." In *Handbook of Child Psychology, Vol. 1: History, Theory, and Methods*, edited by Paul Mussen, pp. 1–40. New York: Wiley, 1983.

Cuban, Larry. *How Teachers Taught: Constancy and Change in American Classrooms, 1890–1980*. New York: Longman, 1984.

Doyle, Walter. "Classroom Organization and Management." In *Handbook of Research on Teaching*, 3rd ed., edited by Merlin Wittrock. New York: Macmillan, 1986.

Elkind, David. *The Hurried Child: Growing Up Too Fast Too Soon*. Reading, Mass.: Addison-Wesley, 1982.

Getzels, Jacob W. "Paradigm and Practice: On the Impact of Basic Research in Education." In *Impact of Research on Education: Some Case Studies*, edited by Patrick Suppes, pp. 477–517. Washington, D. C.: National Academy of Education, 1978.

Good, Thomas. "Teacher Expectations and Student Perceptions: A Decade of Research," *Educational Leadership* 38 (1981): 415–423.

Good, Thomas. "What Is Learned in Elementary Schools?" In *Academic Work and Educational Excellence*, edited by Tommy Tomlinson and Herbert J. Walberg. Berkeley, Calif.: McCutchan, 1986.

Good, Thomas, and Brophy, Jere. *Looking in Classrooms*, 5th ed. New York: Harper and Row, 1991.

Good, Thomas; McCaslin, Mary; and Reys, Barbara. "Structuring Tasks for Small-Group Problem Solving in Mathematics." In *Advances in Research on Teaching*, Vol. 3, edited by Jere Brophy. Greenwich, Conn.: JAI Press, forthcoming.

Haycock, Katie. "Closing Remarks." Presentation at the AAHE/College Board Conference on Mainstreaming University/School Partnerships, Chicago, June, 1990.

Kelman, Herbert C. "Compliance, Identification, and Internalization: Three Processes of Opinion Change," *Journal of Conflict Resolution* 2 (1958): 51–60.

Kelman, Herbert C. "Processes of Attitude Change," *Public Opinion Quarterly* 25 (1961): 57–78.

Kelman, Herber C., and Hamilton, V. Lee. *Crimes of Obedience: Toward a Social Psychology of Authority and Responsibility*. New Haven, Conn.: Yale University Press, 1989.

Kounin, Jacob. *Discipline and Group Management in Classrooms*. New York: Holt, Rinehart, and Winston, 1970.

Lepper, Mark. "Extrinsic Reward and Intrinsic Motivation: Implications for the Classroom." In *Teacher and Student Perceptions: Implications for Learning*, edited by John M. Levine and Margaret C. Wang. Hillsdale, N.J.: Erlbaum, 1983.

Lepper, Mark, and Greene, David. *The Hidden Costs of Reward: New Perspectives on the Psychology of Human Motivation*. Hillsdale, N.J.: Erlbaum, 1978.

Maeroff, Gene. *The Empowerment of Teachers*. New York: Teachers College Press, 1988.

McCaslin, Mary. "Motivated Literacy." In *Literacy Theory and Research: Analyses from Multiple Perspectives*, Thirty-ninth Yearbook of the National Reading Conference, edited by Jerry Zutell and Sandra McCormick. Chicago: National Reading Conference, 1990.

McCaslin, Mary, and Good, Thomas. "Compliant Cognition: The Misalliance of Management and Instructional Goals in Current School Reform," *Educational Researcher*, in press.

McCaslin, Mary, and Murdock, T. B. "The Emergent Interaction of Home and School in the Development of Students' Adaptive Learning." In *Advances in Motivation and Achievement*, Vol. 7, edited by Martin Maehr and Paul Pintrich, pp. 213–260. Greenwich, Conn.: JAI Press, 1991.

McQuaite, MariBeth. "The Value of Peers," *Basic Education* 36, no. 5 (1992): 12–14.

Milgram, Stanley, *Obedience to Authority: An Experimental View*. New York: Harper and Row, 1974.

National Council of Teachers of Mathematics, Commission of Standards for School

Mathematics. *Curriculum and Evaluation Standards for School Mathematics*. Reston, Virg.: National Council of Teachers of Mathematics, 1990.

National Research Council. *Everybody Counts: A Report to the Nation on the Future of Mathematics Education*. Washington, D. C.: National Academy Press, 1989.

Porter, Andrew. *A Curriculum Out of Balance: The Case of Elementary School Mathematics*, Research Series no. 191. East Lansing: Institute for Research on Teaching, Michigan State University, 1988.

Reston, James. *Deadline: A Memoir*. New York: Random House, 1991.

Rohrkemper, Mary McCaslin, "Self-regulated Learning and Academic Achievement: A Vygotskian View." In *Self-regulated Learning and Academic Achievement: Theory, Research, and Practice*, edited by Barry Zimmerman and Dale H. Schunk. New York: Springer-Verlag, 1989.

Rohrkemper, Mary, and Corno, Lyn. "Success and Failure on Classroom Tasks: Adaptive Learning and Classroom Teaching," *Elementary School Journal* 88 (1988): 299–312.

Rose, Mike. *Lives on the Boundary: The Struggles and Achievements of America's Underprepared*. New York: Free Press, 1989.

Sarason, Seymour. *The Predictable Failure of Educational Reform*. San Francisco: Jossey-Bass, 1990.

Stevenson, Harold, and Flanagan, Constance. "A Comparative Study of Chinese and Japanese High School Students." Paper presented at a Directors Meeting, National Science Foundation and Human Resources Directorate, Research in Teaching and Learning Project, Washington, D. C., October 1990.

Toffler, Alvin. *Future Shock*. New York: Bantam Books, 1970.

Part IV
Summary and Recommendations

Chapter 12

SUMMARY AND RECOMMENDATIONS

Tommy M. Tomlinson

Among the principal themes evident in chapters in this volume are the following four:

1. *Students have few incentives to study.* Despite growing numbers of chronically underachieving children, and the intense national concern to motivate them, most schools continue to give a majority of their rewards to high-achieving children. Because high-ability students usually capture the best grades and test scores, the labor of less-talented students is seldom acknowledged, much less inspired by their grades. If this arrangement is discouraging for children of middling academic aptitude—the majority—it is the undoing of many children who labor under the burden of low ability or the handicap of disadvantage. These children, who need to work harder for small accomplishments than those of higher aptitude, perversely have the least incentive to do so. They often find this relationship between low grades and high effort unacceptable, something to be evaded if possible. Some express their displeasure by simple indifference, others by disruption and deception.

2. *School policies and practices discourage student effort.* Many public policies at the federal, state, and local level and many school and classroom practices have worked unwittingly against the best interests of learning. Some of these policies and practices have allowed students to evade difficult academic tasks; others have undermined the need to make the effort; still others have merely substituted the appearance of educational attainment for its substance. For example, in just fifteen years, from 1960 to 1975, as standardized test scores plummeted from their zenith to their nadir, high school completion rates jumped 32

265

percent for whites and 91 percent for blacks. Students were staying in school longer, but learning less. The growth in the rate and parity of high school graduation was being undercut by practices that appeared to contribute to the decline in achievement. Among these were schools that allowed students to design their own courses of study, offered credit for less rigorous alternatives to core subjects, and awarded diplomas to students who merely stayed the course and accumulated credits. Many schools still do these things. Students at all levels of ability have taken advantage of these educational gratuities, virtually all of which were well-intentioned steps to boost the educational progress of the nation's neediest students.

3. *Peer pressure may discourage effort and achievement.* Peer pressure exerts great influence on the academic behavior of students. In most schools, this pressure defines the stance students will take toward academic achievement and academic effort. Typically, pressure is exerted to stay in school and graduate, but high grades as well as low can be a source of embarrassment. Moreover, even as they frown on failure, peers may also restrain high achievement, and some student crowds may even impose strong social sanctions on high achievers. In these instances, effort is hostage to peer pressure, and students work to meet their crowd's expectations rather than those of their teachers or parents.

4. *Good intentions often backfire.* Coping with the problems caused by seemingly intractable performance differences on the one hand, and the imperative to successfully educate ever larger numbers of disadvantaged students on the other, schools have adopted a number of compensatory practices in the interests of its low-achieving students. Many of these practices have had the ironic and unintended effect of compromising the standards and the consequent level of achievement of a wide range of students, but particularly those for whom the help was intended.

Furthermore, many teachers are at cross-purposes about setting higher expectations for low-achieving students, especially those who are disadvantaged. Simply put, teachers seek to reconcile the added student effort that higher expectations require with their concern that disadvantaged and low-ability children may be excessively burdened. Thus, in seeking to be fair and to protect their pupils' self-esteem, many teachers excuse disadvantaged children from the effort that learning requires. This well-intentioned practice obscures the connection between effort and accomplishment, and shields the children from the consequences. The practice also sets the stage for later failure.

RECOMMENDATIONS

Where Do We Go from Here?

Plainly the obstacles to learning far exceed those imposed by the limits of student ability and background. Left to their own devices and absent any incentives to do otherwise, most children treat learning as but one of many things to do—and among the least pleasant of the alternatives. Almost endless opportunities to avoid hard work in the classroom are provided to most of our students, and while understanding the source and nature of these experiences sets the stage for change, it alone will do little to alter the situation. Other steps must be taken:

- We must make learning the highest priority in our children's lives; they have no future without it.
- We, as a nation, must act to focus the attention of students on the educational substance we agree is critical to the nation's future as well as their own.
- We must define the skills we expect and believe all our children should develop and all our schools must teach.
- We must act on the knowledge that the connection between learning and academic effort is powerful, and, with proper support, within the reach of all students.

Help is available. As the papers contained in this volume indicate, education researchers across the country are generating new knowledge about why children do not, and often cannot, work, and are developing classroom strategies that can invigorate academic motivation and effort. The work reported in this book illuminates several sources of student motivation and their consequent effects on achievement. It also suggests steps that teachers and their students can take to improve the returns on their effort. Among the most promising ideas are the following seven.

1. *Move to a schooling format that establishes a better balance between ability and effort in the distribution of rewards and incentives.* Both effort and

ability are, after all, the child's tools for learning, and one must be encouraged with the other and not at its expense. In the early grades, emphasize and demonstrate the relationship between effort and achievement so that children understand and appreciate the importance of effort in learning. Set goals for each child that can be achieved with high effort, and reward their attainment.

Schools can engage children who are less talented and motivated by devising alternate incentives that reward study and personal accomplishment as well as high scores and class standing. Rewards distributed only according to achievement level will invariably favor the brightest children, especially those who work hard. Alternative rewards that emphasize and reinforce effort will be necessary to engage children who are less talented and motivated lest they give up in the face of relative failure.

2. *Teach children how to learn.* There is more to effort than spending time on task. The quality of effort is even more important than the quantity. Schools often offer a class in study skills, but still few students learn how to study effectively by themselves. Insufficient classroom time is spent helping children learn to develop an effective approach to learning. John Thomas noted that teachers can assist students in their studying by requiring proficiency in a number of learning skills, for example, notetaking, producing integrative summaries, self-testing, creating study plans, and time management.

As with most academic tasks, high-ability students have the advantage in picking up these tools of the trade. Nevertheless, efficient and time-saving methods are especially important for slow learners, who are less likely to pick them up from experience, especially if they abandon learning early on. Moreover, many, perhaps most, students enter college still unprepared to engage in effective academic work. Even the most elementary skills may be lacking. For example, one student participant in the conference that led to this volume commented that students were seldom taught to take notes. In contrast, Lois Peak (see Chapter 3) observed that one of the distinctions between the practices of Japanese and American teachers is their emphasis on the acquisition of these skills. Japanese students are introduced to note-taking in the first grade, and by the fifth or sixth grade they are keeping notebooks filled with the results of their studying. In fact, "Japanese students use these notebooks as conscientiously as most American graduate students," said Peak.

3. *Provide supports matched to course demands.* The returns to student effort will be increased if teachers do the following simple things:

- Explain clearly to students what is expected of them, how much work it will require, and how they will be graded.
- Guide students in how to carry out homework and study for tests.
- Give extensive practice on instructional objectives.
- Give extensive feedback on quizzes, homework, and tests.
- Give significant credit for successfully completing homework.

4. *Enhance the status of "doing one's best."* Rewarding high academic achievement alone will seldom enhance the appeal of learning. It merely turns learning into another competition with rewards and the incentives they provide available only to a few. Public recognition of individual excellence, regardless of its nature, may be the most obvious way to accomplish this goal, but it is also perhaps the most overlooked. Accordingly, schools should take care to recognize outstanding performances in areas outside the core curriculum but consistent with goals of schooling. "Trade fairs that feature the products of students in vocational classes are as important as awards assemblies for top math and English scholars," Bradford Brown said (see Chapter 4).

5. *Send the right signals about the comparative importance of academic and nonacademic achievement.* Schools should insist, for example, that athletes meet the same standards as the other students. This can help brighten the image of effort-based learning as well as improve the athletes' preparation for college. It can also reduce student cynicism about the integrity of academics and help convince even varsity football players that learning is the most important activity they can embrace.

6. *Adopt incentive systems that encourage students to strive toward a standard of knowledge instead of competing against each other.* Instructional practices that associate effort with success encourage initiative and persistence as well as a growing sense of personal competence. The result we seek is less that children realize the role and limits of their ability than they accumulate a sense that they can solve a problem and master a subject. As John Thomas (see Chapter 7) noted, "evaluation systems that de-emphasize competition, provide feedback on individual progress, and minimize public comparability have . . . been found to facilitate student learning, motivation, and effort,

especially for students possessing a low self-concept of academic ability."

7. *Eliminate obstacles to innovative classroom practices, most notably school policies that are inconsistent with the development of self-regulated student behavior.* Avoid practices that undercut student initiative, offers of help where none has been requested, for example, or help that offers a solution rather than a method to figure out the answer. Instigate opportunities for students to seek and provide help to one another in developing an effective exchange of ideas, learning strategies, interests, and goals.

When students believe that their ability can be enhanced by effort, said Sharon Nelson-LeGall, they are likely to work harder and more persistently to complete a task (see Chapter 10). They are also likely to look actively for the help they need to complete the job, an important form of student initiative that should be encouraged.

All of this is, of course, easier to say than to do. For one thing, teachers need exposure to good training. But teachers cannot be expected to solve problems of motivation single-handedly. Many of the school and classroom practices and behaviors that undermine the students' desire to achieve academically result, directly or indirectly, from the conflicting messages embedded in our cultural values and educational goals and policies. If reform strategies aimed at lowering specific barriers to academic motivation are to have any wide success, our society's ambivalence and uncertainty about the legitimacy and purpose of academic achievement, especially high achievement, as well as the role and responsibilities of students in their education, must be resolved. Neither high expectations nor sweeping reforms will produce the results we seek unless the students respond with the necessary hard work. Accordingly, the untapped power of student effort must be engaged on behalf of learning if we are to realize the enduring goals of either equity or excellence, much less meet the educational aspirations that the nation has set for the next century.